Imaginary Betrayals

Imaginary Betrayals

Subjectivity and the Discourses of Treason in Early Modern England

Karen Cunningham

PENN

University of Pennsylvania Press
Philadelphia

Printed in the United States of America on acid-free paper

10 9 8 7 6 5 4 3 2 1

Published by
University of Pennsylvania Press
Philadelphia, Pennsylvania 19104-4011

Library of Congress Cataloging-in-Publication Data
Cunningham, Karen.
Imaginary betrayals : subjectivity and the discourses of treason in early Modern England / Karen Cunningham.
p. cm. —
Includes bibliographical references and index.
ISBN 0-8122-3640-8 (cloth : alk. paper)
1. English drama—Early modern and Elizabethan, 1500–1600—History and criticism. 2. Treason in literature. 3. English drama—17th century—History and criticism. 4. Trials (Treason)—England—History—16th century. 5. Law and literature—History—16th century. 6. Subjectivity in literature. 7. Sex role in literature. 8. Betrayal in literature. 9. Law in literature. I. Title. II. Series.
PR658.T77 C86 2001
822'.309358—dc21 2001041541

For my Mom and Dad

Imagination is funny

Contents

Introduction 1

1 "Fugitive Forms": Imagining the Realm 23

2 Female Fidelities on Trial 40

3 Masculinity, Affiliation, and Rootlessness 77

4 Secrecy and the Epistolary Self 110

Conclusion 141

Notes 145

Works Cited 187

Index 203

Acknowledgments 215

Introduction

Think not the King doth banish thee,
But thou the King. . . .

SHAKESPEARE, Richard II

Whether we look to government records, to legal histories, or to theatrical representations, we find ample evidence that treason was perceived as an increasingly serious threat, policed with a new urgency, and publicized with fresh intensity during the sixteenth century. To ensure that trials would gather attention, the Crown convened open arraignments, offered evidence into the record even when the accused had pled guilty, employed circuit judges and preachers to provide official accounts of traitors' misdeeds and convictions, and published pamphlets.[1] In explaining these events, scholars have tended to identify treason more with a political than with a cultural story. The discursive energies of the cultural story, however, are my interest. In discourses of treason, elusive, troublesome conceptions of gender, affiliation, and homeland were repeatedly argued. And although prosecutors attempted to establish a definitive point of view—in Pierre Bourdieu's formulation, "to impose a universally recognized principle of knowledge on the social world"[2]—they did not necessarily succeed. What we find is that in legal proceedings and in dramatic writings, flexible forms of "imaginary practices" (a phrase adopted from treason prosecutions) were continuously contested. Instead of being dominated by one voice and perspective, the trial genre is characterized by disagreement and dispute. Because these legal discourses were widely circulated and consumed through all levels of society, treason trials provide us with an important site for analyzing the volatile discursive relations among the Crown, subjects, and writers for the stage in early modern England.[3] Both the legal and the literary disciplines are devoted to representing ways of "knowing" the English subject, and both claim to represent the truth about that inscrutable figure. Nicholas Udall, William Shakespeare, Christopher Marlowe, and Thomas Kyd, to name only a few, employ elements of contemporary treason discourses to reinterpret categories of national identity. As they construct their conflicts, these writers turn to an issue treason consistently troubles over: personal and political fidelity.

The overarching context for this study is recent work on the notion of subjectivity in the English Renaissance. After a number of works denying that the concept was available in the Renaissance or that it signified anything related to our modern concept of inwardness, there has been a revival of interest in considering the ways interiority was imagined.[4] Often recent work is framed in terms of the problem of knowing one's own and others' minds, and related to the religious and philosophical currents in the English Renaissance that would have made full knowledge both imperative and impossible. My interest is in the intersection of law and literature: in the ways the lawcourt dramatizes legal notions of evidence and persuasion, in the ways it stages assumptions about the possibility of knowing other minds, and in the ways plays engage in conversation with trials.[5] Since treason was defined as compassing the king's death in the imagination, trying a person for the crime would mean discovering or constructing an inward truth as it was manifest in the character and words of the accused.

Until recently, literary scholars have tended to enclose the issue of the relations between plays and trials within biographies of authors. We have, for example, studies of what William Shakespeare knew and treatises on his legal professionalism; of John Marston's life and writings about the Middle Temple; and of Thomas Sackville and Thomas Norton's lives as aspiring benchers, members of Parliament, and authors of *Gorboduc*.[6] These studies provide much useful information, and my debt to them is recorded in the notes below. In illuminating the author, however, these studies have tended to limit the scope of investigation, minimizing the legal story by positioning it as a supplement to an individual writer's interests. My own argument is not fundamentally author-driven, although it may be in any specific instance. I assume that dramatists and legal practitioners respond to and influence their contemporary discourses, in particular those associated with legitimate and illegitimate forms of imagining the nation, though these exchanges may not be conscious or deliberate.

In many studies of law and literature, scholars from both disciplines have tended to use a broad legal statute as a backdrop to support a literary theme. Legal historian Cynthia B. Herrup has noted that "scholars have generally treated the procedures of the law as background. . . . Too frequently legal process appears collapsed from a series of decisions into one judgment and from a multivoiced production into the solo of a single genteel tenor."[7] In foregrounding a codified legal history at the expense of an often inconsistent legal practice, studies may bestow an image of unity on something called "the law" that is at odds with highly flexible early modern legal customs. Legislative history provides us with a partial, particular view of legal-literary relations and of the historical processes and discursive work performed in trials. I want, however, to complement that work by bringing the trial genre into focus.[8]

If, as I and others have argued, public executions were (among other things) formal cautionary rituals staged for various audiences, what legal stories led up to those extreme conclusions?[9] What narratives were necessary to justify the ways of monarchs to men? One of my most surprising discoveries is the extent to which an early modern treason trial is a permeable form, open not only to political agendas and putative facts, but to rumor, scandal, and innuendo. And as in plays, so in trials particular questions of the relations between subjective and national identities emerge repeatedly: what notions of feminine and masculine, of affiliation and differentiation, of homeland and homelessness are crafted in these narratives?

In *Forms of Nationhood*, Richard Helgerson identifies a growing anxiety during the sixteenth century about England's cultural identity: "England was now calling itself an empire. Where were the signs of imperial stature?"[10] For Helgerson, those signs are apparent in the varied, generationally specific writings of such figures as Edmund Spenser, William Camden, John Speed, Michael Drayton, Richard Hakluyt, William Shakespeare, and Richard Hooker. The law, too, is a theme-making system, Helgerson argues, and its archetypal themes are cataloged in the work of such great codifiers as Edward Coke. Rather than turn to the early codes, however, I turn to individual trials and attainders for treason. Close reading of the trials and plays allows us to see developing forms of Englishness as they are more fully represented in legal and dramatic practice; it allows us to subject the historical processes within these texts to closer analysis; and it allows us to explore relations between trials and plays in more particularity. Read dialogically within themselves and against a range of plays, these trials reveal competing discourses in which fluid categories of "legitimate" citizenship are redefined and reassociated with equally fluid forms of evidence that must meet the difficulties of revealing an elusive self and a loyal subject.[11]

Conventionally, drama was granted only a peripheral claim to truth-telling in such formulations as Sir Philip Sidney's in "An Apology for Poetry": the poet "nothing affirms."[12] Sidney was both differentiating and defending the art of the "maker" by sketching a generic distinction between his own discipline and those of his contemporaries: "The lawyer saith what men have determined; the historian, what men have done . . . and the rhetorician and logician, considering what in nature will soonest prove and persuade, thereon give artificial rules, which still are compassed within the circle of a question according to the proposed matter."[13] Reserving his highest commendation for his last figure, Sidney clears a unique space in the realm of imaginative discourse: "Only the poet, disdaining to be tied to any such subjection, lifted up with the vigor of his own invention, doth grow in effect another nature, in making things either better than nature bringeth forth, or, quite anew, forms such as never were in nature, as the Heroes, Demigods, Cyclopes, Chimeras, Furies, and such like."[14] Like all the others not called to the vocation of "maker" in Sidney's value-infused cosmos, the lawyer is a recorder condemned to wander within the boundaries of a preformed Nature and banished from the realm of creative imagination.

What is striking about Sidney's literary taxonomy is that it is belied by legal practices and rhetorical handbooks from the law's earliest days to Sidney's moment and beyond. Perhaps Sidney's emphatic delineation was in part precipitated by his growing awareness of the ways other nascent early modern disciplines, law among them, were impinging on the poet's conceptual space. In his *Arte of Rhetorique*, written in 1560 and reprinted throughout the latter part of the century, Thomas Wilson argues the case for poets as truth-tellers specifically in the context of instructing young lawyers how best to craft arguments:

> The saiynge of Poets and all their fables are not to be forgotten, for by them we may talke at large, and winne men by perswasion, if wee declare before hande that these tales were not fayned of suche wise menne without cause, neither yet continued untyll this tyme, and kepte in memorie without good consideration, and therupon declare the true meanynge of all suche writings. For undoubtedlye there is no one tale emonge al the Poetes, but under the same is comprehended some thinge that perteyneth, eyther to the amendemente of maners, to the knowledge of the trueth, to the settynge forthe of Natures woorcke, or elles the understandinge of some notable thynge done. . . . The Poetes were wise men.[15]

If Sidney gives us a glimpse of poets transcending the limitations of history, Wilson gives us a glimpse of them modeling a rhetoric of persuasion. Both characterize early modern literary and legal theory, in which verbal strategies, persuasive techniques, and imaginative improvisations were basic elements.

As they were theorized, forensic and mimetic rhetorics both were designed to persuade, though each had a different end: the forensic was designed to achieve condemnation or approval of a person's actions, particularly in judicial situations; the mimetic was designed to imitate an action, to achieve an effect of verisimilitude, and to move one to imagine.[16] By emphasizing poetry as a means of achieving instructional effects on an audience, however, Horace had obscured this traditional Aristotelian distinction: "The aim of the poet is to inform or delight, or to combine together, in what he says, both the pleasure and applicability to life."[17] In attending to poesie's mimetic role—"it is that feigning notable images of virtues, vices, or what else, with that delightful teaching" that identify the poet—Sidney extended the Horation vision: "the poet, with that same hand of delight, doth draw the mind more effectually than any other art doth."[18] In early modern legal and dramatic practice, the forensic and the mimetic employ each other, and a continuing theme of my study is the exchange between them.

In a series of recent essays on Shakespearean drama, Patricia Parker has formulated an important challenge shared by early modern courts and theaters: the demand to provide a credible story. Parker writes:

> The obsessively staged desire to see or spy out secrets, or in the absence of the directly ocular, to extract a narrative that might provide a vicarious substitute . . . implicates both *show* and *tell*, eye and ear, in the broader sixteenth- and early seventeenth- century problem of testimony and report . . . a theatrical problem shared by the law courts and other contestatory sites of epistemological or evidentiary certainty, of what might be reliably substituted for what could not be directly witnessed.[19]

Law courts and theaters employed what Parker provocatively calls the "motivated rhetorics" of gender, order, and rule that are rooted in a tradition at least as ancient as Cicero and Quintilian. These "motivated" verbal strategies "point not only to the new social mobility" of the early modern era but also "to rhetoric itself as an instrument of civil order."[20] No where is that instrumentality more evident than in the rhetorical battles waged in the trials and plays that make up this study.

As unstable as the notion of nationhood itself, even the term "treason" comes into use in legal rhetoric not to describe a specific act, but to single out a position relative to others and to competing ideas about the emerging English nation—that is, to make an argument. In the stories told in trials, the traitor is a figure accused of seeking to supplant one ideal of a homeland with another. He or she is brought into being by a dominant culture and is positioned as one who implicitly contests an ideal of nationhood as natural, unified, and self-defining. Although most traitors are officially positioned against the Crown, the figure could also be used by the Crown for its own interests.

This was the complaint of John Ponet in his pamphlet against the absolutism of Mary I published in Strasburg in 1556. In *A Short Treatise of Political Power*, Ponet devoted a chapter to "What confidence is to be given to princes" and concludes that very little confidence is merited. Objecting to the ways rulers might extend their power, Ponet writes that princes employ "traitors" to advance their "policy," then "cast them out on the dung hill."[21] Ponet's complaint clarifies the position of "traitors": they are perceived only relationally, in so far as they differ from a particular and often only partially articulated politics. Variously cast as those who resist or enable royal policy, traitors trouble conventional categories of allegiance. They call into question preexisting frames of reference, many of which are unspoken but which nonetheless to a large extent shape the outcomes of legal proceedings. They repeatedly work to undercut the ostensible monovocality of a discourse of nationhood, attacking in different ways some of the conceptual oppositions—masculine/feminine, friend/enemy, countryman/exile—from which this discourse takes its meanings. Put another way, treason is a discursive category in which certain cultural anxieties emerge into visibility and language, engage with diverse and unpredictable forms of maintenance and resistance, and resolve temporarily into a verdict. And although a verdict puts an end to a particular legal procedure, it activates other legal and social discourses in the continuing work of cultural self-renovation. The form of national identity perceived as threatened in these trials may be as explicit as that symbolized by the life of a particular queen or as implicit as that conveyed in an unspoken teleology of marriage for women. In treason trials, mutating attributes and signs of loyalty or disloyalty, as well as the very thoughts that a subject might appropriately entertain, are continuously reformalized in official narratives.[22]

Although I assume a reciprocity among cultural representations, I also want to draw a distinction: in a treason trial, there is at the end of the line a human being who either lives under a promise of death or who dies. The same cannot be said of the dramatic trial, and this crucial difference is obscured by collapsing legal practice into theater. Trials and plays are instances of what anthropologist Mary Douglas terms "cultural bias," that drape of a national fabric that gives a society its peculiar slant or angle during a particular period.[23] Yet starkly different consequences attend on these intersecting practices. At the end of a treason trial, real people died. What was at stake in every rhetorical move and textual manipulation was a life. At the end of a play, on the other hand, regardless of the fate of the character, the actor lived. In a treason trial, conviction was a death knell; in a drama, a curtain call. It is not that theater stands outside legal discourse, but that its ways of being in that discourse are particular and partial; it could, for example (as my argument implies throughout), help condition ideological forms of gender, affiliation, and homeland as well as lend imaginative credibility to specific versions of "permissible" death. Yet whatever the shared operations and values of a play and a trial, at the end of one an audience attended, at the end of the other, an executioner.

To be accused of treason was to be at the receiving end of a terrifying exercise of government power, and this inequitable relationship makes it tempting to ally the law with the instrumental purposes of absolutist monarchies. Since the penalty for conviction of treason could include not only execution but also forfeiture—that is, the loss of possessions on the part of the person found guilty and the "corrupting of his blood" (the disinheriting of his heirs)—the Crown might gain both political and real currency as a result of a prosecution.[24] Yet although the Crown brought charges and ran the courts, no single figure or office wholly controlled proceedings. Under the Tudors, the monarch's authority was perceived as absolute in some realms and as limited in others. The general concept that rulers received their authority from God extended back at least to the Middle Ages, and as the Tudors strengthened the power of the royal office in the sixteenth century, their supporters heightened the claims of divine right. Yet many English subjects, including many who subscribed to the principles of divine right, also believed that the monarch's authority was limited by the common law, the constitution, and the consent of Parliament.[25] This notion of a limited monarchy relied on two key ideas: "the notion that the king derived his power from the commonwealth, not immediately from God, and that the king and people were bound by reciprocal conditions," effectively an early conception of a social contract, and the notion that there existed "an immemorial common law which had been created by neither king nor people and stood above both."[26] Common law, which was the indigenous case-law based on custom, was understood not as the will of the ruler but as the property and birthright of the very subjects who might be accused in treason prosecutions of violating its strictures.

Because individual trials were engaged in a dialogue with the general laws under which they occurred, an overview of treason legislation might provide coordinates for listening to some of the disputes. At the time Henry VII ascended the throne, definitions of treason rested primarily on a highly serviceable medieval statute. In 1352, Edward III had redefined treason (25 Edw. III st.5 c.2) from behavior to thought, from a physical to a mental action, and from an overt into a covert violation of royal prerogative, extending his control over even the "imaginings" of subjects.[27] Although the adjectival form "high" treason did not appear regularly before the end of the fourteenth century, the crime was understood to include offenses against the king's person and his regality, which were specified as:

to compass or imagine the death of the king, his queen or the royal heir; to violate the king's consort, his eldest daughter or the wife of his eldest son; to levy war against the king in his realm or adhere to the king's enemies and be provably attaint of it by men of the offender's own condition; to counterfeit the great or privy seal of the king's coin, to introduce counterfeit money into England knowing it to be false; also to kill the chancellor, treasurer, or a justice of either bench, of eyre, or assize or of oyer and terminer while executing his office.[28]

According to legal historian John Bellamy, "the most important development in the interpretation of the law of treason between 1352 and 1485 concerned the clause in the Edwardian act about imagining and compassing the king's death. Apart from those based on the offence of levying war against the king, . . . indictments concerned with 'imagining' were dominant."[29] In theory, when "doubtful" cases of treason arose, justices were to delay giving judgment until the question was brought before the king in Parliament and it was determined whether the crime should be classified treason or the lesser crime of felony. In practice, however, the Crown and Edwardian royal justices seem most often to have used a wide interpretation of "imagining and compassing" and to have acknowledged few "doubtful" cases.

By extending treason to "imaginings," Edward III had opened up the category of "constructive" or "presumptive" treason, under which such things as words and writings that commented on the king and his behavior in what could be construed a "malicious" manner became the basis for indictments. Even if a subject's words did not express a direct intent to bring about the king's death, they could be interpreted as having malicious intent indirectly and the accused could be found guilty of treason.[30] The king's lawyers justified these prosecutions in the late fifteenth century on the grounds of intention: such things as approving of a sermon, crying out commentaries about the king's personal behavior in the streets, repeating gossip, or practicing prophetic arts were interpreted as intended to destroy the cordial love which the people had for the king and thereby shorten his life by sadness.[31]

The preeminence of the Edwardian act was unchallenged from 1352 to roughly 1530–36, the years of the Henrician Reformation Parliament, when changes occurred in the scope of treason for which there were no parallels in earlier law.[32] In early 1534, the first act of succession (25 Hen. VIII c. 22) protected Henry's marriage to Anne Boleyn by making into treason deeds or written or printed words imperiling the king's person or prejudicing or slandering his recent marriage. In November 1534, another act (26 Hen. VIII c. 13) again made traitorous words the centerpiece. To wish or attempt bodily harm to the king, queen, or royal heir or to try to deprive the king of his title by malicious deeds, writings, or *spoken* words was now laid down as treason. In the earlier succession act (which had been repealed) it had only been misprision of treason (a lesser crime) to speak words to the peril of the king's person or the hurt of the recent marriage; in the second succession act (28 Hen. VIII c.7) spoken words became actual treason, as deeds and written words had been in the earlier act.

All these new laws are related to a fascinating recurring theme of Henrician treason legislation: matrimonial arrangements. Late in 1534 an unusual act appeared (28 Hen. VIII c. 24) that made it treason in the future to marry the king's sister, niece, or aunt without royal consent or to "defile or deflower" them. Apparently derived from Lord Thomas Howard, Duke of Norfolk's contracting a marriage to Lady Margaret Douglas, natural daughter of the Queen of Scots, this act had no precedents; no earlier king had considered a subject's matrimonial plans treason. Within a few years the Henrician Parliament followed with an act making a new treason (33 Hen. VIII c. 23) concerning women the king might take to wife. A product of the Howard treason, which I take up in detail in Chapter 2, the act centers on a striking theme: what the king knew. It stated that if a woman the king should intend to marry "esteeming her pure and cleane maide" was in fact otherwise, and willingly espoused him without revealing her unchaste past, she was guilty of high treason. Furthermore, if the queen or the wife of the prince of Wales were to "move by writing or message or token persons to have carnal knowledge of them or someone to procure the same," then the queen, the wife of the prince, or the procurer was to be guilty of high treason. Finally, any subject who failed to report to the council or the king any knowledge of "lightness of body" of the queen was to be punished with the same penalties as the actual offender. The act did not try to construe the cuckolding of the king as in some way endangering his health and thus his life, nor as leading to bodily ailment as in the case of Anne Boleyn; it seems to have ignored the principles that had guided prior legislation.[33]

The legislation propagated by the Henrician Parliaments is striking for its lack of precedents: the construction of treason used in the trial of Anne Boleyn; the attainder act against Katherine Howard; and the general act concerning the moral conduct of royal brides, which was joined to it, were without substantial precedent. Nonetheless, they were part of a sustained pattern of making new laws that runs throughout the century. In general, the Tudor era is distinguished by "the large amount of legislation which concerned itself with [treason]. Between 1485 and 1603 . . . there were no fewer than sixty-eight treason statutes enacted, though there had been less than ten in the period 1352–1485."[34] The proliferation is variously attributed to new forms of royal concern over the succession; anxiety about the monarch's ecclesiastical supremacy; reluctance of rulers to trust judicial constructions of existing statutes; and fears of social mobility associated with slippages in traditional hierarchy. Yet the large number of acts did not necessarily imply a ruler's success in enforcing the reach of law. How the law was interpreted—in indictments, in trials, in informal and formal comments by judges, justices, ministers, and defendants—was as important as any statute in making treason.

Side-by-side with the proliferation of laws was the development of another category of treason, common law treason. According to Bellamy, Mary I's judges delved into the past and discovered "for the first time in that century" this new source of law. The exemplary trial was Nicholas Throckmorton's in 1554. Throckmorton was accused of compassing to deprive the queen of her crown and dignity and destroy her, and to take the Tower of London and levy war against her. Though adhering to the queen's enemies or destroying her were treason under prevailing law, compassing to levy war was not. According to Holinshed, who recounts the trial in some detail, Throckmorton challenged the authority of the indictment on the basis that it relied on statutes that had been repealed; only the 1352 Edwardian statute applied, he argued. But Sergeant Stanford answered for the Crown that "there doth remain divers other treasons at this day at the common law, which be not expressed by that statute, as the judges can declare." Because it was not mentioned by the Edwardian statute, Stanford reasoned, common law treason—which Stanford implied predated the 1352 statute—survived and covered crimes not specifically stated in legislation.[35]

The phrase that drew me to this project—"imaginary practices"—was included in the charges repeated during the proceedings against the youthful defendants in the Babington trials of 1586. It also identifies more generally what attracted me as a literary scholar to the crime of treason: its position as an aspect of the imagination. Defined as a function of imagination, treason participates in the contestatory relations that characterize the stage and the political arena as sites of ideological production.[36]

The Edwardian emphasis on "imagining" had created the legal space for new conceptions of patriotic or treacherous character, the former founded on an ideal of intellectual and emotional unity, the latter on a notion of subjective dualism. The true citizen of England was the loyal, integrated subject whose imaginings were understood to issue directly in "honest" and observable actions; continuity between an honest heart and a speaking body was assumed. In contrast, the traitor was a disintegrated dissembler whose behavior was not to be taken at face value, but as a mask for a buried, criminal self, in which "Rank corruption, mining all within / Infects unseen."[37] Whether cast in terms of contests between madness and reason, personal conscience and public confession, or an inward and an outward self, the errant history of treason trials is also a history of competing notions of subjectivity.[38]

This proliferation of selves was cause enough for legal intervention: the law claimed the territory of "imaginings" as its field of investigation, claiming to penetrate the intent of the accused. Richard Firth Green has recently shown that thoughts and intentions first began to come under legal scrutiny specifically in treason rather than felony cases. Although in the fourteenth and fifteenth centuries judges were refusing to consider a would-be felon's thoughts, they were quite willing to try a traitor's: "if a man imagines the death of the king, and does nothing more, he shall be drawn, hung, and disembowelled," said Justice Newton in 1441.[39] At the trial of the Duke of Buckingham in 1521 Chief Justice Fineux stated that between felony and treason there was a clear difference: there could be no felony without some act done, but merely to intend the king's death was high treason and such intention was proven by words alone.[40] At the trial of Sir Thomas More in 1535, the king's attorney general argued that "even though we should have no word or deed to charge upon you, yet we have your silence, and that is a sign of your evil intention and a sure proof of malice."[41] Writing for the popular audience in the 1580s, Holinshed expressed a similar understanding of the crime:

> Oh with what severitie did the ancients punish offenses of this nature! And not without cause. For besides that nothing is more usual in all the whole scriptures, than prohibition to kill or to seek the life or honor, not only of the prince, but also of inferior magistrates, although they be wicked . . . so is it provided by the laws of nations, that not only he that hath killed his sovereign, but he also that made the attempt, that gave counsel, that yielded consent, that conceived the thought, is guilty of high treason.[42]

Defined as transgressive imagining, and focused on exposing the hidden intent of the accused, treason necessarily encounters the problem and affords itself the privilege of characterizing and exposing a subject's interior. In cases where a crime left material traces, such as coining or faulty cloth-making, we might assume (wrongly, I would argue) that establishing evidence was a relatively straightforward matter because proof was embedded in an object. But without material evidence, where no discernable action may have occurred, how were jurists to prove outlawed behavior? What a trial set out to prove it also presupposed and produced: the self-estrangement of the accused. The task of trial participants was to overcome the obstacle of invisible action; in Edward Coke's terms during the trial of Sir Walter Ralegh in 1603, the goal was to "make [the crime] appear to the world" as self-declaring in two senses[43]:

it must appear so obvious as to seem irrefutable, and it must reveal a hidden self that was both different from the observable self and against the law.

In practice, however, this semiotics of the heart was as variable and troublesome as the social and political bases from which it took its meanings. Evidentiary uncertainties were prevalent in the recurring debates throughout the century over requirements for and number of witnesses, and they were compounded by the Tudor historical habit of not distinguishing clearly between witness and accuser. After Henry's death, the first Edwardian act (1 Edw. VI c. 12) required the accusation of two "lawful and sufficient witnesses" or the suspect's own confession for indictment, arraignment, or conviction for treason; it did not say if the witnesses were necessary in person at the arraignment or if their testimony could be presented in writing, that is, in an "examination," which was one of the conventional forms of witnessing. The second Edwardian act (5 & 6 Edw. VI c. 11) demanded two "accusers" (they were not called witnesses), but said more clearly that they should be brought face to face with the accused at the arraignment and maintain the charge stated in the indictment. The first Marian treason act (1 M. st. 1 c. 1) omitted any mention of witnesses at all. Two Elizabethan statutes (13 Eliz. c.1 and 23 Eliz. c.2) specified that two accuser-witnesses were necessary for a treason conviction, but another in 1585 (27 Eliz. c.2) specifically waived that requirement for indictments against Catholics.[44] Court authorities had the right during trials to specify the statute on which proceedings rested; often they strengthened their cases by deciding in favor of the 1352 Edwardian statute, which did not mention witnesses.

Also contradictory were the interpretations of the "overt act" necessary for proving treason: to what, exactly, were the accusers or witnesses testifying? The 1352 act did not require an overt deed for imagining or compassing the king's death, but it did require an overt act for adhering to the king's enemies or giving them comfort.[45] A 1460 act formally recognized that words were the equivalent of an overt deed, a change that influences the form of treason indictments. Formerly, indictments had given a description of a crime followed by a statement that it amounted to compassing the king's death. After 1460, indictments adopted a formula: "*A* had imagined to destroy the king, . . . and to attain that end had committed *X*, *Y*, and *Z*, which were clearly specified acts," including merely speaking or listening to words.[46] As we saw earlier, a further change in what constituted an act came with Henrician legislation in 1534 (26 Hen. VIII c. 13), which included spoken words along with written or printed words as deeds that in themselves could constitute treason. Words, then, might be the crime or they might be evidence of the crime in any given prosecution. What these trials illuminate is that in Tudor legal practice, what counted as an "overt act" was unpredictable and frequently turned on reports one had listened to seditious talk, read suspect books, written lost letters, or spoken one's mind.[47]

Often what was to be proved in these trials of the imagination was less that one had *done* something than that one had *thought* something, although neither act was understood as wholly separable from the other. Commenting on the Babington treasons of 1586, Holinshed explained:

> There is no action but hath his original intention, no intention but issueth from a premeditation, no premeditation but proceedeth from a conceipt: all these concurring with their accessaries, make a complete action. . . . And therefore let men take heed how they give place to a wicked thought, much more to a mischeefous deed.[48]

Undoubtedly the search for inwardness, or the interpretation of its signs, was aggravated by the loose evidentiary rules of the lawcourt. Moreover, since the thing to be proved was an idea or act of intellection, rhetorical strategies weighed heavily in the courtroom.[49] Over and over, what we find in treason trials are signs of rhetorical and social instability and along with those signs, the deliberate production of evidence, including a credible story, as a social and epistemological anchor.[50]

For every apparently "self-evident" case, such as Essex's riding through the streets of London toward the queen in 1601 with drawn sword, there were many in which the incident and its evidence were the object of heated interpretive contests. What counted as persuasive evidence in a particular trial or from one trial to another was variable and unpredictable, and was argued again and again during proceedings. In the attainder of Katherine Howard (1542), for example, a centerpiece of testimony was a "privy mark" on Howard's body; in the trials of Anthony Babington and his comrades (1586), it was the authority of precedents and presence of witnesses; in the trial of Mary, Queen of Scots (1586), it was the authenticity of a packet of encrypted letters; and in the trial of Walter Ralegh (1603), it was the legitimacy of words as evidence. In every case the means of making the crime materialize were rhetorical, and proof was contingent on the effective use of language in a particular situation. Yet the truth-value of speech was itself uncertain, a topic of disagreement in the culture at large and often explicitly contested in trials.

Protestant ideology had circulated beyond itself the notion that truth and plain-speaking were identical. According to Martin Luther, truth seized people's minds: "the mind is so laid hold of by the truth itself, that, by virtue of that truth, it is able to reach certainty in any judgment. . . . The fact is that, rather than being itself the judge, the mind has been taken captive, and has accepted a verdict pronounced by the Truth herself sitting on the tribunal."[51] This theory of plain-spoken truth extended outside the church to political writing, in which claims to plainness *are* claims to truth, to its self-authenticating nature (people recognize it as familiar) and to its implicit appeal to a higher authority. In *The Performance of Conviction*, Kenneth J. E. Graham cites Dudley Fenner's hope in 1588 that "the simple playnes" of *The Artes of Logike and Rethorike* will "drawe men to no curiouse or doubtfull discourses, but onely put them in minde of that which they may easilie seeke and knowe in most familiar examples with great fruit and delight." Truth, Graham points out, is what everyone already knows.[52] Some legal theorists continued to assume the truth-value of speech in revealing the hidden heart: Sir Thomas Egerton pronounced during the Babington trials that "Whoso is guiltless will speak truly and directly, but the counterfeit must speak untruths."[53] Prosecutors, however, typically posited a gap between the speech of the accused and a truth embedded in his or her deviant heart, and proceeded to create suspicion by associating verbal skill with deception. During the Ralegh prosecution, for example, Coke turned Ralegh's rhetorical skill into a sign of guilt and discredited his "wit" as political cunning: "Oh, sir! . . . I know with whom I deal," Coke declaimed, "for we have to deal to-day with a man of wit."[54]

The credibility of witnesses was also complicated by the early modern habit of conflating economic with evidentiary value. "The equation of wealth and worth was effected through reputation," writes Susan Amussen.

> The key concept in this process was "credit." The term is ambiguous: from its Latin root meaning "to believe" comes its use in court testimony referring to the truthfulness of witnesses; but it had also long been used in trade, where letters of credit assured merchants of buyers' ability to pay. By the late sixteenth century "credit" described both honesty and solvency; wealth and virtue were joined. Thus, in 1580 Margaret Guybon said in Bury St. Edmunds that John Smythe "was of no more credit than one that was in the alms house."[55]

The term "credit" was sometimes used with conscious ambiguity, as in this testimony in 1617:

> Susan Wylie is a woman of single ability and dwelleth upon the Common and liveth partly by her own industry and partly by the relief of her neighbours. And such a one as is of very small credit or estimation and one to whom very little or no credit is to be given to her testimony.[56]

Confirmed by the additional attribution of literacy, credit and reputation reinforced each other as modes of distinguishing among the perceived worth of witnesses' testimonies.[57] In many cases, legal decisions turned on such things as the relative "trustworthiness" of the participants and on the "impression" they made on a jury. "No jury, however, tried cases in a social vacuum; character was a composite of social position and demeanor. What a jury saw in the behavior of a defendant reflected its expectations of what was appropriate to a specific person."[58]

These social and rhetorical variables contribute to the epistemological uncertainty that characterizes trials. Typically trial narratives address this uncertainty through a strategy of revelation: adopting a form that suggests an accommodation between providential and skeptical humanist theories, they represent human intervention as the agency of divine will or unpredictable chance. The pervasive logic was tied up with perceptions of God's plans for England. After the collapse of the Wyatt rebellion against Mary in 1554, for example, John Christopherson in his *Exhortation to all menne to take hede and beware of rebellion* (1554) drew the clear conclusion: if the queen "had been an adversary of His truth and of His holy word," God "would never have so aided her" in discovering the plot.[59] In addition, trial texts register the developing legal protocols, which were themselves coming under fire. Michel Foucault lays out the relations between disciplinary protocols and "truth": "Within its own limits," he writes, a particular discipline "recognizes true and false propositions" and repels whole other taxonomies of learning according to whether the propositions "fit into a certain type of theoretical field." A proposition may be *dans le vrai*, "within the true," but it will not be recognized as "true" until it fulfills preconditions specific to its disciplinary situation.[60] In legal practice, "truth" comes into visibility because of the procedures and contexts that define it. It rests on the sort of equivocal base formulated by Thomas Hobbes: "*True* and *False* are attributes of Speech, not of things. And where Speech is not, there is neither *Truth* nor *Falshood*. *Errour* there may be."[61] Within this thoroughly rhetorical framework, appeals to "what really happened" are no more nor less persuasive in themselves than any other linguistic maneuvers.[62] Achieved in rhetoric, justice is not only a social abstraction but also the product of a narrative, a belief in the certainty or probability of something. Like other narrative effects, it is vulnerable to mutations and appropriations over time.

Early modern Britons were avid consumers of legal stories in oral and written forms. Although the precise composition of audiences for these stories remains elusive, it is likely that it included groups interested in both old and new thinking, lawyers and law students, gentry with business interests in London, the greater gentry, well-to-do citizens and merchants, and the greater nobility. To these we must also add the playwrights and other writers of the period, who repeatedly people their works with characters drawn from legal practice and who find in trials considerable dramatic material. It seems equally likely that such a diverse group would not be of the same opinion, orthodox or subversive, about the issues raised in any one case. Whatever the challenges in establishing the composition of the audience, we do know that written, oral, and ceremonial forms of legal practices were circulating among a varied and variously interested audience.[63]

Throughout the sixteenth century, emerging legal discourses were also available more and more widely to official and unofficial readerships in the form of a new written genre: the law report. Sparked by the rise of the legal profession, the second half of the century saw an enormous increase in the printing of law books. Each new generation of lawyers made their own copybooks, and there was a thriving group of professional writers and scriveners of law manuscripts.[64] Coke recognized this popular interest when in the *Institutes* he defined the law report as

> a publike relation, or a bringing againe to memory cases judicially argued, debated, resolved, or adjudged in any of the king's courts of justice, together with such causes and reasons as were delivered by the judges of the same.[65]

In Coke's description, law reports offer a memorial reconstruction ("a bringing againe to memory") of the important events in the nation's legal history and help rationalize (in "causes and reasons") the form that reconstruction takes. Like the chronicle histories they parallel, the law reports did not remain formally fixed. As the legal profession changed, the law reports changed, responding to and influencing their authors' individual or collective sense of social order. Throughout the history of the genre, the very idea of "report" included selective adaptation and emphasis. They were understood not as records in the narrow sense of repetitions of all that was said, but as registers of selectivity, in which particular political themes and national values came into prominence. Discourses of a developing national identity, the law reports provided a range of stories about how England might legitimately view and discipline itself.

The earliest Tudor Yearbooks were economical documents that outlined fundamental issues, generally listing the complainants' names, the legal question, and the judgment. Eventually, "private" law reports, based on notes taken by anonymous students at the Inns of Court, superseded the Yearbooks. These private reports swiftly became public and circulated in printed and manuscript forms. And along with this increasing public circulation came changes in style among individual reporters, particularly a tendency toward summarizing all sides of a judicial argument that marks Edmund Plowden's touchstone of sixteenth-century reporting, the *Commentaries*.[66]

With Plowden's death in 1585, the formative phase of law reporting ended. Yet during "the last fifteen years of the century a striking increase occurred in the number of practitioner-reporters and the volumes they produced: fully two-thirds of the surviving manuscripts so far discovered which relate to the Tudor period cover the years from 1575–1603."[67] Rather than reading like coherent codifications, these texts reveal a spirit of flexible inquiry, conjecture, and imaginative scope at the heart of legal thinking about any subject under adjudication:

> Subjects as diverse as the authenticity of Henry VIII's sign manual and the impounding of a copyholder's livestock, Queen Mary's "pregnancy" and the depredations of mice upon court records, and Queen Elizabeth's use of "etc." in the royal title and whether peacocks were classified as domestic animals— all basked equally in the light of judicial scrutiny.[68]

The reports generally concentrated on land-law cases, which were crucial markers of a subject's traditional liberties. Other kinds of cases also appeared, however, involving parliamentary privilege, majority principle of election, and royal supremacy—as did a description of Anne Boleyn's treason trial that was later cited by Coke, and an extract detailing "the manner and attendance of the Judges at the Coronation of Queen Anne."[69]

The personal opinions registered in reports varied widely, and informal opinions of respected men were sought and recorded. The colloquial readily passed into legal authority. Cases were disputed at various informal sites, especially what came to be called "checker chamber cases," which were suits referred from other courts to the Exchequer for resolution. Wherever lawyers gathered, they put cases to each other, developing and extending the practice of arguing suits and issues beyond the confines of the formal hearing. Among the judicial and extrajudicial sites where legal opinions were often recorded were the two Serjeants' Inns, William Cecil's lodgings, the Holborn Inns, the Inns of Court and Chancery, the chambers of the Chief Justices, and London taverns. In what became known as "table cases" in taverns, "judges and serjeants utilized mealtimes at their hostels to debate current issues."[70]

The conventions of legal reporting reveal a genre committed not to some ideal of empirical accuracy, but to a notion of truth that is selectively shaped. Plowden, who opined that "there are few arguments so pure as not to have refuse in them," operated by selectivity in explaining and reporting significant legal opinions:

> I have for the most part reported cases in a summary way, collecting together the substance . . . of all that was said on one side and on the other, and oftentimes of all that was said by the judges themselves, without reciting their arguments verbatim.[71]

He condensed arguments (telling the reader he had omitted material); included considerations of how to deal with the growing legal conundrums of intention and interpretation of statutes; inserted personal annotations and glosses within the body of various reports; and acknowledged the problem of inscribing what one had heard in oral arguments. If he were unable to be present at a particular pleading, Plowden relied on the report of one who was present.[72]

Describing his own *Reports* as "in the nature of Commentaries," Coke regarded himself as the successor to Plowden, the "one learned & grave man" who first revived the art of reporting.[73] Like Plowden, Coke supplemented his notes by means of "credible relation of others" and conferred with his colleagues to substantiate or discredit a controversial judgment. He advised students to check their work against official records, believing that "taking by ear that which was spoken in court was . . . 'a dangerous kind of reporting.'"[74] Yet Coke also believed, like Plowden, that it was appropriate to alter arguments so long as the "sense and intent" were retained.[75] In Coke's reports, which focused on opinions from the bench, the pronouncements of judges were the heart of the law, and speeches of counsel were often omitted altogether.

Although the primary readers of the law reports would have been lawyers and justices, the sustained appearance of multiple editions suggests a wider audience. Moreover, law reports were not the only genre that transmitted legal stories. Holinshed's *Chronicles of England, Scotland, and Ireland*, for example, which circulated widely late in the century, represented in writing the many oral and ceremonial practices that recapitulated crucial trials and executions. Holinshed reprinted ballads and verses that often followed on arrests or punishments, and included lengthy representations of such celebrated treasons as those of Throckmorton, the Babington conspirators and Mary, Queen of Scots.[76] In her detailed analysis of the Throckmorton trial, Annabel Patterson argues that Holinshed's work educated the public about legal matters:

> not only does the mere presence of the trial in the *Chronicles* serve an educational function, the making of knowledgeable citizens and future jurors; but the reader is explicitly directed to that very source of knowledge of the law that Throckmorton's judges wanted to withhold, the "bookes of the statutes" printed in English, which

had been appearing both annually and in collections, usually beginning with Magna Carta, from the end of the fifteenth century.[77]

Manuals and handbooks also played a part in the popular circulation of law as a vernacular. Wilson's *Arte of Rhetorique*, for example, turns throughout to prosecutions for manslaughter, murder, and treasonous rebellion as the best vehicles for demonstrating rhetorical skill.

What all this suggests is an interested public for whom legal stories were provocative representations of both the legal and the story. Among legal writers, Coke, a common lawyer devoted to indigenous English case law, contributed most substantially to representations of the moral character and authority of the law practitioner himself, linking homegrown morality to the understanding of law. No man of "a loose and lawless life," wrote Coke, ever gained a sound knowledge of the law; those who did achieve such proficiency were invariably "honest, faithful and virtuous."[78]

It is to figures of "a loose and lawless life"—Katherine Howard, Anthony Babington, and Mary, Queen of Scots—that this study in part attends.[79] All were convicted of treason between 1542 and 1587; all were executed for their crimes against the realm.[80] The Howard attainder, embedded in an unprecedented legal situation in which a monarch supports his marriages by exploiting treason laws, marks an early event in the developing gender ideology that would fix women as repositories of secret sexuality. The Babington treasons, which occur at the culmination of a decades-long struggle to dispose of Mary Stuart, represent the deepest known extent of government intrusion into the creation of evidence, the clearest case of the role of forgery in the fabrication of evidence, and the specific challenge of male friendship to political allegiance. The Scots trial, in which a deposed queen is repositioned as a subject of a foreign land, has been noted for its historical significance. But what has been discussed less are the means by which Mary is represented—in letters and in sonnets—as both transcendent "absolute queen" and earthbound femme fatale.

Although the historical position of these figures in a single criminal category might suggest they shared a political view, their similarity is as much an effect of a flexible legal designation as of shared dissent. Despite being attainted of treason, and despite the legal linking of Babington with Mary, no two of these figures were accused of having committed the same act. Katherine Howard was found guilty of having had sexual relations before she met and married a king. Anthony Babington (and twelve cohorts) were found guilty of "having met and conferred" about what England might be if it were not ruled by Elizabeth. Mary was found guilty of plotting the death of her cousin, Elizabeth. The law of treason positioned each of these figures as a fearsome border-dweller; each, in turn, required the crown to reinterpret political and geographical boundaries. Perhaps that was among the most serious crimes each committed: by imagining another England, each made visible the arbitrariness of positions that the Crown strove to make appear natural.

Before turning to the trials and plays that are my main focus, I want to pause initially to bring into more prominence the imaginative bases of legal practice. In many literary-legal studies, two things have traditionally escaped notice: first, the activities and influence of the Inns of Court, where court-centered authority was contested sufficiently to prompt Henry VIII to complain about the Inns and to prompt Elizabeth to try to shut them down. And second, the central pedagogical practice, mooting, through which law was taught not as a uniform code nor (and perhaps more importantly) as a reaction to real events, but as a ritual performance and challenge to the imagination. Chapter 1 explores the conditions under which aspiring benchers were called upon to display their developing skills and qualifications by acting out conjectural cases that were drawn typically from laws of property. These, Charles Henry McIlwain explains, were also the laws of "franchises or 'liberties,' of personal status, of public office, and of much more besides."[81] It is to that "much more besides" that I want to attend. The England of moot cases, like the England of treason trials and plays, is subject to continuous challenge and refashioning by would-be proprietors. Holding the soil in place—making it English—is the purpose of mooting.

Chapter 2 introduces the first of my prosecutions, that of Katherine Howard, which turns on the sexually-marked issue of female incontinency and its exposure. The fifth of Henry VIII's wives, Howard was attainted of treason in 1542 for allegedly having had sexual relations with two men before she married. The proceedings formulate uncertainties among epistemology, secrecy, and truth in terms of a dualism between woman's apparent and secret fidelities. As it develops narrative and rhetorical strategies for revealing the "truth" about women's infidelities, the attainder implies a theory of place in which personal identity characterizes space.

Like the Howard story, and written while the attainder was still fresh in memory, Nicholas Udall's *Ralph Roister Doister* (c. 1550–53) relies on a teleology of marriage in crafting its representation of women's domestic life. What was clandestine frolic in the attainder, however, is purged from Udall's work. The play reinstates and revises the representation of an all female household, constructing a narrowed moral biography for its marriage-bound heroine, Custance. The Howard attainder makes its truth claims by doing what legal practice characteristically does, suppressing the notion that proof is something made. In such a logic, what a woman "is," like murder, will out. In contrast, Udall's play finds that knowing the truth about Custance is contingent on male testimony. Here, what a woman "is" will be found in what her husband believes. Much later Shakespeare's *Cymbeline* (c. 1608) again focuses on knowing female fidelity. It claims to tell the truth about Imogen through what appears to be yet another strategy, by unsettling the fictions that generate the "unfaithful woman." When a penitent Iachimo belatedly confesses to having produced only "simular proof" of Imogen's infidelity, he explicates one of the play's central points: proof is a feigned, mimetic version of things. What is true about woman, Shakespeare suggests, cannot be discovered or represented by testimony or report.

In Chapter 3, beleaguered masculinity emerges into competition in trials and plays that enact a process of differentiating among men, of producing what will count as the English man, and of presenting the kind of manhood the law will recognize as belonging to true subjects of the realm. In 1586, the Crown accused Anthony Babington and twelve confederates of plotting with the Spanish to invade England, assassinate Elizabeth, and see Mary of Scotland enthroned. As the trials develop, codes of courtiership mediate testimonies in which male friendship is made to signify the priority of personal companionship and a challenge to political loyalty. At issue legally is the long-held and highly variable status of what had been known as *diffidatio*, the right of a retainer to renounce his allegiance to a ruler without penalty. For the Babington conspirators, however, allegiance is ultimately recast into images of promiscuous travel, and their rootlessness comes to signify internal infidelity.

Like treason trials in general, and like the Babington trials in particular, Christopher Marlowe stages conflicts over loyalty in terms of disputed conceptions of "the country." Recent studies show that Marlowe was among the spies commissioned by Francis Walsingham to infiltrate the Catholics at Cambridge following the exposure of the Babington plot. The earliest of his plays, *Tamburlaine I* (c.1587–88), may have been drafted while he was among those confederates. The play suggests that in discourses of treason, male friendship is superior to other forms of affiliation and is the bond from which new nations are made. On the side of those who renounce their former allegiance, Marlowe's work glorifies what the Babington prosecutors fear: that fidelity to male friends will triumph over fidelity to "the country."

Chapter 4 explores the question of the letter and its relationship to theories of identity. According to the infamous Elizabethan commission that accused her, Mary Stuart had plotted with Anthony Babington in 1586 to see herself enthroned. There is no doubt Mary had been a thorn in Elizabeth's side, and she had served as the motive for rumored treasons throughout her stay in England. What distinguishes the Scots case, however, and what most interests me is the particular form of the evidence: a packet of cryptic letters. Implicated in a larger social discourse on the metaphysics and meanings of writing, the Scots trial is the exemplary epistolary treason. The status of the documents—letters written in cipher, written by secretaries, and intercepted and amended with forged insertions—is a vexed issue, and their authenticity and authorship form the centerpiece of a sustained evidentiary struggle. As the written self is set against the embodied, speaking self as the source of truth, the Scots attainder concludes that no matter how many structures mediate a secret self, ultimately *in letters*, it "will appear to the world," to return to Coke's formulation.

The unsettled principles of epistolary interpretation are also central in Thomas Kyd's *The Spanish Tragedy*, which may have been written soon after the Scots proceedings. Through Bel-imperia's letters, Kyd brings into focus questions about the evidentiary force of written words. Kyd's play probes the meanings of circulating, intercepting, and authenticating documents, as the playwright ties those meanings to conceptions of secret interiority and mutating fidelity. Like the trial, the play offers complex views of an unsettled competitive relationship between writing and selfhood, between letters and persons as sites of knowledge. In Kyd's work, the material self is less authoritative than the scripted self, and the play suggests an increasing Tudor tendency to abstract the inner subject and to externalize her in writing.

Reading these treasons and dramas together, my purpose is not, like that of one strong strain of critical legal studies, to expose the flawed fiction of objectivity at the heart of the law.[82] We cannot "cleanse" the law of its rhetorical and social biases, because those biases are indigenous to its way of being both language and law. Instead, I write as a literary scholar whose issue is (again in Douglas's apt phrase) cultural bias, those ideologically-invested predispositions of thought and act that emerge into visibility in the desperate imaginings of early modern betrayers and players and in the stories by which we know them and ourselves.[83]

1.

"Fugitive Forms": Imagining the Realm

Michel Foucault's generalization that power acts by concealing itself, and that one of its historically persistent masks is the law, has contributed to a tendency in one strain of literary studies to identify early modern legal practices with the interests of court-centered power and political absolutism.[1] In emphasizing court-centered authority, however, these accounts overlook the activities of the Inns of Court. Yet the Inns were perceived as influential sites where law, though not made, was shaped, and where the sway of the monarch might be challenged by the influence of subjects. According to legal historian J. H. Baker, "the law . . . was not confined to pronouncements in court, but was what common lawyers in general believed it to be." This pattern of influence was sufficient to cause Henry VIII to complain about the Inns and to prompt Elizabeth to try to shut them down.[2] Under Elizabeth, judges, who had often considered moot cases in making decisions, acquired increased autonomy from the opinions born in law schools, until "by 1573 the judges had the last word."[3] What the history of the Inns tells us is that relations between their speculative legal work and court-centered pronouncements had long been characterized by competition and conflict.

One side of the competition was represented by the central pedagogical practice—mooting or reading—through which law was taught not as a self-interpreting code nor as a reaction to real events, but as an evocation of the imagination and as a ritual performance. What was it about mooting that made it so troublesome? Cases focused on "a specific problem with hypothetical facts—upon which the question would be framed."[4] The avowed purpose of mooting was to "preserve and elaborate the common learning concerning real property,"[5] and aspiring benchers were called upon to display their developing skills and qualifications by acting out conjectural cases. In this association between learning law and transmitting property, mooting ritualized and emphasized the crucial issue of proprietorship. Certainly these law performances promulgated official monarchical lines. Yet moots were constructed in ways that also admitted other, less constrained interpretations, opening out the conceptual borders of the land to a range of possible meanings. As law teachers conveyed legal principles through extensive discussions of cases that were "sometimes real, sometimes imaginary," the purpose of judicial playing became calling to mind exceptions to traditional frames of reference.[6]

What is striking is that before they settle their issues, these legal inventions, which Baker identifies as "fugitive forms of literature," require the disputants to deliberate a wide range of imaginary, anomalous events. In what we might call an ideology of legal reassurance, moots anticipate threats to laws, process those threats through imaginative discourse, and redefine them as contained within laws. In the process, these imaginative practices introduce into circulation elusive ideas—ideas about affiliations among kin, about sexuality and its management, and about the sudden liquidity of a homeland—that are not wholly contained by the discourse that elicited them. Late in their history, this sense that moots might obscure as much as they illuminated appeared in contemporary commentary. In the estimation of Francis Bacon, himself a resident of the Inns during the sixteenth century, the most visible effect of mooting by the late Tudor era was to cloud rather than to shed light on legal principles. Contrasting what he imagined to have been a superior, objective, ancient practice with that of his own day, Bacon determined

> to revive and recontinue the ancient form of [mooting], . . . being of less ostentation and more fruit than the manner lately accustomed; for the use then was substantially to expound the statutes by grounds and diversities; as you shall find the [mooting] still to run upon case of like law, and contrary law; whereof the one includes the learning of a ground, the other the learning of a difference; and not to stir concise and subtle doubts, or to contrive a multitude of tedious and intricate cases, whereof all, saving one, are buried, and the greater part of that one case, which is taken, is commonly nothing to the matter in hand; but my labour shall be in the ancient course, to open the law upon doubts, and not to open doubts upon this law.[7]

As Bacon frames it, the practice of mooting had shifted from its early, noble end of illuminating the "grounds and diversities" of a reliable, self-evident law, to its late Elizabethan ignoble end of obscuring and undermining that law. Serious consideration had been supplanted by spurious quibbling and gratuitous displays of intellectual gymnastics, a view widely dispersed in popular culture in parodies such as Shakespeare's Dogberry in *Much Ado About Nothing* or Touchstone in *As You Like It*.

An assertion that writers for the stage were involved in an imaginative enterprise needs no arguing. A complementary argument, however, does need making: like dramatists, lawmen—and by that term we should cast our net widely to include most every well-born man in England—were habitually involved in growing "in effect another nature" in the practice of mooting. This routine practice invited a wide range of Englishmen to compete with each other and with the government in envisioning themselves the legitimate proprietors of the realm. The many ways men who read the law exercised great influence on English political life has been well documented, and "in an age when almost every gentleman could expect to be involved in one or more often protracted legal cases, familiarity with the fundamentals of law was inevitable among England's ruling classes."[8] What I want to explore here are the ways these men exercised great influence on English imaginative and ideological life by putting into discourse notions that recur in treasons and plays throughout the century. Residency in the Inns of Court ensured exchanges among members of legal and theatrical disciplines, and the practices of mooting and reveling encouraged innsmen to think of themselves as the proprietors of the realm and to secure their visions by thinking of themselves as outside the law. As those habits of mind migrated, legal talk became part of the vernacular.

Mooting emerged as an identifiable practice in the Inns late in the fourteenth century; it enjoyed its heyday during the decades from 1450 to 1550; it persisted throughout the late sixteenth and early seventeenth centuries; and it slowly faded until its curtailment in 1642.[9] Attempts to revive the practice in 1660 failed, and it never recovered its former importance as a site where doctrine was performed, fabricated, and challenged.[10] At its end, "the age-old obligation to moot [had been] commuted to cash payment."[11] Intellectual currency had mutated into coin, and the bencher, whose very designation insisted that he have his bottom firmly planted on English oak, had become the paid advocate, whose affiliations might shift as readily as two pence changed hands—a metamorphosis bitterly dramatized in Jonson's *Volpone* by the advocate Voltore, a "mercenary tongue" who "For six sols more would plead against his Maker."[12]

The basic structure of moots included four parts: 1) the problem; 2) the question arising from the problem; 3) the disputation, arguments pro and contra; and 4) the solution, any authoritative answer or ruling given by the teacher.[13] According to Baker, the mooters' typical method was to list copious examples to illustrate the subject. The more, and the more comprehensive the examples, the better. Thus, we find cases beginning:

Someone makes a bond to two women; one of them marries an outlaw; the day [of payment] arrives; the husband dies; the escheator obtains the deed.

Or:

A man and a single woman carry off the goods of an abbot; the man marries the same woman; the abbot gives all his goods to the husband; the abbot commits a felony for which he is attainted, and another is elected [in his place].

Or:

Someone makes a bond to another man and a single woman in £20, on condition that if he pays £10 at a certain day the bond will be void; the person who made the bond marries the same woman; the man to whom the bond was made appoints his executors, enters into religion, and is professed.[14]

Baker concludes that there was no necessary relationship between the events represented in moots and their probability of occurring in social life: "It does not seem to have mattered too much whether they were examples ever likely to be met with in the real world, though of course the law teacher's most unlikely academic fantasies have a habit of coming true." Their purpose was "to exercise the mind" by showing how legal principles might work in hypothetical situations.[15]

In *Purity and Danger*, Mary Douglas reminds us that diverse cultures perceive different things as dangerous and react dissimilarly to those perceptions.[16] Both the perception of danger and its solution, according to Douglas, are effects of "cultural bias."[17] What is the "bias" of these legal tales? Like other fictions, specific moots advance plots, suggest character (typically in archetypal terms), arrange space, and develop imaginative landscapes. What do they perceive as the dangers to which laws must respond?

Two often-repeated, classic cases serve as my examples of the England imagined in moots. In each, the central story turns on disturbances to the smooth transmission of land. In order to preserve the distinctive flavor of these imaginary cases, I quote one here at length:

Two brothers, who are villeins, purchase jointly certain land to which an advowson is appendant; the lord enters and leases the same land with the appurtenances to the two of them to hold in villeinage; the elder brother dies, his wife being secretly pregnant; the lord marries the same woman, who is delivered of a son and dies; the lord takes another wife and dies, his wife being secretly pregnant; the younger brother marries the same woman, who has a son, and then the wife dies; he takes another wife, who is pregnant by him before the espousals; the husband dies; the woman is delivered of two twin sons, namely Jacob and Esau; the elder brother's son enters in one moiety, and the three sons in the other moiety, but the attendancy is made to the elder

> brother's son; the three sons enter and make partition among themselves; the [elder] twin son grants what belongs to him and what belongs to his younger brother to an abbot, unto him and his successors; the lord's son brings a writ of right of advowson against him, and after the mise joined he is nonsuited; then the elder twin son enters into religion in the same abbey; the abbot is deposed, and he is elected abbot; then the church becomes vacant; the abbot presents; and he is hindered by the three. Etc. Discuss.[18]

No matter where he intervenes in this case, the mootman enters a long line of memorializing. There is in this depiction, as Glenn Clark has written in another context, "no natural, nonsocialized geography with which to start."[19] Representing a privileged spatial practice, the moot ensures uninterrupted transmission of property by offering verbal sequence as temporal continuity. In this, moots as a genre resemble the popular chronicle histories contemporary with them: organized by temporal sequence and divided into units that represent the ownership of successive husband-fathers, moots tell the histories of the commonwealth in its analogous form of the family.

Entitled "Jacob and Esau," this moot takes its name from the narrative in Genesis in which Esau sold his birthright to his younger twin, Jacob, who became father of the twelve tribes of Israel.[20] It depicts the siblings as rivals, and the rivalry rests on the relationship between birthright and changes in land possession. The recurring legal issue underwriting this pattern here and in moots more generally, is the feudal distinction in inheritance between fee simple and fee tail. Fee simple describes a freehold estate of virtually infinite duration; inheritance is free from conditions, limitations, or restrictions to particular heirs. In contrast, fee tail identifies a conveyance created by a deed or will to a person and "the heirs of his body" specifically. A fee tail establishes a fixed line of inheritable succession and may cut off the regular succession of heirs. It is a limited estate in that inheritance is through lineal descent only, though this can be either male or female (fee tail male, fee tail female). In fee tail, if the family line ends (failure of issue), the fee reverts to the grantor, that is, the person who granted the property initially, or his successors.[21]

What interests me is the stories moots have to tell. "Jacob and Esau" is a particularly competitive vision, one in which alliances shift swiftly, even among brothers, and devotions dissolve one into another. The genre teaches an expectation: that the land will be contested, that there will be conflicting claims to proprietorship. In this, it is an anticipatory genre, predictive and prophetic: there *will* be challenges to a subject's holding property in perpetuity. Where is the subject to look for those challenges? Most often, conflict comes not from outside figures but from those within the family or within members of one's own class. In anticipating these challenges, moots are surprising in allocating an authoritative, disruptive agency equally to a wide range of subjects across genders, ranks, and occupations: nieces, daughters, widows, abbots, strangers, as well as wives, husbands, brothers, and fathers, *initiate actions* in moots. Yet their motives remain obscure, elusive, and inferential: things happen, moots show, and the reasons are inscrutable or irrelevant.

The association between property and family carries us to the depictions of fathers and mothers. Throughout, "Jacob and Esau" specifies the birth father of each child, attributing the position of patriarch to the man to whom each woman was wed at the time of childbirth. In the language of *King Lear*'s Gloucester, sons are differentiated as Edgar and Edmund were, by "order of law" (1.1.19) or by "breeding" (1.1.9). The first son born is the blood son of the elder of the two original brothers who purchased the tenancy, but he is also the legal son (under the marriage contract) of the lord of the manor. When the younger brother's wife bears a son, again the blood father is the lord of the manor, but the contractual father is the younger brother who originally purchased the land. Such issues of bloodline and birth order are the bases for differentiating legally between a child being the product of a father's "body" or not, and thus for differentiating between kinds of inheritance he might claim. What becomes apparent are the operations of the marriage contract: it legitimates whoever is born under its authority. And in so far as it makes a potential "bastard" into a "son" under the law, the contract forges a legal identity.

This association of marriage and property also carries us to the issue of women and chastity. When the female first appears, she is already both married and pregnant: "the elder brother dies, his wife being secretly pregnant," "the lord takes another wife and dies, his wife being secretly pregnant," "he takes another wife, who is pregnant by him before the espousals." When she emerges into visibility, it is as a representative of the category "wife" and, more precisely, as "pregnant wife"; in two cases, she is "secretly pregnant wife." Why does the moot keep these pregnancies "secret"? To whom are they unknown? The husband? The village? In these patterns, the moot demonstrates the remarkable mobility of the law; it is never stagnant. Here it preserves land transmission, wards off the social consequences of adultery and cuckoldry, and sustains the subject's honor and authority. It is as though the imaginative process has taken the legal concept of the *feme covert* and enlivened it, and we witness an endlessly repeatable process of covering or subsuming a wife. Visible primarily as she is subsumed into a husband in marriage, the woman is always-already an element in a teleology of matrimony that not only privileges heterosexuality but also equates it with reproduction.

While the representation of woman-as-wife-mother may be obvious given the topic of the linear conveyance of land, it also enforces an idea already in place in the culture about one role of the female: her position in an order of generation.[22] The moot sees certain possible disruptions—caused by secretly pregnant wives—to linear conveyance of property; it sees those potential disruptions as threatening to erode the legitimacy of the family name from within; and it resolves those questions of legitimacy by including both the pregnancy and its secrecy within the modes of legal succession. If a patriarchal culture fears female adultery, because it could "make a mockery of the whole story of patriarchal succession,"[23] the moot is curiously tranquil: what counts is not the specter of an adulteress but the sequence of spouses and children. Linked in moots to the ideology of uninterrupted land succession, women are represented as "honest" by their links to clear kinship relations and to marriage.

How are we to account, however, for the position of the abbot? There is a provocative ellipsis in our knowledge: while we have manuscripts of moot cases, we generally do not have many of the discussions those cases prompted. We are without the legal points made regarding land ownership, marriage contracts, and the position of monks and abbots. Many moots were formed prior to the Reformation and continued to be used after the Henrician Parliaments had recast the legal position of religious figures. Their fascination with monks and abbots may reflect an earlier anxiety that is, like those associated with pregnancy and marriage, continuously transformed. Baker notes that cases in the moot books "are full . . . of landowners becoming monks and then inconveniently coming back to life when claimed by deserted fiancees."[24] In general, as in "Jacob and Esau," moots represent religious figures as potentially unstable or duplicitous, men who might at any minute renounce a worldly family in favor of the church, then renounce the church in turn. These men, moots suggest, become land grabbers seeking to deprive others of their birthrights. They lose, however, almost inevitably it seems, when another "legitimate" owner asserts a claim.

In my second classic case, certain conventional themes recur, especially those associated with bloodline and legitimate transmission of property: "the son of the whole blood," that is, the son of the husband and wife with whom the case begins, claims property; "the brother of the half blood" also contends for the land; and "the son of the second issue enters" a case.[25] Added to the dynamic of imaging England in this moot, however, is another figure: the stranger. The case begins when a man holding land "marries a wife, they have issue two daughters, and die"; the daughters arrange "partition" so that each holds a portion of the land:

the elder marries; she and her husband have issue a son and a daughter; the husband dies; she marries another husband and they have issue a son and die; the issue by the first marriage leases the same land to a woman for life upon condition that if he grants the reversion to anyone else she shall have fee; he then grants the reversion to a stranger; the tenant for life by his lease recovers; the person to whom the reversion was granted enters upon the woman; she brings an assize and recovers.[26]

Not all blood is created equal ("whole" and "half" characterizing the strength of a relationship to the land), yet the case allows figures of "half blood" to claim land. These designations ensure the smooth transmission of property, but the logic of social legitimacy also works in reverse: bloodline legitimates the son's possession, but his legal possession also implies that he participates in the legitimate bloodline, whatever the biological facts might be. What fascinates me, however, is the stranger. He is a recurring type in moots, and he typically enters late in the process: *after* a landholder has committed a felony, lost his land, had daughters, and died, "the second grantee grants his services to a stranger for the term of his life"; *after* a villein purchases land, has three daughters, bequeaths land, purchases more, marries, has a son, and dies, "the son aliens to a stranger."[27] The stranger's story is a story of belatedness, of deferring to an England that precedes and succeeds him; he always arrives a little too late to possess the realm.

Unlike women, however, the stranger is typically associated with danger of a specifically Calvinist slant: "What will remain safe in human society," Calvin had asked, "if license be given to bring in by stealth the offspring of a stranger? to steal a name which may be given to spurious offspring? and to transfer to them property taken from lawful heirs?"[28] As the moot positions him, the stranger begins as a figure unrelated to recognizable kinship relations—"he then grants the reversion to a stranger"—and his function is to be suspended there unless (or until) he can be anchored in the soil or in sexual fertility.[29] Were he able either to purchase or marry into the land, the stranger would be domesticated and made familiar by his ability to associate with the earth in terms the moot finds acceptable. Here, however, the moot repels the stranger—"the person [stranger] to whom the reversion was granted enters upon the woman; she brings an assize and recovers"—preserving the family's orientation to each other and to the land at issue. Demonstrating the law's capacity to accommodate what it finds disorienting, the representation does significant cultural work: before expelling the stranger, it repositions him from potential threat to potential ally and from intruder to property-owner, a figure whose legitimacy might be subsequently ensured by his right to transmit property. Before the stranger loses the case brought by the woman, the idea of land ownership eases his foreignness. He is suspended, however, in a realm of possibility unachieved, as though possessing the realm *might* have "naturalized" the stranger as one of "us," if only. . . .

In contrast to their sequential momentum, the intellectual or imaginative properties foregrounded in moots are largely non sequiturs, and their themes are the precariousness of life, the vulnerability of marriage, the changeability of the self, and the mortality of humankind. In this series of threshold experiences, brothers die, wives bear children, husbands perish, ad infinitum in endless repetition. The repetition promises to continue beyond the bounds of the school-case, and there is no apparent closure within the moot. It stops rather than concludes. It imagines a place in constant jeopardy from undisclosed pregnancies, from arbitrary deaths, from men suddenly struck by religion. The force of the repetition makes it seem that England will continue well after an individual's claims on it end.

The imaginary worlds represented in moots are ordered by the recurrence of transience. It is not only the student's psyche or the English law that comes to seem mobile, but the land itself, as it is verbally transported from claimant to claimant. This is the universe at its most Faustian, in which allegorical figures and archetypes appear willy-nilly, impinging on the idea of the stability of place. What can the preservation of "real" estate mean in such an imagination-saturated venue?

Although the law in moots does not explicitly proclaim its access to characters' interiors, it assists in forming them as sites of constant vigilance against potential disasters. Behind this lies a process of transforming the remote into the familiar and the improbable into the likely. Yet there is also a complementary counterprocess, that of making the familiar strange and uncertain by calling down into the quotidian world curses, tragedies, and disasters. In this, moots are akin to the genre of romance, which is less a repository of rational than of moral order, and which accommodates the marvelous and unnatural to its morality. Moots can also be said to evoke a need for the vigilance they demand: they produce as problems (or perceive as dangers) events that they also exist to resolve.[30] (We might also note that in this logic, preserving the legitimate transmission of the land is formally coterminous with preserving the Inns.) They accustom mootmen to a view of history in which the nation is always on the brink of dissolution, its continued existence threatened by events that might go unforeseen were it not for the custodial eyes of the members of the Inns of Court.

The practice of mooting provides one arena for exploring what lies latent in legal constructions of the "realm." The England organized in these cases is eternal yet precariously situated; its soil is perpetually in jeopardy of masterlessness, misappropriation, or reversion to wilderness; and its residents are fickle, transient, and mortal. What moots most fear, and what they most often dramatize, is the potential for English soil quite suddenly to become what Douglas calls "matter out of order"—that is, dirt, with all its moral connotations.[31] What holds the soil in place, what "Englishes" it, is one of the least interrogated foundations of legal storytelling: acts of imagination.

The preservation and elaboration of land law at the heart of mooting was predicated on keeping doubts alive and raising queries. Mooters were encouraged to invent what Baker labels "mind-stretching remote contingenc[ies]" and extemporaneous exceptions to pleadings.[32] Moreover, on the one hand, the setting and conventions of the mooting performance accustom young men to the ways that senior benchers "think" the law. That accustoming, in turn, is understood as shaping subjects' behavior. Bacon speaks with a majority in recognizing the importance of these practices. In the essay "Of Custom and Education," he observes that Machiavelli's "rule holdeth still, that nature, nor the engagement of words, are so forcible as custom" in inculcating behavior.[33] On the other hand, however, the content of these cases brings into being diverse notions of England and its inhabitants and requires a speculative play that is consistently at odds with customary social order. As they are structured for performance, the degree of latitude is contained: mooters adopt or are assigned two positions from which to argue. The form itself suggests there may be only two legitimate ways to see the issues. In practice, however, moots demand the multiplication of possibilities and positions. The relative conformity achieved in the ritual performance is continuously eroded by the acts of improvisation demanded by that performance.

The continuous improvisations demanded in mooting sustain one version of patriotism, based on eluding or challenging the reach of traditional authority. The formal conditions of performance, however, circulate another version, one based on adhering to that traditional authority: the performative is as highly ritualized as the intellectual is improvised. It would be a mistake to take either part of the practice as total. In mooting, traditional points of view are continuously subject to refutation, yet in the end the refutations are assimilated into the moot as the "diversities" for which the law is able, after all, to account. Involved in creating a "natural" affiliation among new barristers, as well as among new barristers and those of the distant past, the mooting performance repeats an arbitrary practice and sustains an ideology of sameness and continuity against the changing social conditions of the realm.

The customary practices at Middle Temple, where the same rooms served for solemn legal disputation and for reveling, provide a glimpse of the central themes:

> The new barristers . . . are, for their degree, to perform each of them two several assignments of moots; which exercises are done in the hall in the term-time only, every Tuesday and Thursday night immediately after supper. The case is framed with apt and proper pleadings unto it by the two utter barristers who are to perform the assignment. These pleadings are recited by two gentlemen under the bar, one of which speaks for the plaintiff, the other for the defendant; . . . Immediately after supper the benchers assemble themselves in the bay window at the upper end of the hall; where standing in order according to their antiquity, there repair unto them two gentlemen under the bar whose turn it is to hear the pleadings. Who, after a low obeisance, demand whether it be their pleasure to hear a moot, and depart with an affirmative answer. . . . When it is agreed on who are to argue, all the benchers depart out of the hall, leaving the rest of the company there. The two arguers walk a turn in the court or garden until the hall be prepared and made ready for them; which being done, they return into the hall and stay at the cupboard, demanding if the mootmen be ready. . . . [A]ll parties being ready, the two benchers appointed to argue, together with the reader elect, take their places at the bench table, the ancient bencher sitting in the midst, the second on his right hand, and the reader-elect on his left. Then the mootmen also take their place, sitting on a form close to the cupboard and opposite to the benchers. On the one side of them sits one of the students that recites the pleading, and the other on the other side. The pleadings are first recited by the students, then the case put and argued by the barristers, and lastly by the reader-elect and benchers, in manner and form aforesaid. . . . The moot being ended, all parties return to the cupboard, where the mootmen present the benchers with a cup of beer and a slice of bread; and so the exercise for that night is ended.[34]

The scene is a model of ideal pedagogical form. Time is made regular, useful, and precise: "every Tuesday and Thursday night," "immediately after supper." Rank is vigilantly differentiated and observed in the distribution of tasks: "the new barristers," "two utter barristers," "two gentlemen under the bar." Space is apportioned to replicate wider cultural values: "in the bay window at the upper end of the hall"; "two benchers take their place at the bench table." Bodies are positioned to reproduce a hierarchy of class, seniority, and deference: "standing in order of their antiquity," "after a low obeisance."

In his work on proximity, anthropologist M. J. Abercrombie explains that "spatial relationships of the objects and furnishings . . . convey information about the roles of the people using them." In mooting, benchers are positioned above and below the bar, above and below the cupboard, at the upper end of the hall, or at the center of the table. "Conventions of this kind," Abercrombie finds, "not only demonstrate the roles to be played by people, but support the people in their roles and make it difficult for them to adopt alternative ones." Place signifies status, and figures of higher rank occupy higher spaces, "as though the more important person needs more [rarefied] air to breathe."[35] Further, the process of mooting offers its concluding ritual of fellowship—sharing a cup of beer and slice of bread—as its *achievement*, as though the entire ceremony that preceded it were necessary in order to reach this moment of community. The community mooting achieves is an effect of repetition, of taking the self through the same physical and mental acts that previous generations of students enacted.

In the utopia of embodied status represented in moots, each member of the society becomes a potential relay point in a widely dispersed network of judging and normalizing.[36] The success of the pedagogical strategy depends upon its use of simple instruments, invisible to us now because embodied then, including a raised eyebrow, bemused frown, or encouraging nod. It disciplines by means of observation, integrating the details of surveillance into the teaching relationship. It organizes the minds and bodies of the scholars and constitutes them as objects of political work. Their study is regular and measurable; it is orderly and constant; and it serves both the self and the nation. "Look at the aspiring bencher," the practice seems to say. "In his relation to himself, a relation of discipline and labor, he reveals his relation to the laws of the land and exemplifies yours as well."

As it is represented in these performances, the relation of the subject to the law is one of inserting the self into a vital, continuing tradition. Exercises are regulated and administered with a strong sense of history revived, performed always "by the ancient custom of the house."[37] Even the terms for positioning the agents of the arguments emphasize self-effacement or immersion in a group. They train the subject to discover and realize himself within aggregate designations: "Une gent dient"; "ascuns diont"; "semble a auters"; "moy semble." The effect of this anonymity is to cast the disputes themselves as what "some" and "others" say, normalizing the anonymous speaking subjects as voices of "gentlemen" in a collective mentality.[38] "Our laws are not individual, but communal and positional," this anonymity suggests; "they do not see or make visible prejudices of nature, nurture, and politics." Understood as a pedagogy aimed at inserting individuals into a collective version of law, the practice of mooting supports a conservative agenda. In it, to become an English man means to affiliate oneself with what a historically-generated "some" continue to "say" about the nation as it is represented in legal history. Against this conservatism, however, the speculative play that characterizes mooting creates an ideological instability at the center of the practice. Thematically and theoretically, readings were devoted to collective wisdom and "common learning," yet in practice mooters "were always testing by disputation the borders of that common learning."[39]

As the practice and ideology of mooting make evident, one task of the Inns was to forge affiliations among members of disparate groups, both to each other and to an official idea of English law. Students were encouraged to see themselves as the legitimate proprietors of the realm and as subjects deeply invested in securing its stability. The goal was to make informed courtiers, and a prominent method for achieving that end was to offer the members a privileged relation to legal codes by suspending their reach in the interests of intellectual play. In this way, for a small part of their lives, residents in the Inns lived above the law. This privileged perspective is captured in Philip Finkelpearl's provocative observation: "Frequently Inns writers and lawyers acted as though they lived in a separate kingdom. It is a habit of mind in which they had training."[40] In this "separate kingdom," and particularly in the revels that punctuated its festivities, what was treason in the larger society was intellectual play among mootmen.

Relatively little is known about the Inns of Court until the fifteenth century, when Henry VI's chancellor, Sir John Fortescue, described this "academy": it is "not situated in the city, where the tumult of the crowds could disturb the students' quiet, but is a little isolated in a suburb of the city, and nearer to the aforesaid courts, so that the students are able to attend them daily at pleasure without the inconvenience of fatigue."[41] In their early days, they were perceived by Fortescue as exempla of good government, stability, and internal order. The behavior of the innsmen was a model of brotherhood:

> Scarcely any turbulence, quarrels, or disturbance ever occur there, but offenders are punished with no other punishment than expulsion from participation in their mutual society, which is a penalty they fear more than criminals elsewhere fear imprisonment and fetters. For a man once expelled from one of these societies is never received into the fellowship of any other of those societies. Hence there is continual peace and their conduct is like the behaviour of such as are conjoined in perfect amity.[42]

By the late sixteenth century, however, the Inns no longer enjoyed what to Fortescue had been idyllic isolation, and his contemplative model had yielded to an active and slightly sordid urbanity:

> London had reached out and surrounded the Inns. Across the river was Southwark with its playhouses and stews, readily accessible by boat from the Temple stairs. Next door to the Temple was the old Blackfriars liberty occupied by debtors, cony catchers, and sometimes private theatres. Another immediate neighbor during the 1590's was the Earl of Essex's establishment. . . . In short, the Inns of Court were located in the heart of Elizabethan London.[43]

Elizabethan perspectives vary significantly from Fortescue's, and they describe the Inns quite differently, as places that "harboured a large and shadowy population of non-members; domestic staff, personal servants, lawyer's clerks, seminary priests, 'bankrupts and debtors, . . . make here their subterfuges from arrests.' . . . '[S]undry gentlemen of the country . . . forriners and discontinuers' . . . threatened to turn the houses from "*hospitia* to *diversoria*."[44] These Elizabethan histories remark on "lewd women in the night" entering the chambers; Lincoln's Inn "ordered that no woman should henceforth be entertained in any member's chamber, 'bycause the same is thought to be to the great disworship of the house.'"[45] So, too, the aspiring barrister himself is cast as a threat to the community, one who has separated himself from a powerful affiliation: the houses routinely issued orders disapproving of members "living out 'as forraignors rather than as fellows associated together.'"[46] Moreover, there was a widespread perception that mootmen, too infused with a sense of their privileged relation to law, were not to be trusted outside the Inns. "The junior members of the inns were notorious for their violent behaviour outside the societies; William Harrison, writing in 1577, claimed that 'the younger sort of them abroad in the streets are scarce able to be bridled by any good order whatsoever.'"[47]

In relocating to London to read the law, hopeful barristers did not abandon their ties to their villages, but transported their homelands within them: "students tended to cluster at one Inn or another on the basis of geographical origin." Son followed father, neighbor joined neighbor, and nephew followed uncle. Each Inn had an individual character and a "tendency toward clannishness" that derived from a perceived relation to and superiority of one's place of origin.[48]

Lineage, rank, and status all played a part in making a young man fit for the residences. According to Fortescue's early perception, "there are not many who learn the laws in the inns except the sons of nobles. For poor and common people cannot bear so much cost for the maintenance of their sons. . . . Hence it comes about that there is scarcely to be found in the realm a man trained in the laws, who is not noble or sprung of noble lineage."[49] By the close of the sixteenth century, however, the economic background appeared considerably less uniform: many admissions in the 1590s are to "the son and heir" of men identified as citizen, mercer, or merchant of London. The shift in constituency did not go unnoticed: as late as James I's reign, there was an official attempt to limit admission to the Inns to men who could demonstrate a pedigree for at least three generations.[50] Yet it remained generally true that the Inns were occupied by the sons of the landed gentry, and "from 1550 until 1700 (at least), a period of residence at one of the Inns of Court was a normal stage in the education of the sons of the gentry and would-be gentry."[51]

For some, admission to an Inn was a convenient solution to London's housing shortage; for others, the Inns were finishing schools. By the end of the century, among the population of the city (variously estimated at 100,000 to 200,000), this was the largest group of literate men.[52] The sense of social mobility suggested by legal study was satirically encapsulated in 1583 by Thomas Smith in *De Republica Anglorum*:

> as for gentlemen, they be made good cheape in England, for whosoever studieth the lawes of the realm, who studieth in the universities, who professeth liberall sciences, and to be shorte, who can live idly and without manuall labour, and will bear the port, charge and countenaunce of a gentleman, he shall be called master.[53]

Status among members of the Inns was secured and displayed through leisure activities and the concomitant disposable time and income they represented. Among the most common of these activities was feasting, and the fellowship of breaking bread together was also a means of constructing economic fellowship. If mooting was scheduled for Mondays, Wednesdays, and Fridays,

> the intermediate days were spent in feasting and entertaining as guests lords and other eminent persons, the [mooter] however, taking precedence, whatever were the degree of the guests. The expenses of the [mooters] were great on these occasions; some spent, it is said, above 600£. in two days less than a fortnight. Some outlay in feasting strangers to the society appears to have been expected from them. In the last week of the reading, a great feast was provided for the entertainment of foreign ambassadors, earls, lords and men of eminent quality. The expense of this was imposed on four members of the Inn (two of them barristers and two under the bar), called stewards of the feast.[54]

In addition to the affiliations produced by feasting, others were secured by the Inns' widely-recognized reveling. In the fifteenth century, Fortescue described opportunities to learn "to sing and to exercise themselves in every kind of harmonics. They are also taught there to practise dancing and all games proper for nobles, as those brought up in the king's household are accustomed to practise."[55] Mockeries of legal forms, innumerable jokes about sex, satirical play on the lascivious Inns-a-Court man, wit combats over disorderly use of language—all found their way into the revels. Members of the Inns were immersed in continual carnivalesque festivities, a situation of licensed permissiveness in which an authority permitted its own overturning, but which also already presupposed the re-turning to the authority of the sanctioned.[56] This habit of festive liberty was so intimately linked to the Inns that in Finkelpearl's view, members "seem to have made a deep, if unconscious, connection between reveling and the study of the law."[57]

One of these revels, the Christmas Prince, held during the holidays at

Middle Temple, bears particularly on the special position treason occupied in the legal consciousness. It began with the selection of the leader, or Prince, who was installed at the first Grand night. He and his court ruled for the next few weeks, as ceremony piled on ceremony:

> an elaborate emblazoning of the Prince's titles, a detailed description of the responsibilities of court officers, a conferring of "knighthoods," a declaration of laws and edicts for the Prince's realm, an arraignment of a criminal with his incarceration in "the tower" (that is, the stocks), and many long orations on a variety of subjects. These entertainments were supplemented by the presentation of one or more plays and masques, sometimes acted by students, sometimes by professional groups. Often some portion of the revels were presented at Court. Finally the Prince "died" and the Christmas revels ended, usually with a banquet on Candlemas Night, February 2.[58]

Within the structure of the revels and the sanctioned inversions they entail, imagining the death of the prince is not merely allowed but is an important formal element of the story; it is the event that precipitates a return to normal rule. The revel suspends the law, encouraging benchers to entertain thoughts that in the outside realm are illegal.

If members of the Inns made a deep connection between reveling and the study of the law, they appear also to have made a deep connection between writing of all kinds, including poetry and plays for private and public audiences, and the study of the law. In his work on law reporting, L. W. Abbott finds that the Inns were "the clearing-houses for much of the legal literature produced." Offering close companionship among aspiring legal practitioners and constant circulation of ideas, the Inns were essential sites for "the compilation of private reports throughout the sixteenth century," just as they had been for the preparation and circulation of Yearbooks.[59] Tradition has it that both Chaucer and Gower were members, and whatever the facts (the claim is unsubstantiated), the tradition itself suggests the mythological power of perceived relations between court and writer. Finkelpearl has shown that in the sixteenth and seventeenth centuries, "an astonishing number of important writers" occupied the Inns at some point: More, Ascham, Turberville, Googe, Gascoigne, Sackville and Norton, Lodge, Fraunce, Ralegh, Harington, Campion, Donne, Bacon, Davies, Marston, Ford, Beaumont, Shirley, Davenant, William Browne, Wither, Denham, Quarles, Carew, Suckling, and Congreve, among others.[60] Although Sir Philip Sidney's disciplinary rules limited lawyers to saying "what men have determined," many writers of extra-legal stories lived in the Inns and grew "in effect another nature."[61]

Writers at the Inns produced revels, poems, plays, and masques. They wrote or commissioned plays for revels and holiday performances. In addition to Sackville and Norton's *Gorboduc* (1561–62), for example, another Senecan tragedy, *Gismonde of Salerne* was penned by five young law students and performed before the queen in 1566; and another, *The Misfortunes of Arthur*, by Thomas Hughes and other students of Gray's Inn was penned in 1588 and was performed "for the Queen with dumb-shows conceived by the young Francis Bacon." *The Comedy of Errors* was famously commissioned for Gray's Inn.[62] Members self-consciously produced translations of Seneca from 1558 to 1572, and turned out such guides to governing as the *Mirror for Magistrates*.[63] The Inns were literary and intellectual centers, and members were both creators and consumers of literature who assumed an easy transit between the legal and the literary. In his dedication to the 1616 folio of his play *Every Man Out of His Humour* (first performed in 1599), Ben Jonson offered his paean: "To the Noblest Nourceries of Humanity, and Liberty, in the Kingdome: the Innes of Court."[64]

The exchanges among mootmen and writers ensured that one need not have been at law school to speak the languages of legal practice, nor need he have been in the theater to speak the languages of imaginative fictions. The mootman could expect at any moment to be called on to side alternatively with fathers or sons, wives or daughters, progeny of "whole" blood or strangers. What we see is that legal practice has always included imaginative work. It has always been involved in facilitating the development of a collective identity among men. Its main theme is proprietorship, which mooting shows as tested or challenged by strangers, secretly pregnant women, abbots, brothers, mothers—virtually any person or event that might (or might not) occur. But the mootman need not fear, because these challenges are resolvable through the double application of inventiveness and statute. Nursing Jonson's "humanity and liberty," the practices of the Inns of Court contributed to a discourse of personal proprietorship in which "the realm" was undergoing continual renovation and was as liquid as a mootman's imagination.

2.
Female Fidelities on Trial

Among Henry VIII's contributions to early modern social instability was his dissolving of English Catholicism and his founding of the Church of England, which nationalized religion and thereby nationalized the right of English authority to oversee a subject's interior life. What often goes unremarked, however, is that simultaneous with this religious reorganization was Henry's implementation of matrimonial high treasons. Under the Reformation Parliament of 1530–34, of "the new acts which concerned treason in general, three were the result of the king's matrimonial ventures. . . . Henry had started on the path of supporting his marriages with the sanctions of treason."[1] The first several of these acts were associated with Henry's marriage to Anne Boleyn. They made it treason to slander the marriage or the succession in writing or print (25 Hen. VIII c. 22), to attempt bodily harm against the king or to slander the marriage or the succession by spoken words (26 Hen. VIII c. 7), and finally (in order to prosecute Boleyn) to commit adultery while married to the king, a wholly new form of treason.[2] Henry added another act related to marriage, this one associated with Lord Thomas Howard's betrothal to Lady Margaret Douglas (28 Hen. VIII c. 24), which made it treason to "defile or deflower" or to marry almost any of the king's female relatives without royal consent. Finally, the prosecution of Henry's fifth queen, Katherine Howard, became the source of yet another unprecedented piece of legislation (33 Hen. VIII c. 23) making it treason for subjects to fail to reveal any knowledge they might have of "lightness of body" of any woman the king might intend to marry.

Like treasons in general, the matrimonial treasons register deep anxieties about the existence and implications of a secret self whose loyalties and desires might differ from those of an observable self. Such duplicitous subjectivity would threaten the image of cohesiveness and stability of the social order that authorizes the behaviors of subjects in the first place. Unlike other treasons, however, the matrimonial cases formulate this fear of subjective dualism specifically in terms of women's unobservable sexual fidelity:

variously valued as transgressing social order, as blurring distinctions among conventional categories of mastery and subordination within marriage, and as undermining gendered categories of dominance and submission in the culture more generally, women's unseen fidelity came to signify the potential for errant self-will and personal agency.

Three representations, one drawn from legal practice, the other two from dramatic practice, allow me to illuminate some of the contradictions in the cultural positioning of the "woman problem": Katherine Howard's attainder for treason in 1542, Christian Custance's scrutiny for infidelity in Nicholas Udall's *Ralph Roister Doister* (c. 1550), and Imogen's metaphorical trial for promiscuity in Shakespeare's *Cymbeline* (c. 1608). In all three, women are associated with uncertainties characteristic of early modern English struggles with relations among epistemology, secrecy, and truth. All formulate those uncertainties in terms of a dualism between women's apparent and secret fidelities. Each, however, develops its own means of "knowing" women, foregrounding the rhetorical and narrative strategies necessary to producing and proving that knowledge. The Howard attainder makes its truth-claims by doing what early modern law characteristically does, suppressing the notion that proof is something made. *Ralph Roister Doister*, written perhaps in response to the attainder, claims to "know" Custance by gendering the sources of truth-telling and linking possession of the truth about women to the interpretations of men. *Cymbeline*, however, claims its truth by what appears to be an opposing strategy: it wears its status as a simulation on its sleeve, aggressively destabilizing the fictions that generate the "unfaithful woman." When a penitent Iachimo belatedly confesses to having produced only "simular proof" of Imogen's infidelity, he is not only clearing his own character but explicating one of the play's central points: proof is a feigned, mimetic version of things whose believers are, at best, victims of folly. Although they are separated by time and by genre, all three works illuminate the artifice involved in making what counted as knowledge of early modern women.

What could Katherine Howard have thought that chilly afternoon in October 1541, as she and her husband Henry VIII returned to Hampton Court after a progress to the north that had lasted three months? Perhaps she had hoped to console Henry, who arrived to find his son seriously ill with fever. Perhaps she had hoped to repair her relations with an anxious group of Protestant reformers, led by Archbishop Cranmer, who feared she might return the nation to papal dominance. Perhaps, worn down by the bad weather and tensions of the journey, she simply hoped to rest. Howard's own voice on these events remains elusive, lost to the historical habit of not recording women's words. Whatever her intentions, the longed for respite quickly culminated in the event that shaped the remainder of her short life: her attainder for treason. A brief entry in Charles Wriothesley's chronicle of 1541 reads:

> This yeare, the 13th daye of November, Sir Thomas Wriothesley, knight, and Secretary to the Kinge, came to Hampton Court to the Quene, and called all the ladies and gentlewomen and her servaunts into the Great Chamber, and there openlye afore them declared certeine offences that she had done in misusing her bodye with certeine persons afore the Kinges tyme.[3]

Initially Howard was indicted for her crime. In the usual procedure, once charges had been made, the accused and witnesses were part of a somewhat public process of examination and jury trial that included appearing in court to defend oneself. For reasons that remain obscure, however, Howard was not brought to trial. Instead, she was attainted of treason by an act of Parliament, which evaded both the need for court appearances and the possibility of public resistance.[4]

Why did the law take an interest in Howard? The modes of explanation are less personal than national. The fifth of Henry's six wives, and a well-connected niece of the Norfolks, Howard was a pawn in a high-stakes game of political dominance between partisans of reform and revolution on one side and religious and political conservatism on the other. On the side of reform and revolution, Thomas Cromwell, the king's vicar-general, had gained influence over Henry by finding the means of Henry's divorcing Catherine of Aragon and marrying Anne Boleyn, and by subsequently bringing about the Cleves marriage. Allied with him was his protege Sir Thomas Audley, the Lord Chancellor, who presided at a series of high-profile trials including those of Thomas More and Anne Boleyn and her associates. Audley was continuously involved in Henry's "matrimonial projects. He helped make the marriage treaty between the king and Anne of Cleves; he attended Henry at her reception in England; he was sent to tell Anne of the king's 'alteration of countenance,' and he rendered depositions during the annulment proceedings."[5] Against the reformers, on the side of the ancient prerogatives of the nobility and Catholicism without a Pope, Stephen Gardiner, bishop of Winchester, and his ally, the duke of Norfolk (Howard's uncle) were working diligently behind the scenes for a return to the old orthodoxy and the institution of a new wife to replace the protestant Anne of Cleves; Howard was their candidate.[6] Howard first became important to the realm not as a criminal, but as a vehicle for averting political crisis and stabilizing local political alignments. Her nation, in this case identified with feudal leanings and conservative ancient prerogatives, had need of her.

Less than two years after her marriage in 1540, Howard found herself charged with treason. The initial claims against her depended on two issues: her having engaged in sexual activity some years earlier with Henry Mannock, who is identified in all the historical accounts as having taught her the virginals, and her having engaged in sexual activity and contracted marriage with Francis Dereham. Relatively late in the investigations a third lover was named, Howard's distant cousin, Thomas Culpeper, for whom it was rumored she had finally cast off Dereham and to whom it was also rumored she had been affianced. It was alleged against Culpeper that he had held secret, illicit meetings with the queen, who had "incited him to have intercourse with her, and insinuated that she loved him better than the King and all others."[7] The attainder declared that Howard, "whom the King took to wife, is proved to have been not of pure and honest living before her marriage, and the fact that she has since taken to her service one Francis Dereham, with whom she used that vicious life before, and has taken as chamberers a woman who was privy to her naughty life before, is proof of her will to return to her old abominable life."[8] The Crown contended that Howard had "offended in incontinency": under the Act of Succession used to convict Anne Boleyn in 1536, she had slandered her children and the succession by engaging in sexual activity with anyone other than the king.[9] But whereas the Boleyn treason was founded on adultery during the marriage, the Howard attainder addressed *pre*marital behavior. There was no law—or rather, there had not yet been a construction of treason—that made female sexual activity itself traitorous. Howard was attainted, then, outside any existing law. Her attainder marks a distinct moment in the early modern discourses of female sexuality when a woman's premarital sexuality becomes legally identified with her marital sexuality. Ironically, after her conviction, the same Parliament that made her a traitor made the laws that criminalized her.

Here is the official version of the story:

While the King's Majesty was in his Progress, one John Lassells came to the . . . Archbishop of Canterbury and declared unto him that he had been with a sister of his married in Sussex, which sometimes had been a servant with the old Duchess of Norfolk, who did also bring up the said Mistress Catherine, and being with his . . . sister, chanced to fall in communication with her of the Queen, wherein he advised her, because she was of the Queen's old acquaintance, to sue to be her woman. Whereunto his sister answered that she would not so do, but that she was very sorry for the Queen. "Why?" quoth Lassells. "Marry," quoth she, "for she is light both in living and condition." "How so?" quoth Lassells. "Marry," quoth she, "there is one Francis Dereham, who was servant also in my Lady of Norfolk's house, which hath lain in bed with her in his doublet and hose an hundred nights. And there hath been such puffing and blowing between them, that once . . . a maid which lay in the house with [Katherine] said to me she would lie no longer with her because she knew not what matrimony meant."[10]

What is fascinating here, above the tale itself, is the power of these rumors to elicit wonder and conjecture: when Lassells reported this family chatter to Archbishop Cranmer, Cranmer "was marvelously perplexed therewith."

Cranmer transmitted the tale to Audley and Seymour, the Earl of Hertford; they too "marvelled" at the tale. As history, this conjunction of Cranmer, Audley and Seymour boded ill for Howard; they were all in sympathy with the reformed religion and bringing down Howard could serve their political ends.[11] As rhetoric, however, these reported reactions are difficult to assess; one historian asserts that it was a "matter for amazement that not a whisper as to the unsuitability of the new union [had] reached the king. So many people seem to have been aware that Catherine Howard was a woman with a past."[12] And *Hall's Chronicle; Containing the History of England* reports that the queen "was accused to the Kyng of dissolute liuyng, before her marriage . . . and that was not secretly, but many knewe it."[13] Yet however widely knowledge of Howard's past had circulated, the attainder represents that knowledge as a shocking revelation, a "marvel" whose rhetorical effect is to convey a sense of the uniqueness of the information and to imply a prior belief about Howard with which this tale is incompatible. Although the response to the news is naturalized in terms of emotions, there is art here that is not nature's. Reared on Aristotle, every schoolboy knew the rhetorical force of wonder in provoking and directing speculative thinking: "It is owing to their wonder that men both now begin and at first began to philosophize."[14]

Spurred to action by Lassells's perplexing tale, the counselors agreed that the king must be told, and Cranmer undertook the task. Yet in a move as multivalent as it is significant, "because . . . [he] could not find it in his heart to express the same to the King's majesty by word of mouth, he declared the information thereof to His Highness in writing."[15] Unable to repeat the rumors "by word of mouth," Cranmer (reportedly following Audley's advice) reworks Lassells's oral saga into a document, subjecting it to the strictures of scripted narrative. And as she is written, Howard is situated in a complex historical process in which documentary evidence is gaining authority and becoming institutionalized as the more persuasive form of testimony. In earlier years, the famous court reporter Edmund Plowden had pronounced that "our law says that nothing is true but what may be tried, for truth never wants trial."[16] By the late seventeenth century, English law will suggest that whatever is true is "truer" if it is in print.[17] In the interim, trials continuously include debates about what will count as evidence, sometimes taking writing as more legitimate than speaking, sometimes demanding oral validation of written claims. As late as 1603, Walter Ralegh challenged the prosecution, "your words cannot condemn me," "your phrases will not prove it," which the prosecution countered with its own insistence, "the denial of the defendant is no evidence."[18]

The effect of transforming the accusations against Howard into a document is to distance the author from the tainted behavior inscribed in the text: represented as a man distracted by heart-felt sympathy for the pain the news may bring Henry, Cranmer disappears into the written report, reinforcing the sense that the tale speaks in its own voice, that the voice is unmediated, and that the truth is unmuddied by personal interests. Yet paradoxically, the document acquires an added aura of credibility precisely because of Cranmer's personal position: its written form is attributed to the self-negating figure of a faithful "secretorie." Angell Day, laying out the secretary's relationship to what he writes, explains that "His pen in this action is not his owne" and his task is "utterlie to relinquish anie affectation to his own doings" or admixture of his own will in bearing messages.[19] The oral claims against Howard were a melange of rumors from widely dispersed witnesses, the sort of anecdotes that might at best issue in a disjointed, multivocal work.[20] The written charges imposed material and thematic unity on the fragments and produced a univocal story with a pointed theme—Howard's moral weakness and Parliament's legal triumph—all the while making the events appear to narrate themselves. The "guilty" Howard comes to exist in writing, in the form of evidence whose truth-claims are growing increasingly persuasive. And the inscriber's extra-legal status as a reliable "secretorie" lends the charges additional credibility.

The Howard attainder stakes part of its claims to truth on its status as an official document, offering the palpable reality of paper as the substantial reality of a "criminal record." How else does it generate conviction? By structuring its moralities as mutually contingent, defining, and exclusive. It discredits Howard by crediting her accusers, exempting them from the taint of personal malice in the process. Although Lassells was widely known to be a zealous anti-Catholic working on the side of the reformers, the source-story represents him as a man removed from court politics, an average citizen who heard of Katherine's behavior only by accident. The revelation of the crime appears as a spontaneous event; it is a quasi-miraculous eruption into an occasional conversation between siblings, for he only "*chanced* to fall into communication with [his sister] of the Queen" (emphasis added). In diction that suggests a perception that self-interest is at odds with truth, Lassells is cleared by the operations of accident of any hidden motives. He is, instead, allied with the good of the nation and shown as one whose personal and national devotion are identical: asked why he came forward, he vowed it was his duty as a citizen.[21] Mary Lassells Hall, too, is represented as free from self-interest, for she refuses to trade on her prior relationship and seek a position with such a tainted queen. In a sustained process of differentiation between the two women, Mary Lassells Hall's moral rectitude becomes the condition for Katherine Howard's moral turpitude: that Mary "feels very sorry for Katherine" distinguishes the noble country wife from the voluptuous queen along sexual and moral axes. Hall's authority is legitimated here by her recognition (or more accurately, her reproduction) of an official ideology that takes unmarried female sexual activity as "light" behavior, and her tender emotions serve as a standard of female conduct against which Howard is measured. Focused on matrimony, the discourse of treason develops a narrative of pity that indicts one woman by constructing a morally acceptable and superior "other," in this case a monogamous country wife who "knows" what marriage is.

Within three days of reading the initial charges on November 2, 1541, Henry had left Hampton Court for London; he never saw his wife again. What replaces him in the accounts is a body of textual evidence that rhetorically generates the corroboration it needs, minting "truth" and coherence from disparate elements. The procedure reveals the unstated order of criminal investigations more generally: it is not that a random batch of "facts" lead inquisitors to the right conclusion, but that conclusions guide the search for corroborating "facts" and bring the potentially useful to light.[22] An instance of the trope metalepsis, which governs historical discourse, cause (which here is the inquisitors' interests) and effect (evidence, proof) are joined while the intervening steps in the causal chain are jumped or compressed. When Henry's representatives examined Lassells, his sister Mary, Mannock, and Dereham, they found these witnesses "constant in [their] former sayings" or congruous with each other. When Sir Thomas Wriothesley interviewed Mannock, he heard

> that [Mannock] had commonly used to feel the secrets and other parts of [Katherine's] body, ere ever Dereham was so familiar with her; and Dereham confessed that he had known her carnally many times, both in his doublet and his hose between the sheets, and in naked bed, alleging such Witnesses of three sundry women one after another, that had lain in the same bed with them when he did the acts.[23]

"Then the rest of the witnesses, eight or nine men and women, were examined and agreed in one tale."[24] Again late in the proceedings, Culpeper confirmed the depositions of his private conversations with Katherine, though probably under duress and torture in the Tower.[25] In legal discourse, as this piling on of a master narrative reveals, to corroborate is in part to *re*produce a fact that already exists and also in part to *produce* a fact. Perhaps most important, corroboration produces the effect of "corroboration." The weight of persuasiveness is on the congruity of the stories, on producing from ostensibly unrelated people and events a tale in which repetition serves as both narrative and subjective unity. The congruity testifies both to the truth of the stories (they match because they are all objective observations about an independent fact) and to the interior of the accused (they match because they are all accurate reflections of a specifiable, although invisible, interior). The diction of discovery obscures the presence of the interrogators in their interrogation: the witnesses were "found" to tell the same tale. In the Howard case, as in treasons more generally, prosecutors enhance their claims to reliability by allying themselves with natural or divine evidence, discredit the defendants' credibility by allying them with intentionally crafted artifice, and produce an official document that eclipses the agency of human authors. However, Stanley Fish has argued persuasively that

> similarity is not something one finds, but something one must establish, and when one establishes it one establishes the configurations of the cited cases as well as of the case that is to be decided. Similarity . . . is not a property of texts (similarities do not announce themselves), but a property conferred by a relational argument in which the statement *A* is like *B* is a characterization (one open to challenge) of *both A* and *B*.[26]

Relating one tale to another is not a process of perfect matching but of continuous revision, as different details are foregrounded and others dropped. In the discourse of treason, as elsewhere, the very process of corroboration is the process of producing narrative consistency.

In a text that repeatedly grounds its authority in its power to forge continuities, Howard's body submits to the demands of narrative signification and testifies against her. According to Lassells's sister, "one Mannock . . . knew a privy mark of [Katherine's] body."[27] Dereham too confessed to knowing the "privy mark." Through exchanges of partners, in diverse places, and across passages of time, Katherine could be identified as herself by this single material fact. These substantiating details rest uneasily amid a transition from medieval evidentiary symbolism, in which marks on the body speak in God's voice, to early modern juridical practice, in which marks on the body serve as visible, objective evidence of criminal identity. What is striking is that the privy mark is evoked as something "self-evident" in two senses: it is evidence of a guilty self and it is evidence so self-declaring it appears to need no supplemental explanation. What is equally striking is that the verbal description produces the phenomenon that it also purports merely to record: there is no perspective from which to observe this "privy mark" neutrally, before it receives an interpretation as the sign of Howard's promiscuity. To see it as "privy" is already to have assigned it an interpretation according to a context (assumed, though not argued, during the proceedings) that differentiates private from other parts of the body; to see it as a "mark" is already to see it as a mark *of* something.[28]

Some decades later Edmund Coke will remark that of all forms of evidence, witnessing is the least reliable, "seeing such variety amongst witnesses are about [the event], as few of them agree together."[29] But here the claim to eyewitnessing is the source of Mannock and Dereham's official authority. The privy mark enters the narrative as the sort of "ocular proof" that Othello longs for, substituting a bodily detail for acts that cannot be seen. It puts the accusers in the possession of a particular kind of knowledge, persuasive because private, and it undermines the wife's credibility, for she has failed to prevent penetration by the piercing gaze of any man except her husband. Described as something the alleged lovers saw, the mark proves Howard's double violation of marital conventions, her transgression of rules of property (for her body is her husband's) and of hierarchies of agency (for she acted as though she possessed the authority to dispose of her body according to her own will). The testimony reveals an ideology of bodily evidence which assumes rather than describes a "normal" body against which it measures deviations. This bodily deviance metonymically implies a sexual and subjective deviance. More specifically, the mark signifies Howard's failure to conform, body and soul, to the norms of a dominant social order. As though by magic, the law has made apparent an external, embodied sign of internal, moral corruption.

In the Bakhtinian sense, this marvelous detail transforms Howard into a grotesque body, a degraded figure whose openness and accessibility radically jeopardize patrilinear authority and social organization.[30] The relevant historical contrast to this representation of Howard's promiscuous body is that of her immediate predecessor, Anne of Cleves. With haste only Hamlet could properly describe ("the divorce baked-meats / Did coldly furnish forth the marriage tables" [1.2.180–81]), Henry wed Katherine within three weeks of the Cleves annulment. Yet Anne remained in England, officially repositioned as "the King's adopted sister, with precedence before all other ladies but the King's wife and daughters." She swore in a letter to her brother that "my body remaineth in the integrity which I brought into this realm."[31] An essential element in the Howard story, Anne emerges as a necessary other against whose bodily and spiritual "integrity" Katherine's promiscuity could be built.[32]

Armed with the mutually corroborating texts and the crucial bodily detail of the privy mark, Henry's representatives interrogated the queen.[33]

At the first she constantly denied it, but the matter being so declared unto her that she perceived it to be wholly disclosed, the same night she disclosed the whole to the Archbishop of Canterbury [Cranmer], who took the confession of the same in writing subscribed with her hand. Then were the rest of the number, being eight or nine men and women which knew of her doings, examined, who all agreed in one tale.[34]

Although Howard's initial position is resistance (she "constantly denied" the charges), by the account's end she has become a final instance of belated corroboration. The job of the accused is to validate the legal procedure in such instances, to demonstrate that law did, after all, ferret out the "truth." In this case, the problem is that we have no precise record of what Cranmer "declared" to her nor what she "disclosed" to him, and we have no precise record of what the "eight or nine men and women which knew of her doings" had "agreed" on. What we have is an official version of a figure who comes to recognize herself in a story authored by her prosecutors.[35]

The section of the account dealing with Howard's attainder closes by activating an influential logic of sustained unified identity and self-continuity that comes to characterize discourses of treason throughout the century: "Now may you see what was done before the marriage; God knoweth what hath been done since."[36] Positing a God not in evidence, who sees into the recesses of the hidden heart, and evoking the idea of a permanent, unchanging selfhood, the account refashions the queen along the outlines of a memorially reconstructed "Katherine Howard": the Katherine Howard who married Henry is continuous with (continued to be the same as) the one who was between the sheets huffing and puffing with Mannock, Dereham, and Culpeper.

At its culminating moment, the Howard story conflicts not over the issue of whether Howard is a criminal, but over the issue of what crime she acknowledges as her own. In both versions of her execution, she is represented has having embraced the decorum of formal death: on the night before she died, she had an executioner's block brought to her room, "that she might learn how to dispose her head upon it." She then "calmly and smilingly rehearsed her part in the tragedy of the morrow."[37] The official version of her scaffold speech, delivered on February 13, 1542, as she faced beheading on Tower Green, is recorded in the *Letters and Papers of the Reign of Henry VIII*. It reports that she "spoke shortly. She died . . . in full confidence in God's goodness."[38] As it does in numerous contemporary scaffold testimonies, Howard's speech as reported lends the attainder credibility by corroborating it; her penitent demeanor reflects the successful display of official power in overcoming traitors; and her beheading testifies to the success of the law in penetrating and punishing even the "imaginings" of its subjects.

There is, however, a competing unofficial version of the speech, recorded in the *Spanish Chronicle of Henry VIII*, in which Howard is represented as resisting the abject position of the condemned. In this text, instead of complying with the terms supplied by convention, Howard redraws the contours of her identity: although she admitted that "she had grievously sinned and deserved death," she denied having "wronged the King in the particular way that she had been accused of."[39] Seizing authority not to proclaim her innocence but to define her guilt, Howard shifts the grounds of her criminality from the legal verdict to her own desires:

> She proudly and calmly gloried in her love for her betrothed Culpeper, whom she knew she soon would join in death. . . . Even as he, with his last breath, had confessed his love for her, and had mourned that the King's passion for her had stood in the way of their honest union, so did she . . . proclaim that love was victorious over death; and that since there had been no mercy for the man she loved she asked no mercy for herself from the King. . . . If she had married the man she loved, instead of being dazzled by ambition, all would have been well; and when the headsman knelt to ask her forgiveness, she pardoned him, but exclaimed, "I die a Queen, but I would rather have died the wife of Culpeper."[40]

The moral of every confession, writes Christopher Pye, was the condemned's self-negating inscription within the law: "I see I must die, because I have not been constant to myself."[41] Howard's second confession, however, raises the question of which "self" she has betrayed. It sparks an alternative logic of self-continuity, re-identifying Howard with the theme of fidelity, but tying that fidelity to her nonroyal lover. The former scaffold speech imagines her as the source of Henry's personal victimization and the nation's political jeopardy; her reputed promiscuity represented the delegitimation of monarchical succession. But the latter imagines her as an individual agent clinging faithfully to her role as Culpeper's wife, despite having been led astray by the flatteries of an overly-amorous king. As represented in this second scaffold speech, the king was an obstacle to her "honest union" with Culpeper. Perhaps this is Howard's more serious crime: shunning the putative privileges of royal matrimony to reclaim the supremacy of her own domestic imaginings. To do so was to envision a different England, one in which a teleology of royal marriage did not govern all premarital sexuality, in which marriage might be a matter of personal consent rather than national proclamation, and in which emotional fidelity, volatile and invisible, claimed its own authority.

Howard's attainder redefined her into a system of sexual promiscuity and concealment. Her body was remade into a repository of secret places and privy marks; her mind was reformed into a site of pure willfulness (her motto had been "No other will than hers"[42]); and her past was rewritten as a sequence of encounters with doublets and hose between the sheets. At the time she married, she was assessed as "a hazel-eyed, auburn haired beauty"; "the radiant hope for a strong Tudor succession"; the child of a "noble and illustrious family"; a woman with "a notable appearance of honour, cleanness, and maidenly behavior"; a "jewel" of womanhood and virtue.[43] By parliamentary decree, she became, instead (or, in the logic of self-continuity, she reverted to being) a woman who "led an abominable, base, carnal, voluptuous and vicious life, like a common harlot, with divers persons, . . . maintaining however the outward appearance of chastity and honesty."[44]

Although I asserted earlier that Howard's "nation had need of her," what the attainder makes evident is that one *version* of the nation had need of her. In her attainder, we see competing visions of nationhood and competing interests construed as "national": her marriage signified the political ascendancy of an idea of England that was conservative, Catholic, and feudal in its leanings, and it promised through the legitimating power of patriarchal succession to transmit that England to future generations. Her body became a site of competition not as "her" body, but, under the marriage contract, as the property of her royal husband. She figured in the perpetuation of the nascent Tudor dynasty at a time when social and political stability was typically anchored in representations of genealogical succession. Like the wives figured in moots at the Inns of Court, Howard is positioned within the confines of a national project in which any assumed act of female adultery "could at any moment make a mockery of the whole story."[45]

When she was interrogated as a witness in the Howard attainder, Catherine Tylney, a servant, reported that at least twice during a recent progress to the north with the king, the queen had left her own chamber at night and "had gone on two occasions to Lady Rochford's room, which could be reached by a little pair of back stairs near the Queen's apartment."[46] Tylney and another servant, Margery Morton, reported having been sent by Howard on mysterious secret errands to Lady Rochford, the accused go-between with Howard's lovers, with messages they could not understand. Lady Rochford herself deposed that the queen had held many interviews in her rooms with Thomas Culpeper for several months: "But as Culpeper stood at the farther end of the room with his foot upon the top of the back stairs, so as to be ready to slip down in case of alarm, and the Queen talked to him at the door, Lady Rochford professed to be ignorant of what had passed between them."[47] "One night, she recalled, the Queen and herself were standing at the back door at eleven at night, when a watchman came with a lantern and locked the door. Shortly afterwards, however, Culpeper entered the room, saying that he and his servant had picked the lock."[48] Punctuated with images that elide the material differences between entering a woman's body and entering her rooms, these articulations of architecturally unconfined and undefined behavior register a popular, patriarchal anxiety: "the fear of a house that is too open, penetrable by and hospitable to any number of disorderly and masterless men, analogized implicitly with the female body in its stubborn resistance of male control."[49]

More than merely circulating the ideological resonances of female accessibility, however, Tylney's testimony foregrounds the priority of Howard's association with women over her relationship with her husband. The cultural commonplace was that with marriage a woman transferred her loyalty and possessions from father to husband, forsaking the former to unite with the latter. These parallel relocations of loyalty and household are treated widely in such popular theater as *A Midsummer Night's Dream*, where Helena and Hermia reject not only their fathers' wills but also their female friendship in competing for men. Earlier in the century, as it is represented in the Howard attainder, a woman's relocation from one household to another does not bring with it any reduced sense of personal authority, a self-possession the trial seems to comprehend as the root of Howard's criminality. In the identity crafted for Howard, her "crime" is a result of her upbringing: a childhood and adolescence lacking what counted as effective discipline. Both the attainder and the early biography entwined with it lay that lack and its consequent promiscuity at the door (or, more accurately, on the back stairs and in the bedchamber) of a household of women which Howard had only imperfectly forsaken.

Katherine was a child when her mother died. When her father remarried, she was placed under the care of her grandmother, the Dowager Duchess of Norfolk, with whom she lived, "in common with the women-servants," in Norfolk and later in Lambeth.[50] Inserting Katherine among the servants, the biography immediately places (or, according to a logic of hierarchical status, misplaces) her in the household. Moreover, whatever the condition of the Duchess's household prior to Howard's entry, her insertion into it initiates accounts of domestic space overrun with female eroticism: one by one wooers inside and outside the Duchess's immediate household approach the young Katherine. In "The Refuges of Intimacy," Orest Ranum has shown that early modern households were undergoing a long-term transformation in the conceptualization of space.[51] One aspect of that transformation was that shared spaces became demarcated by association with the activities that took place within them, and their meanings became increasingly contingent as much on moral as on architectural distinctions. In the Howard attainder, these conceptual transformations are brought about by the descriptions of Howard's trysts, which characterize (in the root sense of "lend her character to") each area she occupies. Yet as the assignations recur, the paradoxical effect is to obscure Howard as an individual and to replace her with an atmosphere of amorphous sexuality.

According to the treason depositions, soon after Howard moved into the Norfolk household, Mannock became her tutor. On at least one occasion, the Duchess discovered Mannock hugging Howard and upbraided him, beat Howard, and forbade any future meetings.[52] Mannock later deposed that he "fell in love with [Katherine] and she with him, but the Duchess found them alone together one day and gave mistress Catherine two or three blows, and charged them never to be alone after."[53] Despite the Duchess's subsequent intermittent punishments and beatings, Mannock and Howard continued to meet.

With Mannock still in the household, a rival, Francis Dereham, entered, trailing his own erotic power: "Dereham, with the lovers of two of the [Duchess's] women, used to obtain access almost nightly to the dormitory, where they remained feasting and rioting until two or three in the morning." Although "the old Duchess always had the keys of the maids' dormitory, where Katherine also slept, brought to her chamber after the doors were locked," Dereham and the young women apparently circumvented the Duchess's discipline.[54] The deposition of a servant in the household, Catherine Tylney, claims, "Once she [the Duchess] found Dereham embracing Mistress Catherine Howard in his arms and kissing her, and thereat was much offended and gave Dereham a blow, and also beat [Katherine] and gave Joan Bulmer [a servant] a blow because she was present." Finally, as we saw earlier, during the treason interrogation, "Derrham confessed that he had known [Katherine] carnally many times, both in his doublet and his hose between the sheets, and in naked bed, alledging such Witnesses of three sundry women one after another, that had lien in the same bed with them when he did the acts."[55]

In repeating the detail of Howard's sleeping in the maids' dormitory, the accounts suggest an uneasiness about a reciprocal leveling of class and morality that is here expressed erotically, in the sharing of beds and the proximity of bedpartners. Although the visibility of the bed at the center of the chamber may surprise a reader more accustomed to modern structures of intimacy, Lena Cowen Orlin explains that "household inventories of the sixteenth and seventeenth centuries list beds in nearly every conceivable space

—halls, parlors, stair landings, outbuildings, and kitchens, as well as bedchambers proper—in houses of all sizes, status, and regions."[56] "The basic distinction available to early moderns," Orlin writes, "was not that of the public and the individual space but that of the public and the shared."[57] What characterizes the Howard story is not a demarcation of space into particular rooms where acts understood as "private" or "secret" might occur, but the threat of an extension of indeterminate, unbounded sexuality into all the surrounding space. Positioning the trysts in group and public situations ("three sundry women one after another, . . . had lien in the same bed with them when he did the acts"),[58] the narrative sustains a link between Howard's presence and a pervasive eroticism. To put it more directly, where Katherine Howard goes, there goes sex. Here, that sex eludes containment, and refuses to remain not only in one place, but in one form: the description of Howard's activities includes the potential for a man and a woman, a man and several women, or a woman with other women to be sharing in sexual activities.

It is not primarily, however, the kinds of sexuality that are relevant but the links to a wider cultural discourse on the meanings of place. The Howard attainder, like virtually every treason trial throughout the century, registers anxiety about a shifting sense of spatial meanings. In his study of geography and meaning in drama, Glenn Clark has argued that early modern conceptions of space are "rhetorical" in the sense of socially-encoded, and that "Such rhetoricization may be possible in part because of the contemporary deterioration of the conception of the hierarchical universe itself, and the substitution for it of a voidlike, homogenized space" vulnerable to transformation by or into nostalgic rhetoric.[59] By the early 1590s, this notion of the vulnerability of space to rhetorical transformation will be captured in *Doctor Faustus* by Christopher Marlowe's Mephistophilis, with his pronouncements that *what* one is characterizes *where* one is: "Why this is hell, nor am I out of it" (1.3.76); "Hell hath no limits, nor is circumscribed / In one self place, but where we are is hell, / And where hell is, there must we ever be" (2.1.119–21).[60] Yet whereas Marlowe's play evokes an emergent discourse in giving priority to the consciousness of individuated characters, the Howard attainder reflects an earlier ethos in which the person is subsumed into the concept: rather than an individual consciousness reforming space (and it is important to note that we hear nothing of Howard's voice in these accounts), an idea of disembodied sexuality permeates every place Howard occupies. Increasing the amount of space perceived as erotic, the discourse saturates sites that had carried other domestic designations—a tutoring corridor, a dormitory, a maids' chamber, a back stair, and so on.[61] In the trial, Howard's omnitopic eroticism is presented as a claim on shared space, and that space is made sexual and disorderly by the intrusive acts of hedonistic women, who threaten to transform every place into a site of pleasure. Put another way, in this ideology of space, affiliations among women produce sites of unsanctioned erotic activity.

The popular image of the sexually inexhaustible woman, which traced its origins to Greece and Rome, was not new, of course. Its familiarity conditioned the persuasiveness of the claims against Howard, and its fantasy of women's households as sites of male sexual victimization contributed to the "believability" of those charges and to the more widespread social imaging of the masterless house. Howard's behavior was described in ways that matched and met expectations circulating in contemporary tracts and literatures. During Howard's marriage to Henry, for example, both Edward Gosynhill's *Mulierum Paean* (c. 1542) and the anonymous *Schoolhouse of Women* (c. 1541) appeared. Taking what Katherine Henderson and Barbara McManus call "a cook's tour of the conventional stereotypes of women—their love for fashion, their spendthrift ways, their vanities, their sexual voraciousness, their infidelity, their shrewishness, and so on," the *Schoolhouse* imagines "women's households as a forum for training women in gossip and male manipulation": "Thus learn the younger of the elders' guiding; / Day by day, keeping such schools, / The simple men they make as fools."[62] Such misogynist tracts do not only emphasize women's duplicity and envision their conversations as male-centered; they also characterize the spaces where women gather as sites of social subversion.

Unlike the *Schoolhouse*, which represents women's affiliations as violations of household discipline, the Howard attainder puts conventional, hierarchical discipline at its center. That discipline is gendered, however, in a way that further discredits the female of the house: as administered by a woman to women, it fails completely. "Even if the woman tries to produce domestic order," the Howard story claims, "she cannot succeed." Despite the Duchess of Norfolk's efforts in withholding the keys to Katherine's rooms (with their conventional significance of locking the woman's chastity), in berating would-be lovers, and in repeatedly beating Katherine and any servants unfortunate enough to have been within reach, assignations continued (if the transcriptions are to be believed) nearly without interruption. Tylney's deposition reports that if someone asked where Dereham was, "the Duchess would say, 'I warrant you if you seek him in Catherine Howard's chamber ye shall find him there.'"[63] Neither woman nor space yields to physical, moral, or conceptual discipline.

Ultimately the embattled Duchess dismissed several servants who appeared to have been involved in Howard's trysts and moved Howard to Lambeth to live among a new set of people. Yet what is striking about this part of the story is that the erotic imaging relocated with the members of the household: once they settled at Lambeth, it was rumored that Dereham attempted clandestinely to renew his relationship with Howard, but that she rebuffed him; that Howard was seduced by and betrothed to her third lover, her cousin Thomas Culpeper; and that the affair ended when Henry was taken with Howard during a visit to Lambeth.[64]

What is represented as being at stake in this failure to rule is social stability itself. In the decades following the Reformation, the individual household became the primary unit of social control and the male householder became "responsible for the maintenance of moral order in his immediate sphere" not only for himself or his village but "to macrocosmic benefit."[65] When only a woman is present to administer that order, however, as in the Howard attainder, her efforts emerge as lesser versions of an elusive, authentic power, which appears always to reside just outside the boundaries of the household. Historical evidence suggests that fully half the widows of the sixteenth century did not remarry and maintained their own households after their husbands' deaths.[66] Yet, as Linda Woodbridge has shown, the widow in Renaissance literature is represented as "unregenerately lecherous," an imaging that appears as a reaction to widows' relatively independent status.[67] This popular imaging appears in the Howard case: centered on an unruly household run by a female, the attainder implies that only the male-headed home can achieve domestic and personal order and effectively enclose sexuality within the bounds of propriety.

According to one logic, a household of women produces and spreads an atmosphere of unbridled eroticism; sexual activity is its "way of being" a women's household. The solution to such pervasive sexualizing is the reorganization of the household and its hierarchy by the introduction of a male head. Given the orthodoxies of the day, Howard's relocation from the Duchess's to the king's household when she became his wife "ought" also to have repositioned and contained her sexuality. Instead, however, the attainder produces an alternate logic that it ultimately criminalizes with post facto legislation: despite her position in a male-headed household, Howard is represented as acting in Henry's domain no differently than she acted in the Duchess's, overriding the ordering authority of even the highest earthly patriarch. Moreover, that self-authorized persistence is attributed not to the inadequacy of a male householder but to the triumph of an association among women.

Although much has been made of Katherine Howard's position in the Henrician treasonous adulteries, little has been said about the female fidelities that were intertwined with her conviction. Both, I believe, were discursive necessities in producing evidence of her "criminality." Officially, Howard was convicted of having jeopardized the nation by jeopardizing the king's well-being and succession; ideologically she was convicted of having been sexually active when she lived in a community of women: "Actual adultery is not alleged, . . . The *liaison* with Dereham before the marriage was not denied; nor were the meetings with Culpeper after the marriage. This and the concealment were sufficient."[68] Considerable responsibility for that "concealment" is placed at the threshold of a women's house. Howard,

> whom the King took to wife, is proved to have been not of pure and honest living before her marriage, and the fact that she has since taken to her service one Francis Dereham, with whom she used that vicious life before, and has taken as chamberers a woman who was privy to her naughty life before, is proof of her will to return to her old abominable life.[69]

Written while the Howard attainder was still fresh in memory, and circulated within a few years of her brief marriage and swift execution, Nicholas Udall's *Ralph Roister Doister* (c. 1550–53) can be understood as the playwright's reply to the Henrician discourse of matrimonial treason. Udall's work shapes its logic of female fidelity by purging the home of clandestine frolic and introducing an ideologically-narrowed revision of female constancy. Custance, a young widow overseeing a household of women, like Howard finds her honor suspect and her character contingent on the testimony of others. Unlike the historical Katherine, however, the fictional Custance brings conventional order to the domestic scene. As Udall stages it, her ability to secure that order is contingent on the testimony of male protectors and the (re)institution of a temporarily absent male householder. In place of the pervasive eroticism that infiltrated the architectural and conceptual space in the attainder, however, is a dramatization of repetitious boundary drawing. Put another way, where the attainder was devoted to expanding erotic space, Udall's domestic comedy is devoted to building doors. As they publish ways of imagining the structures, themes, and events of women's domestic life, both works contribute to the circulation of notions about what can be recognized as "in the true" (to return to Foucault's phrase) about women, and both reveal elements of what women's households were made to mean in early Tudor writings.[70]

An eminent clergyman and scholar, Udall was favored by Henry VIII, Edward VI, and Mary. Once headmaster of both Eton and Westminster schools, he was well-connected at court and may have been quite familiar with the Henrician matrimonial treasons in general and with the Howard attainder in particular.[71] Relatively little is known of Udall's dramatic activities except that they appear to have been extensive.

> He wrote verses for London pageants at Anne Boleyn's coronation in 1532; was perhaps the author of a late miracle play called *Placidas alias Sir Eustace* in 1534 at Braintree, Essex (of which he was vicar, 1533–7); . . . brought his Eton boys to play before Cromwell in 1538 (nothing is known of the play, which may have been in Latin); and perhaps at this period composed the lost *Ezekias* which was later acted at the sister-foundation King's College, Cambridge. He had produced court "dialogues and enterludes" before Mary "at soondrie seasons" before 1554, when he was authorized to receive "apparell" for his forthcoming "devises" at Christmas. He died in 1556.[72]

Traditional scholarship about *Ralph Roister Doister* has generally emphasized generic conventions and focused on its place in the history of early English theater. According to these interpretations, Ralph, a transplanted Plautine *miles gloriosus*, is a stereotypical self-deluded braggart driven by lechery. Custance, "a virtuous English widow," is a displacement of "the familiar courtesan of Greek and Latin comedy," who in Udall's play "runs an English household with her vivacious English servant women." She "is wooed by a worthy English merchant [Gawyn Goodluck] who takes the precaution of assuring himself that she is an innocent party after she has been maligned. These are not frivolous characters but representatives of the solid British middle class upon which depended the prosperity and power of Elizabethan England."[73] Within that class-representation, "The heroine . . . could not have been allowed to act with the independence of her prototype in Terence, the courtesan Thais, if Udall had not made her a widow, free from parental authority."[74] Custance, in this view, occupies a liminal thematic space, detached from her father's and dead spouse's households and not yet married into Goodluck's. Norman Sanders identifies the limiting framework of the play—"the absence of Gawyn Goodluck"—as that which makes possible Ralph's self-deceived courtship.[75]

More relevant to its proximity to the Howard treason, Goodluck's absence also focuses Udall's work on the representation of beleaguered fidelity in a household of women. In the play, however, unlike in the attainder, the audience always knows the truth. The focus is not on the determination of Custance's honesty, but on the conditions for interpreting her fidelity. Such a structure places Udall's comedy firmly within the gender work of "anxious masculinity" analyzed by Mark Breitenberg: sexuality and knowledge are "in a reciprocal dynamic of mutual power and legitimation for men," one which also suggests "almost an interchangeability between carnal and interpretive knowledge." While the carnal is prominent in the Howard attainder, the interpretive is prominent in Udall's play. In it, as Breitenberg writes about later sixteenth-century plays, "the staging of false accusations . . . prolongs and intensifies the interpretive suspicion."[76] False accusations legitimate masculine authority not only to settle the "doubt" projected on to women, but also to establish the *means* of settling that doubt and to determine what will count as the evidence for or against her.

The claims against Custance are less charges than suspicions. After dedicating acts 1 through 3 to Ralph's comic wooing, Udall devotes much of acts 4 and 5 to accusing, "trying," and clearing Custance of the taint of emotional disloyalty. In this discursive situation, Udall demonstrates that the accusations spring from prior (and, in Udall's work, unmerited) doubt, and that doubt in turn seeks the signs or evidence that will justify it. Act 4 opens with the return of Sim Suresby, who has risked "an outrageous tempest" to come ahead of his master, Gawyn Goodluck:

> Now the first point wherefore my master hath me sent
> Is to salute Dame Christian Custance, his wife
> Espoused, whom he tendereth no less than his life.
> I must see how it is with her, well or wrong,
> And whether she for him doth not now think long. (4.1.1–5)[77]

Suresby's task is double: "to salute" Custance and to determine "whether she for [Goodluck] doth not now think long," that is, to investigate woman's intellectual fidelity. Rhetorically, Udall signals that Goodluck and Custance are a perfect match: to Suresby's message from Goodluck Custance replies with identical language, "I think now long for him" (4.1.7). Structurally, however, Udall pits Custance's vows against Suresby's suspicions. Roister Doister and his wily servant Merrygreek interrupt the reunion with another round of wooing; Ralph declares, "Well found, sweet wife, I trust, / for all this your sour look!" (4.3.29–30); Merrygreek refers to letters from Roister Doister to Custance; and she acknowledges that the would-be spouse has sent "tokens." The discourse of doubt Udall is dramatizing allows Suresby to take these references as the signs of Custance's dishonesty: "Somewhat there is, I fear it" (4.1.6); "this gear goeth acrook" (4.1.32).[78]

By positioning Suresby to read the tokens as signs of Custance's inner infidelity, Udall evokes a wider cultural discourse on the meanings of souvenirs within which tokens function as multifaceted evidence of an elusive intimacy. And like treason, such intimacy need not involve a bodily act to be represented as transgressive; it has an intellectual setting. Juan Luis Vives admonished in *Instruction of a Christian Woman*, "Be not proud, maid, that thou art holy of body if thou be broken in mind, nor because no man hath touched thy body if many men have pierced thy mind."[79] The Howard attainder took gifts as evidence of intimacy in reporting that Francis Dereham, among others, bestowed them on Katherine: "artificial flowers, articles of dress, or materials for them, trinkets and adornments," and food and drink for the nightly tables. Culpeper, too, deposed that Katherine when queen had given him a velvet cap.[80] Suresby sees would-be lovers and hears of letters and rings. Like intimate spaces, souvenir objects, Orest Ranum points out, were sites that lent themselves to "intimate uses" and to provocative "thoughts" whose social significance and value extended beyond simple ownership. Conduct books make it clear that the thought associated with tokens was gendered and tied to conceptions of selfhood: "A woman that giveth a gift, giveth her self: a woman that taketh a gift, selleth her self. Therefore an honest woman shall neither give, nor take," wrote Vives.[81]

Knowing the truth about women's hearts, as Udall shows, becomes a problem not because of women's actions (Custance, true to the allegorical implications of her name, never waivers in her devotion to Goodluck) but because of the misinterpretations that attend on male doubts. The resolution of the problem cannot be provided by the woman (since it is not caused by her) but only by reaffirmations of complex male-male loyalty. Suresby's first scene sets in motion a rhetoric of such loyalty. Having risked a tempest to come ashore ahead of Goodluck—"Is there any man but I, Sim Suresby, alone / That would have taken such an enterprise him upon, / In such an outrageous tempest as this was? (4.1.1–3)—Suresby allies his risk-taking with his loyalty to Goodluck: "But fie on that servant which for his master's wealth / Will stick for to hazard both his life and his health!" (4.1.9–10). Tasked later with telling Goodluck his suspicions, Suresby vows:

To report that I heard and saw, to me is ruth,
But both by my duty and name and property
Warneth me to you to show fidelity.
It may be well enough, and I wish it so to be;
She may herself discharge, and try her honesty,
Yet their claim to her, methought, was very large,
For with letters, rings, and tokens, they did her charge. (5.1.4–10)

Tristram Trusty, too, promises to help Custance and to testify for her out of loyalty to Goodluck: "For my friend Goodluck's sake, ye shall not send in wast" (4.5.22).

In this show of male-male loyalty, doubt demands report, and report is a means of cementing relations among men.[82] Despite Suresby's claims that it may be dangerous and painful to report what he believes he saw (as it was dangerous for him to risk the stormy seas), "duty," "name," and "property" all demand that he do so "to show fidelity" to Goodluck. Again the play is usefully related to a crucial issue in the discourse of treason. When Cranmer first learned of the rumors about Howard, he "could not find it in his heart to express the same by word of mouth," yet loyalty demanded he "tell" the king. Ultimately, he wrote to the king about the claims. Later, following Howard's execution, Henry demanded legislation that made it treason to fail to tell the king one's suspicions about a woman's fidelity:

> An Act was also passed, declaring that it shall be lawful for any of the King's subjects, if themselves do perfectly know, or by vehement presumption do perceive any will, act or condition, of lightness of body in her which shall be the Queen of this realm, to disclose the same to the King or some of his Council. But they shall not openly blow it abroad or whisper it, until it be divulged by the King or his Council. If the King or any of his successors shall marry a woman which was before incontinent, if she conceal the same it shall be high treason, &c.[83]

The effect was not only to make it a man's duty to report his suspicions but to make it a capital crime for him to fail to do so, a view Udall approves of in Suresby's vows. Like the law, Udall's work suggests that loyalty among men is contingent on their reporting suspicions about women to each other. In this dynamic, the culturally diffuse notion that a woman is concealing something is a useful tool in developing affiliations among men; failure to report such suspicions is both a political and a domestic crime. Loyalty to the male householder, like loyalty to the monarch, could be demonstrated by offering a report of a disloyal wife.

Although trial texts aim to forge a unified story from disparate elements, Udall's play is committed to no such cohesiveness. Instead, the playwright mines discrepancies between what he can *show* and what Suresby *tells*, interrogating the value of report and exposing a consequential gap between the imperative *to* report and the truth represented *in* a report. The issue, as Udall understands it, is a gendered concept of knowledge: what men know becomes the ground of what counts as "knowledge," and both the trial and play are engaged in circumscribing what will count as true "knowledge" of woman. Goodluck responds to Suresby's initial report about Custance with a slipping fidelity of his own: "All things that shineth is not by and by pure gold. / If any do live a woman of honesty, / I would have sworn Christian Custance had been she" (5.1.14–16). For him, Suresby's report and true knowledge of Custance are at this moment the same thing. Suresby, however, urges caution about such easy equivalencies: "Sir, though I to you be a servant true and just, / Yet do not ye therefore your faithful spouse mistrust; / But examine the matter" (5.1.17–19). As Udall problematizes it, report is only one way among a possible range of ways of "knowing" the truth about a woman, and each of those is to be greeted with some skepticism. While the reporter's heart may be true, his interpretation may be wrong, as Custance acknowledges when she forgives Suresby, "because to thy master thou hast a true heart, /. . . / I forgive thee for my part" (5.4.22–24). Udall perceives a breach here between the motives of the witness, in this case the loyal Suresby, and the accuracy of his report.

The playwright's skepticism here aligns him with Coke in the contemporary debates over forms of evidence. Coke, as I noted earlier, argued for discrediting eyewitnesses because they produced too many different stories. Passed through an observer's imagination, the self-evident is neither so much "itself" nor "evident." Thomas Wilson, however, in the *Arte of Rhetorique* cites a proverbial preference for an observed truth: "I will soner truste mine eye, then myne eare."[84] In the attainder, reports of Howard's actions were converted to written documents. Perhaps Udall is exploring the nascent capacities of the stage to make its own truth claims, for he begins to mine the discrepancies between the seen and the reported. Ultimately, he suggests that "first hand" or "empirical" knowledge of woman's fidelity cannot be gained by observation, interpretation, and report.[85]

In dramatizing female fidelity on trial, Udall develops a complex view in which the female both reads herself in terms of what report will say about her *and* self-consciously views herself as differing from that report. No sooner do Ralph and Merrygreek approach than she worries, "What mean these lewd fellows thus to trouble me still? / Sim Suresby here, perchance, shall thereof deem some ill, / And shall suspect me of some naughtiness" (4.3.3). As Suresby awkwardly hurries to flee the chaos, Custance fears, "Surely this fellow misdeemeth some ill in me" (4.3.52). It is not enough to say that Custance has merely absorbed a prevalent ideology that positions her in a particular way, though her recitations of the place of women make it clear that she has:

O Lord! How necessary it is now of days,
That each body live uprightly all manner ways;
For let never so little gap be open,
And be sure of this—the worst shall be spoken. (5.3.1–3)

There is, however, more here than reproduction of a dominant ideology: Udall uses Custance as a means of qualifying a code's absolute hold on interpretation. She calls attention to her own perspective, and implies that different perspectives are possible; to adapt Jean Howard's formulation, in Custance, Udall reveals that this way of perceiving women is *somebody's* way of perceiving women.[86] And whereas in part she legitimates Suresby's reading of events by anticipating how he will see them, in part she also undermines the authority of that reading by insisting that his interpretations do not reflect reality. This is not to suggest that Udall is a protofeminist, but to recognize that his destabilizing of the easy equivalence between report and interpretation opens other aspects of this ideology of female fidelity to interrogation.

What is secured as documentary evidence in the Howard attainder is questioned as opinion in Udall's play. Custance contrasts what Goodluck ought to know with what he heard reported: "Could any man's report your mind therein persuade?" (5.2.14). She dresses down Suresby in similarly contrasting terms: "is this the honesty that ye have / To hurt me with report, not knowing the thing?" (5.2.17–18). Though Suresby reports what he "saw" (unlike, for example, a figure who merely lies), Udall shows that a report is always an interpretation and that any single interpretation is not necessarily authentic knowledge. What he adds to the mix is the importance of the male's knowledge of the woman's prior life: how Custance behaved in the past, Udall says, *ought* to enable Goodluck to believe her in the present.

As they were in the Howard attainder, spaces in *Ralph Roister Doister* are demarcated by association with the activities that take place within them, their identities contingent less on architectural than on moral distinctions. In fact, one of the ways theatrical and legal practices overlap is in their comprehension of space: both acknowledge considerable anxiety about undefined spatial meaning and both conceive of particular places facilitating particular behaviors. In the Howard household these conceptual demarcations were brought about primarily by the comings and goings of men into the women's domain: Howard reportedly told Culpeper, "if I had tarried still in the maiden's chamber I would have tried you."[87] In Udall's play, however, they are brought about primarily by the comings and goings of Custance's women servants. Recasting the attainder's spatial anxieties in simpler terms, Udall's play is embedded in the cultural work of testing woman's domestic authority and encouraging her to identify herself and her household with her spouse—even a dead or absent spouse.

Udall immediately images Custance's household as overflowing its architectural boundaries, and just as the servants overflow the building, their garrulous talk overflows the limits of appropriate conversation and impedes their work. Margery Mumblecrust, Tibet Talkapace, and Alice Alyface spin and sew in a public area in front of Custance's house, chatting of ale, of other tasty drinks, of their nimble tongues, and of the fun of clever argument. This is a "merry," humorous, and witty household; it buzzes with domestic labor; and it is sometimes disorderly and contentious. The servants quarrel over completing their work, sing about it, and intermittently fail to complete their tasks. In this domestic environment, the play valorizes Custance as a force of conservative order. Although the eavesdropping Ralph bemoans the very idea of discipline—"It would grieve my heart to see one of them beaten" (1.3.40)—Custance scolds, prods, and beats her servants into their proper "places," morally and physically. Unlike Howard, to whom no distinction from her servants is attributed in her private life, Custance is differentiated from the other women in her household by her acute sensitivity to public condemnation, her status—widow, householder, betrothed—and her habits of discipline. Yet although Udall casts Custance as a disciplining woman, his theme is the ineffectiveness of that discipline. Though Custance's ordering efforts may demonstrate what the play takes to be her proper relations to her servants, they also demonstrate that despite good intentions, a woman's household success is limited by the absence of the male householder. Talkapace, for example, scorns the beatings (the "curried coat") with which she is already familiar: "There it lieth! / The worst is but a curried coat, / Tut, I am used thereto; I care not a groat!" (1.3.76–78).

Where the Howard attainder is devoted to expanding erotic space, Udall's play is devoted to building a door beyond which to pass is to trespass.[88] Historically, women's lives spilled out of the household and extended to the washhouse, the fountain, the oven, the mill. "Doorways, streets, even public squares were taken over by women working—a world that cannot be called strictly domestic, in which barmaids washed their glasses in public waters, and which had not yet been contained by official regulations."[89] Dramatically, however, the door becomes both symbol and reality of entrance and welcome, a threshold and liminal space of morality. We might here recall the door-pounding scene in Shakespeare's *Comedy of Errors*, where the conceptual difference between hospitality and whoring shifts with each character's point of view. As Udall represents it, the interior of Custance's house is a repository not of expanding eroticism, a la Howard, but of discipline. Being outdoors translates into all sorts of behaviors that are either inappropriate or (more importantly for the play's quasi-legal constructions of knowledge) misapprehended; if a woman is outdoors, she is vulnerable not only to unsought advances, but to misperception and misinterpretation. Thus, Custance chastises her servants in terms that slur their gender—"Is all your delight and joy / In whisking and ramping abroad like a tomboy?" (2.4.5)—and embarks on a set-piece in which she frames women's place: "Good wenches would not so ramp abroad idly. / But keep within doors, and ply their work earnestly" (2.4.29–

30). According to this discourse of spatial meaning, to protect herself from misapprehension, the honest woman (whatever her status) "places" herself indoors, beyond the observations of intrusive and misguided eyes.

Yet what the eyes cannot penetrate, the tokens can, and it is the demarcation between indoors and out that Ralph's gifts threaten to blur. Ranum points out that "a souvenir was unique and intimate and yet immediately recognizable by society as such."[90] It was a socially-coded sign of a unique intimacy and of "inner consent," the crucial condition for authentic marriage. Custance attempts to prevent gifts from crossing her threshold, and the door to her house is the boundary to this kind of imaginative entry and to the kind of "piercing the mind" Vives cautions against. The play imagines Custance redirecting the misdirected servants from their errant ways to the path of spousal teleology: "I am bespoken; / And I thought, verily, this had been some token, / From my dear spouse Gawyn Goodluck" (1.3.7–9). She chastises Mumblecrust: "And see thou no more move me folly to begin. / Nor bring me no more letters for no man's pleasure, / But thou know from whom" (1.3.20–22). When another of Roister Doister's emissaries, Dobinet Doughty, later approaches Mumblecrust with a ring and a token for Custance, a chastened Mumblecrust (who earlier accepted a letter from Ralph to Custance [1.4.125]) this time refuses the mission: "Now, by the token that God tokened, brother, / I will deliver no token, one nor another!" (2.2.11–12).[91]

Despite the multiple perspectives on women's place Udall voices, he brings his play to the conventional ending toward which it was going from its beginning: Custance is reunited in every way with Goodluck. Perhaps one of the most unsettling aspects of this conclusion is the extent to which the play comprehends knowing female fidelity as a product of male testimony. Custance explains the jesting with Roister Doister to Goodluck, "Truly, most dear spouse, nought was done but for pastance" (5.2.22); Goodluck rebuffs her, "Yea, Custance, 'Better,' they say, a bad 'scuse than none'" (5.2.28); and Custance recruits Trusty to speak for her in this court of male conscience, "Why, Tristram Trusty, sir, your true and faithful friend, / Was privy both to the beginning and the end. / Let him be the judge and for me testify" (5.2.29–31). It is the superior credibility attributed to Trusty—by virtue of both his being a man *and* his having personal knowledge of "the beginning and the end"—that elicits Goodluck's confidence: "I will the more credit that he shall verify. / And because I will the truth know e'en as it is, / I will to him myself, and know all without miss" (5.2.32–34). The order and honesty of the fictional household is contingent on the thoughts of the male protagonist: as his mind is cleared, the moral atmosphere of the household is cleared.

In his introduction to *Ralph Roister Doister*, John Gassner states that the play offers conventional themes: "the spectacle of vanity suffering reproof and folly receiving correction."[92] In both cases, Ralph is the target. However, if we consider Udall's domestic comedy in relation to such contemporary events as the Henrician matrimonial treasons, in which each woman's personal history was transmuted into material for popular consumption and political advantage, and in which officials represented women's households as vulnerable, chaotic, and immoral, we might also conclude that the play was deeply engaged in doing other important cultural work. Udall's play is embedded in a historical transition when credibility in testimony is shifting from that associated with personal knowledge of the character of the accused to adjudication and interpretation of "facts" of a case; it recognizes the emergence of the interpretive model, even as it calls up personal knowledge of an individual's history as a crucial component. Tainted by Suresby, cleared by Trusty, and credited by Goodluck, Custance becomes in the play's final testimonials a figure of "constant fidelity" (5.4.11), "the pearl of perfect honesty" (5.4.12), and "a true wife" (5.4.14). The plot apportions to her and characterizes through her what will count as acceptable "domesticated" English space. Creating what will count as useable knowledge of the faithful English woman, Udall lends credibility to a gendered system in which the truth about a woman will be recognized primarily through transactions of loyalty among men. Within the dynamics of marital submission, however—"To your will I assent" (5.4.19), Custance promises Goodluck—the playwright also injects subversive glimpses of a woman's self-knowledge beginning to find a brief authority: as Custance tells Suresby, "I know mine own truth" (5.4.24).

Although the Henrician matrimonial treason acts were repealed under Edward VI in the late 1540s and under Mary I in the early 1550s, their social and discursive force endured. Displaced into "petty treason," matrimonial trials continuously reiterated and published official equivalences between an ordered, hierarchical marriage and an ordered England.[93] Put another way, the process of "knowing" the truth about women in legal and literary works became a way of "knowing" the state of the nation as it was perceived to be reflected in traditional gender categories. And just as concerns about patrilinear succession, unified loyal subjectivity, and stable gender assignments persisted in legal venues, so too did the reproduction of these tensions in a range of popular genres. Throughout the century, Tudor-Stuart dramas are full of stagings of female fidelity under scrutiny, and many plays could be used to study theatrical truth-telling.[94] Shakespeare's *Cymbeline*, in particular, puts Imogen on trial when the probing of female fidelities was once more acute: early in James I's reign, the nation was undergoing a political conversion from Elizabethanism to Jacobeanism, legitimate succession was again a controversial topic, and prosecutions for treason and its sister crime, witchcraft, had risen.[95] Both kinds of cases addressed problems of discovering an inward truth.

Although law courts claimed authority to establish officially the guilt or innocence of a subject's hidden self, the theater was leveling its own claim to telling reliable stories. Jean-Christophe Agnew has shown that during the early modern decades, "traditional social signs and symbols had metamorphosed into detached and manipulable commodities," and "professional theater offered itself, ironically, as the most credible instrument with which to visualize, so to speak, the lost transparency of other acts."[96] In order to assert its credibility, the theater can embrace what the law must suppress: the self-conscious display of its own processes, especially the processes of human mediation and intervention. In the courtroom, apparent evidentiary constructedness tends to make jurors skeptical about the legitimacy of a prosecution. In the theater, on the other hand, evidentiary constructedness is not necessarily good or bad; its moral and thematic effects depend on its specific dramatic contexts.

In Christopher Marlowe's *Doctor Faustus*, for example, theatricality affirms its credibility by appearing to critique the very notion of the authority of visible evidence, exposing that evidence as fictive and illusory. Foregrounding the problem of developing authoritative interpretations, Marlowe's play returns to an overdetermined element of bodily evidence, a privy mark, to ground a moment of verification. It briefly focuses on a German Emperor, at whose request Faustus has conjured Alexander and his paramour. The persuasive, ordering force of the scene is a detail derived from an old rumor about a clandestine lover:

EMPEROR: But, Faustus, since I may not speak to them,
To satisfy my longing thoughts at full,
Let me this tell thee: I have heard it said
That this fair lady, whilst she lived on earth,
Had on her neck a little wart or mole:
How may I prove that saying to be true?
FAUSTUS: Your majesty may boldly go and see.
EMPEROR: Faustus, I see it plain,
And in this sight thou better pleasest me
Than if I gained another monarchy. (4.2.58–67)

What is the truth about the paramour's past and how does one know it? The Emperor recalls having heard of the private mark, but he also mistrusts both his own memory and the truth of what he remembers. Perhaps it was only gossip. What, then, is the authoritative status of gossip? (In the Howard case, for example, Mary Lassells Hall was gossiping.) In *Doctor Faustus* the paramour's corpse corroborates the Emperor's memory; the memory corroborates the rumor; the rumor corroborates the historical reality of an anonymous paramour who is a staged delusion; and that delusion proves that a particular hero once lived. Marlowe's scene is deliberately equivocal in making sight the site of conflict, where a fabricated, memorial reconstruction bestows "eyewitness" validity on an absent past.

Like Marlowe's play, which derives much of its energy from mining the instabilities of theatrical illusions, Shakespeare's *Cymbeline* wears its simulation on its sleeve.[97] But what had been harmless (or more accurately, desired) within the frame of Marlovian magic turns potentially tragic within the darker frame of Shakespeare's work. The play dramatizes a range of ways that figures "know" what they know, attending self-consciously to the uncertainties of getting at the truth. In the process, it embeds the tainting of its heroine in a pattern of quasi-legal language that foregrounds problems of "knowing Imogen," ultimately linking authentic knowledge to the reestablishment of legitimate dynastic succession.[98]

In *Ralph Roister Doister*, the inquiry into Custance's loyalty is preceded by male mistrust, which seems to be a masculine prerogative. Doubt comes first; misinterpretations of behavior follow. In contrast, in *Cymbeline* the investigation into female fidelity appears to surface independently of the lover's doubt. It gains a halo of objectivity and a claim to be truth-seeking by appearing initially to surface independently of personal motives. Just as in the Howard attainder Lassells only "chances" to take up the issue of Howard's sexuality with his sister, so in *Cymbeline* Posthumus, Iachimo, and their French, Dutch, and Spanish interlocutors, only randomly and coincidentally revisit a conventional argument about ladies:

> FRENCH: It was much like an argument that fell out last night, where each of us fell in praise of our country-mistresses; this gentleman at that time vouching—and upon warrant of bloody affirmation—his to be more fair, virtuous, wise, chaste, constant, qualified, and less attemptable than any the rarest of our ladies in France.
>
> IACHIMO: That lady is not now living, or this gentleman's opinion by this worn out.
>
> POSTHUMUS: She holds her virtue still, and I my mind. (1.4.58–69)

Phrased in familiar patrilineal terms that repeatedly link each lady's virtue ("more chaste") to each man's legitimacy, the wager polices national boundaries by policing female sexuality: on the assured sexual virtue of each woman rests the superior political *virtu* of each country.[99]

Like the Howard-Cleves linkage, the Imogen-Ladies linkage forged here circulates a persuasive mode of thought: that the superior virtue of one woman is contingent on the inferior virtue of another. Structured as a contest between mutually exclusive moralities, the wager reiterates the trope of alternativity that characterizes discourses of treason and that here functions to differentiate and dissociate women from each other. In the attainder, either Howard or Mary Lassells "knows what marriage is"; again, either Howard or Anne of Cleves "retains her body in integrity." With quasi-legal precision, the "either-or" rhetoric limits the vantage points from which one might imagine the questions, narrowing the scope of conjecture. In the play, similar logic aims to control the play of the imagination and constrict the ways one might think about womanhood: Posthumus began

His mistress' picture; which by his tongue being made,
And then a mind put in't, *either* our brags
Were crack'd of kitchen-trulls, *or* his description
Prov'd us unspeaking sots. (5.5.173–78; emphasis added)

Unlike the attainder, however, the play undermines the limiting force of alternativity by shifting the ground of competition from what the Ladies *are* to what the men are *doing*, interjecting into the argument what the law struggles continuously to reformulate and displace, the problematic question of intention. In general, legal records limit and shape the voices and perspectives they include to a unified, conclusive version of events and the criminal. They are engaged in producing a "conviction" in both the legal and intellectual sense about the condemned's hidden and therefore presumably criminal character. That narrowing is helped along in the Howard attainder by the absence of Howard's voice, which might cause one to assume that the charges were not contested because they could not be contested. (In this context, Howard's absence might be taken as guilty silence, implicitly becoming additional evidence against her.) Shakespeare's play, however, displays Imogen's tainting dialogically, as a multivocal competition in which various voices, proofs, and motives contest and qualify each other. What the attainder unifies, the play multiplies, particularly the operations of personal motives in producing credible stories.

Shakespeare lays out the wager as a competition among the men to dominate the imaginative and verbal space, as they strive to avoid appearing as "unspeaking sots." In an evocative pun, Posthumus swears to hold his mind "*still*" (emphasis added), continuing in his belief and sustaining his mental calm. By the scene's end, what is under interrogation is not Imogen's fidelity but Posthumus's, Iachimo's target: "I make my wager rather against your confidence than [Imogen's] reputation" (1.5.120–21). The challenge, as Shakespeare writes it, is to belief itself, to the capacity to sustain an imagined relationship in one's own mind without evidence to confirm it.

That such interior activity is sustainable is the point of Imogen's skeptical resistance to Iachimo. Prior belief enables her to reject Iachimo's conversion of the Posthumus she knows into "the Briton reveller" (1.6.61), to refuse to be "reveng'd" on him, and to turn the tables on the teller of the tale. Her complex reaction collapses the distance between making a "true report" and being an honest man. It is Imogen who makes explicit the argument that the validity of the evidence rests on the purity of the evidence-giver's heart and that honest testimony springs from a desire not for personal gain but "for virtue": "If thou wert honorable, / Thou wouldst have told this tale for virtue, not / For such an end thou seek'st,—as base as strange. / Thou wrong'st a gentleman, who is as far / From thy report as thou from honour" (1.6.142–46). Reiterating Egerton's conservative comments in the Ralegh trial, that the truth of the tale is guaranteed by the internal integrity of its teller ("whoso is guiltless will speak truly and directly, but"),[100] Imogen distances the "report" from the figure it describes by making an issue of intention: in Iachimo, interiority, staged as troublesome and elusive in its morality, slips easily into an even more elusive ulteriority, staged as insistently immoral.

In the mid-1550s *Ralph Roister Doister* attributes false reports to error and misinterpretation; even the most loyal servant can misread what he sees and transmit his misreading. By the turn of the century, the intentions of the reporter are themselves objects of suspicion, and evidence of infidelity in *Cymbeline* acquires a new aggressiveness as the play attributes false reports to personal malice. *Cymbeline* identifies them as kinds of "assault" (1.6.150) and associates their violence with Iachimo in references to literary and legendary rapists. The act of assault is not physical but rhetorical: constructing a new Imogen identical with the idea of infidelity.[101] As many scholars have noted, Iachimo's secret entry into Imogen's private bedchamber evokes an atmosphere of physical and emotional violation and penetration, as his eye moves from a general view to the room's tightest corners:

I will write all down:
Such and such pictures; there the window; such
Th' adornment of her bed; the arras, figures,
Why, such and such, and the contents o' th' story. (2.2.24–27)[102]

Explicitly acknowledging the central importance of the "contents o' th' story" (the one Imogen was reading and the one he is writing) in constructing his persuasive image of Imogen-incontinent, Iachimo makes visible both the act of writing and the decorative details that will lend credibility to his having occupied private territories, appropriating ornamental elements to the needs of corroboration.

The scene self-reflexively exposes the operations of intention in building disbelief: this accuser begins with his conclusion ("but to my design"), collecting those "facts" that will best fit the story he plans to tell, and he transforms his story into writing, creating a substantial written record as a substitute for imaginary bodily acts. The theory of substitution operating here, in which writing bestows sustained "life" on words, is familiarly expressed in Castiglione's *The Book of the Courtier*: "writing is nothing other than a kind of speech which remains in being after it has been uttered, the representation, as it were, or rather the very life of our words."[103] Yet what is distinctive in the theater is the body on stage, which in *Cymbeline* contradicts rather than confirms written and oral report. What this tale of infidelity records—Imogen's promiscuity—the staging refutes: as Iachimo writes, Imogen lies sleeping, a body of evidence that is, to recall her words, far from report.

When, on his return to Posthumus, Iachimo claims to have found a secret Imogen quite different from the faithful mistress Posthumus imagines, he offers that discovery as though it were self-evident. The clearest thing about evidence in *Cymbeline*, however, is that it is neither stable nor self-pronouncing, its meanings open to resistance and reformulation. In her symmetrical account of "belief and resistance," Barbara Herrnstein Smith describes two views of knowledge: traditional, rationalist accounts "insist on the possibility of the *correction* of prior belief by present evidence," whereas constructivist accounts "stress the *participation* of the prior belief in the perception of present evidence."[104] In Udall's play, Suresby plays the rationalist, suggesting that Goodluck's prior belief in Custance has been misplaced, and Goodluck swiftly slips into that same rationalist mode, for which Custance chastises him: "Could any man's report your mind therein persuade?" (5.2.14). As swiftly as it is compromised, however, Custance's honesty is restored by the smooth operations of the system of male credit and verification. Shakespeare devotes more time to the dialogue between these stances, finding in them a challenge to belief that indicts both accuser and defender. Each time Iachimo (the rationalist here) offers his evidence, Posthumus (the constructivist) recontextualizes it, relying on his prior belief in Imogen's character to plant the ostensible fact in another explanatory field where it does not mean what it would (promiscuity, adultery) if it were left undisturbed in the contexts Iachimo controls.

When Iachimo accuses Imogen, Posthumus challenges him to "make it apparent"; when Iachimo describes her bedchamber, Posthumus discredits the details as "things [Iachimo] might have heard of here, by me / Or by some other"; when Iachimo describes the furnishings, Posthumus grants his having seen them, but denies their status as proof of sexual activity: "Let it be granted you have seen all this . . . the description / Of what is in her chamber nothing saves / The wager you have laid" (2.4.91–94). When the bracelet momentarily influences Posthumus, Philario reinterprets the meaning of Iachimo's possession: "It may be probable she lost it" (2.4.115). In Posthumus's resistance, Shakespeare temporarily lays waste to two powerful conventions of female infidelity, both of which appeared in the Howard attainder and in *Ralph Roister Doister*: the associations between access to the household and dishonesty, and the association between possessing a token and sharing intimacy. However, Iachimo overcomes Posthumus's resistance by expressing his knowledge as *visual* memory: as he offers the apparently irrefutable material evidence of the bracelet—"She stripped it from her arm. I see her yet" (2.4.101)—he represents the moment as an observed event whose meaning is as visible as the act itself.[105] Slipped from Imogen's body, the bracelet metonymically and visibly evokes the slippage of her chastity.

The bracelet enters the scene as substantial evidence designed to enable resolution; instead, its meaning becomes the source of further irresolution, as it spawns multiple alternative explanations and reveals the peculiar ambiguous status of objects in a trial.[106] Imogen prophetically identified one of the stories the bracelet might tell when she discovered its loss: "I hope it be not gone to tell my lord / That I kiss aught but he" (2.4.152–53). Iachimo's own version of the bracelet's meaning depends on adopting the view that there is only one explanation for his possessing it, one order of truth: Imogen permitted him access to her private self, signified by this personal ornament, and removed from her body (detached from herself) her fidelity to Posthumus. When the witness finally swears, "By Jupiter, I had it from her arm" (2.4.121), Posthumus revises his belief to fit Iachimo's version of the story: "The cognizance of her incontinency / Is this. She hath bought the name of whore thus dearly" (2.4.127–28).[107] Through Iachimo's interventions, the multiple meanings of this piece of evidence come to corroborate one another, as contrived proximity slips into willful promiscuity. Shakespeare seems quite concerned about the theory of knowledge these characters share: the rivals express a complex dynamic of legal belief and resistance as a mere *transference* of what is empirically knowable from one knower to another. In this view, there is no mediation by the interlocutors' motives or by language itself.

One of the curiosities of Shakespeare's play is that although Posthumus had earlier demanded more material evidence—"Render to me some corporal sign about her, / More evident than this; for this was stolen" (2.4.119–20)—it is the bracelet that wins him over. In *Cymbeline*'s sources, as in the Howard attainder and *Doctor Faustus*, a mole proves the female's promiscuous identity, and it does so by assuming a normative virtuous body: irregular markings imply irregular desires. In Shakespeare's play, only after Posthumus believes that Iachimo "hath enjoy'd her" does additional evidence appear:

> If you seek
> For further satisfying, under her breast—
> Worthy the pressing—lies a mole, right proud
> Of that most delicate lodging. By my life,
> I kiss'd it; and it gave me present hunger
> To feed again, though full. (2.4.133–36)

The redirected import of this mole is less to prove the claims against Imogen than to punish Posthumus for "holding his mind" by graphically representing Iachimo's knowledge of "Imogen-incontinent" as physical knowledge. In the reference to the mole, with its associations with "her breast" and the "present hunger / To feed," Iachimo's proof crosses over into what Patricia Parker elsewhere describes as a "pornographic doubleness": it both opens up and denies to the eye the "secret" part of woman.[108] The potential meanings of that opening up are multiplied by the roles bodily marks play in the widespread contemporary practice of witch-hunting. Linking witchcraft trials to the ambiguous, contradictory position of women in post-Reformation culture, Christina Larner has shown that these popular legal events continuously reproduced the patriarchal practice of differentiating between women on the basis of conformity to dominant social codes.[109] And Gail Paster has explained that these trials introduced "the witch into the category of the sexually deviant and transgressive female," subjected the woman's body to a "shameful transformation," and found "in the apparent objectivity of bodily evidence a means of occluding the ideological grounds for social division."[110]

In *Cymbeline*, the objectivity of that bodily evidence is never at issue; rather, its meanings shift and multiply with the contexts in which it appears. As Iachimo crafts it, Imogen can be identified as "herself" and that self can be aligned with "the name of whore" by a private mark that is offered as though it were self-interpreting. As Shakespeare crafts it, however, the self-identifying body is neither gender-specific nor uniform in its meanings, and the feature designed to cement the representation of "Imogen-incontinent" becomes the means of destabilizing her identity again and of effecting social and political transformations none of the play's characters could foresee. In the play's final scene, the mole is recast from the sign of corruption and transgression into the sign of royalty and legitimate dynastic succession: King Cymbeline's long lost son Guiderius is revealed as a nobleman and reinserted into the royal lineage through a mole he shares with his sister:

> This is he,
> Who hath upon him still that natural stamp.
> It was wise Nature's end in the donation,
> To be his evidence now. (5.5.365–68)

Repositioned by the operations of patrilinearity from potential queen—"O Imogen, / Thou hast lost by this a kingdom" (5.5.372–73)—to loving wife and sister, Imogen aligns herself with those operations by embracing domesticity and reconceiving it as sovereignty: "No, my lord; / I have got two worlds by it" (5.5.373–74).

It is here that the God-not-in-evidence who haunts treason trials, evoked in order to testify to the internal honesty and subjective integrity of the participants, appears in the form of the playwright. Throughout, Shakespeare has positioned the spectators along side himself as possessors of divine knowledge, equally privy to the truths that Imogen is faithful, Iachimo a hypocrite, and his reports sinister falsifications of sustained chastity. In a final turn, however, Shakespeare claims still superior knowledge by bringing to light what no character and no spectator could foresee, Nature's hand in marking the royal siblings' bodies. As they do in the Howard attainder, so here, the meanings of the "natural stamp" mutate with the interpretive contexts in which it operates *as* evidence. Yet what the law obscures, this play foregrounds: the hand of the author in providing proof.

Taken as a theatrical deliberation on the uncertainties of early modern struggles with epistemology, theatricality, and truth, *Cymbeline* makes its claims to credibility through the strategy of an exposé, revealing the intentions of men in the operations of persuasion: representing motivated evidence, Iachimo confesses

> my practice so prevailed
> That I return'd with simular proof enough
> To make the noble Leonatus mad,
> By wounding his belief. (5.5.199–202)

In formulating its claims to truth-telling, the play raises the specter of a threatening dualism between women's apparent and secret fidelities—"Your daughter's chastity—there it begins" (5.5.179)—but it exposes that dualism not as a fearful truth or accidental error but as a deliberate and powerful fiction.

The Howard attainder, *Ralph Roister Doister*, and *Cymbeline* are among the clusters of tales told in trials, plays, ballads, and pamphlets that conditioned the idea of female fidelity in early modern English culture. Each is an instance of the repetitious cultural activity of playing out belief, and each formally posits a crucial moment in a woman's history when (due to the machinations of fate, chance, or nosy neighbors) her observable character suddenly appears to be a deception and a corrupt interior becomes visible. In these texts, female fidelity exists within a more general theory of nationhood and identity—one organized around ideas of the legitimacy of patrilinear purity, unified subjectivity, and secure gender hierarchy—that was asserted, interrogated, and reasserted again and again in law courts and theaters.

In producing its credible story, the attainder tends to minimize the effects of human agency and intervention, whether in something so elusive as personal motive or so apparent as a material document. It formulates the force behind legal proceedings as God's hand in the lives of men and women: "Now you may see what was done before the marriage; God knoweth what hath been done since."[111] The theater, on the other hand, might draw on any notion of evidence, natural, human, or divine, to make its claims. *Ralph Roister Doister* streamlines its interventions: there is misinterpretation that is readily solved by brief testimony among men. *Cymbeline*, in contrast, maximizes human intervention in Iachimo's production of "Imogen-incontinent." In the process, it identifies evil motives with individuals, making those motives the personal contrivances of villains: "*my* practice" prevailed, confesses Iachimo; "*I*" produced "simular proof enough" (emphasis added). One effect of that displacement is to confine the scope of "ill will" to an individual and prototypical Machiavel. Evil is attributed to one man. A concomitant effect, however, is to obscure the operations of dominant social codes and political discourses in bringing about "convictions."

During the sixteenth and early seventeenth centuries, law courts and theaters are formalizing their respective disciplines as professions, in some ways competing with each other to offer the more reliable version of things. To claim their respective credibilities, each repeatedly activates its epistemological rules for limiting what will be seen as "in the true," to return to Foucault's terms.[112] Yet whatever the terms of the contest, it is important to remember that the consequences for constructing credible stories of female fidelities on stage and in court were quite different: in the plays, the unfaithful female is cleared of all offenses and shown to be the victim either of mistaken interpretation (as in *Ralph Roister Doister*) or personal malice (as in *Cymbeline*); in both cases, she lives to embrace a socially- and theatrically-sanctioned domesticity. Even if each had not been cleared, however, and had gone to her death like Desdemona, the boy who played her would nonetheless have revived and survived to play another day. In the attainder, the unfaithful female is convicted of all offenses and shown to be an agent of malice and national instability. We do not know Katherine Howard's precise birthdate. We do know that in the discourses of treason she became a sign of the subversive dangers of affiliations among women and a legal prompt for unprecedented legislation against them. We know also that she had been queen of England for less than two years when she was beheaded on Tower Green February 13, 1542.[113]

3.
Masculinity, Affiliation, and Rootlessness

Although the nation is in some way at issue in all treasons, it is not always foregrounded in the same terms nor identified with the same cultural work. In the Howard attainder, Howard's having had at least one sexual partner prior to her marriage to Henry VIII was cast as treason. Her body became an object of legal knowledge, and female sexuality was embedded in new laws that retroactively criminalized both the sexual activity of unmarried women and any failure to report that activity. To explain Howard's adult behavior, prosecutors developed an implied theory of domestic associations among women: in the absence of a male householder to dispense discipline, female attempts to assume authority prove ineffective, which leads to the expansion of erotic behavior throughout all the architectural and imaginative space. More generally, the key themes of matrimonial treasons were transformed by law into national issues: women's associations with women and men were seen as threats not only to domestic but to government stability; their potential to disrupt the government justified heightened official interventions in women's activities from birth to death.

Men's activities evoke a different discourse of association and fidelity. As treason is recast from Howard's female crime of "misusing the body" (as Wriothesley had put it) to a male crime of misusing the mind, men are indicted for discussing "by what means and ways [their] false traitorous imagined practices might be brought to pass."[1] In this chapter, I want to focus on two well-known stories of masculine alliance and betrayal from the late 1580s: the infamous Babington treasons of 1586 and Christopher Marlowe's *Tamburlaine I*, written in 1587 or 1588. Like all treasons, the Babington trials structure their contest explicitly over the "forms of nationhood," to borrow Richard Helgerson's evocative title.[2] Their specific trouble point, however, is the role of male friendship in sustaining, renovating, or destroying that nation. These trials enact a discursive process of differentiating among "men"—of producing what will count as the English "man," of including the kind of "manhood" the law will recognize as belonging to true subjects of the realm, and of helping fabricate a stereotype of the "treacherous man."[3] That treachery is developed in part as a result of discursive links forged among courtiership, "the country," and rootlessness.

Like treason trials in general, and like the Babington accounts in particular, Marlowe's dramas stage conflicts over legitimate proprietorship in terms of disputed conceptions of "the country." The earliest of these plays, *Tamburlaine I*, may have been drafted while Marlowe was acting as a spy at Cambridge following the revelation of the Babington plot. The play is positioned directly against the themes of the Babington treasons, and in it Marlowe suggests that male friendship is superior to other forms of affiliation; it is the stuff from which new nations are made. What the Babington prosecutors fear and find treacherous—that fidelity to unauthorized male friendship will triumph over fidelity to the sovereign and "the country" she represents—Marlowe's play exalts.

It has become something of a commonplace in early modern English studies to observe ambivalent male feelings of subjection and mastery and to identify them with the provocations of a female monarch. According to these arguments, Barbara Correll writes, "as monarch and as woman, Elizabeth exploited and provoked psychological anxieties in her male subjects, anxieties of male selfhood which reflected the political tensions of a society in transition."[4] But in a powerful reading of Erasmus's discourses on civility, Correll has shown that even when there is no female monarch there is nonetheless widespread anxiety about "beleaguered masculine identity." Such anxiety can be understood not necessarily in terms of a unique female in a position of authority, but alternatively in terms of a social conflict "between hereditary and intellectual or bourgeois claims to power" that "reveals sexual anxiety in shifting notions of subordination and superiority."[5]

Treason trials, where natural and divinely ordained bases for ordering hierarchies were topics of continuous talk, are particularly rich sites for studying the cultural formation of masculine identity. I use "masculinity" here to designate a range of discursive positions a figure might occupy relative to cultural codes and assumptions that, though they often go without saying, underwrite and secure hierarchies. Narrowing the range of positions to a binary formulation of masculine versus feminine can obscure the subtle differentiations within the group of masculinity itself. Instead, my aim is to bring into visibility a range of discursive acts that inform the kinds of manhood these trials assert, challenge, and reject. In this view, not all that is designated "not masculine" designates "feminine," nor is all that is positioned as failed masculinity identical with effeminacy.

How did a group of thirteen young men, most of whom were Catholic though not particularly partisan about it, end up convicted of treason? They were linked inextricably to the anxieties in England about the imprisoned Mary Queen of Scots. Evidence of their treason was the means of justifying proceedings against her, and their prosecution was preceded by a series of unusual documentary events: the famous Papal Bull in 1570 excommunicating Elizabeth and allowing subjects to depose a ruler who had violated divine law; the ban on reforming princes in 1580 by the Brussels government forbidding princes from instigating religious conversions in their countries; and the "Statute of Silence" (28 Eliz. c. 2) in 1581 making it punishable by death to discuss the rights of any heir to the English throne and specifying that Elizabeth's successor would be named by a vote of her Privy Council. Evidence of heated international and domestic conflicts, these contributed to a climate of suspicion and resistance that surrounded the Babington prosecutions.[6]

What I am calling the Babington trials occurred over several days and involved thirteen defendants. Anthony Babington, a member of an ancient family with considerable wealth, was accused of recruiting a dozen like-minded friends to kill the queen and to rescue Mary.[7] According to historian Wallace MacCaffrey, the conspiracy was "a highly amateur, almost freelance affair."[8] The whole thing might have begun and ended with talk, were it not for the constant intervention of Francis Walsingham, who spearheaded the operation against the defendants and prodded his spies to keep the plot alive. Walsingham, strongly anti-Catholic and aggressively working to preserve England as a stronghold of Protestant orthodoxy, was appointed Secretary in Elizabeth's council in 1573, where he became a kind of de facto foreign secretary and the organizer of an intelligence network, which he enlarged during his years of service. During the years spying was most active (1582–88), the Babington conspiracy came to light.[9]

Around eleven o'clock on the morning of August 4, 1586, John Ballard, a recusant priest, was captured by the queen's guard and stowed in the Tower, where, according to Walsingham, he was to "be examined out of force by torture to utter that which otherwise he would not discover."[10] According to the Crown, Ballard had plotted with the Spanish and with a group of disaffected young Englishmen to invade England, assassinate Elizabeth, and see Mary, Queen of Scots, rescued from custody and enthroned.[11] Rumors of Ballard's capture spread swiftly among his cohorts and sent them fleeing in all directions. Chief among them was Anthony Babington, who rushed to Chidiock Titchburne's lodgings, only to find them deserted. Scurrying from Titchburne's to a barber's near Bishopsgate, Babington made a terrifying discovery: three official sketches—of himself, Titchburne, and a third confederate, John Savage—had already been posted there in anticipation of his arrival; each bore scrawls demanding information about the criminals.[12]

Again Babington fled, this time to Smithfield, where finally he rendezvoused with Titchburne. Their reunion, however, only added to Babington's growing troubles: as Titchburne would later testify, because one of his legs was injured, he could not ride well enough to meet his fellows. Cursing this bad luck, Babington complained: "I had rather than 500£. thy leg were whole, for then this matter should be dispatched."[13] Had it not been for a lame leg, it appears, the nation would have been lost and Elizabeth would have faded into history in the twenty-seventh year of her reign. But Titchburne was lame, and within ten days all thirteen of the men named as Ballard's conspirators had been swept up by the efficient hands of the law.

On Wednesday, September 14, 1586, Babington stood among his cohorts and listened to the charges: that Bernardine de Mendoza, a Spanish ambassador to King Philip, and Charles Paget, Mary Stuart's confidant in Paris, "maliciously and wickedly devised by what ways and means this realm of England might be invaded, and by what ways and means Mary queen of Scots might be delivered"; that they passed this on to Ballard, who would go to England "to understand and know what ports and landings might be procured and provided" for the invasion; and that Babington and his confederates "as false traitors against the crown and queen's most excellent majesty, your true and natural sovereign; intending to put away the love of her majesty's most loving subjects . . . did falsely, horribly, traitorously, and devilishly conspire, conclude and agree, the queen's most excellent majesty not only from her royal crown and dignity to depose, but also her to kill and slay."[14]

The Crown called the members of the Babington group rebels; the accused identified themselves as loyalists; both sides legitimated themselves by referring to a range of shared cultural codes and positions. The struggle at the center of these courtroom maneuvers suggests a profound competition among men over traditional male privileges and, more subtly, over what counts as legitimate masculine identity. What role do these competitions play in structuring relationships among masculine identity, affiliation, and the homeland in early modern discourses?

In numerous repetitions throughout the trials the prosecution takes "the country" as having a transparent referent, speaking as though "the country" were a stable entity with a specifiable, self-pronouncing identity. The idea of "the country" hovers over the testimony, serving as motive and rationale for prosecutors and defendants alike: "his country," "your country," "the country"[15]—these are the terms of traitors and loyalists, each transformed by a simple pronoun, adjective, or article into a shifting signifier of an unstable nation. Like Shakespeare's John of Gaunt, who eulogizes "this blessed plot, this earth, this realm, this England" (*Richard II*, 2.1.50), the Crown's rhetoric stabilizes and sustains a vision of "this realm of England" in dense repetitions, which work to bestow an almost material reality on a conceptual "realm."[16] To the Crown, abstract patrilinear legitimacy is expressed in terms of demonstrable, proximate geography: "this realm," "this isle."

It is precisely the stable referentiality of such phrases, however, that figures accused of treason call into question. In giving voice to a vision of "this realm" that differs in significant ways from the vision perpetuated by the Crown, the traitors undermine and contest the naturalness or self-evidence of the term's meaning. To the Crown, "this realm" means traditional prerogatives of the monarchy, obedience of the subject, and Protestant behaviors if not beliefs. The Babington conspirators see another country, however, one ruled by an unlawful monarch who had been excommunicated in 1570. They resist the Crown's identification of them as "rebels," and they do so by pitting a discourse of affiliation against the Crown's language of partition: they adopt a rhetoric of chivalry to identify themselves with their countrymen and to transform "treason" into "loyalty." In their testimony, imagining another monarch is not "rebellion," that is, resistance to a legitimate authority, but submission to "duty." Defendant Gifford, for example, expresses his intentions in chivalric terms, as "honourable and meritorious," setting an enduring idea of "better service" against suspect, temporary allegiances. Defendant Titchburne insists "he should never do more good" than to join the plotters, arguing that "to do so were a far better service than to study divinity." Babington himself swore "for the deliverance of [his] country" and "with the hazard of [his] life" to "do [his] sacred majesty one day's good service."[17] Adopting the language of service, representatives on both sides of the bench compete not only to define an abstract "realm" but also to designate what counts as "service" within it.

The precise terms of service are as familiar and accessible as the early modern code of courtiership. As Count Ludovico puts it in Castiglione's *The Book of the Courtier*, the "first and true profession" of the ideal courtier "must be that of arms"; his chief end ought to be service to his monarch;

> and this above everything else I wish him to pursue vigorously. Let him also stand out from the rest as enterprising, bold, and loyal to whomever he serves. And he will win good reputation by demonstrating these qualities whenever and wherever possible.[18]

Similarly, in Thomas Wilson's *Arte of Rhetorique*, aimed at would-be legal practitioners and courtiers in 1560, "Fortitude or manhode" are interchangeable terms, both defined as "a considerate hassardyng upon daunger, and a willyng harte to take paines in behalfe of the right."[19] Wilson takes his cue from Cicero, who urges that "it be made to appear that the law has to do with matters of the highest importance, advantage, honour, and sanctity."[20] Through the language of chivalric service, the defendants claim kinship with the prosecutors, taming the perceived threat of rebellion and invasion by recasting it as a political disagreement among men of the same kind. The Crown positions itself as the conservator of a self-defining, unified community faced with treachery; the accused position themselves as the self-sacrificing hope of that same nation in jeopardy. "Like you," the accused imply, "we recognize and enact the standards of performance demanded of the English courtier." But there is no space for loyal opposition in the discourse of treason, and the prosecutors perform a continual process of "othering" that makes alien the values and behaviors of the accused. From their point of view, the accused are not fellow gentlemen offering welcome counsel but a band of rogues voicing dangerous ideas. What becomes apparent in the contest is that both sides in this legal warfare occupy imaginary communities, and, depending on his place of residence, one man's rebellion is another's rescue mission.

The accused pitch their claims to affiliation on the ground of the shared values of chivalry. The prosecution resists on that same ground; it rejects the defendants not on the basis of their exclusion from chivalric codes per se, but on the basis of their failing to meet the historically-legitimated standards of those codes. To the Crown, it is "ease" the conspirators sought, not heroic glory, and "ease" that taints them. Defendant Savage is recast from aspiring hero to coward, his claim of having discussed "exploits of service" betrayed by the recorder's tag line, "but Savage seemed to object how dangerous and difficult it was." Similarly damning terms taint Ballard, who, when conferring with an ally in France, said, "It is now more easy to invade the realm than before, because the earl of Leicester, with the best of our captains, were in Flanders."[21] (Holinshed reports that Ballard commended "the murdering of her majesty as a deed of great honor, singular merit, and easy to effectuate.")[22] Planning to invade when a nation's reputed general is away might signify expert military strategy in a world of Machiavellian real politic. In the claims of the prosecution, however, the plan is discredited by being associated with the conspirators' having sought the "easy" way to accomplish their goals. By transforming heroic service into "ease," the prosecution positions the challengers as inferiors, paints them with the colors of cowardice, and undermines the force of their claims to shared nobility. Lacking specifically Leicestrian virility, the Babington defendants are stigmatized as lacking the kind of masculinity the nation will recognize as its own.[23]

The conventions of chivalric courtiership evoked in these trials were enjoying a revival in the late sixteenth century in the tilts and tournaments staged to confirm Tudor sovereignty. As Helgerson has recently argued, chivalry was a self-divided code, its rituals deployed to mediate between rival English loyalties: "each [participant] is torn between a private code of honor based on a combination of noble lineage and individual military accomplishment and the public duty he owes his sovereign."[24] The Crown exploits these conflicting elements by adopting a position of subordination to public duty while placing the accused in a position of willful individual self-estrangement. In the Crown's view, the accused were acting as dissenters rather than as servants. They were operating not out of loyalty but out of a desire to assert their own power. Although they prompt prosecutor Hatton to repeat his lamentation—"you could have done your country good service"—what counts as "good service" is rhetorically secured by an implied identification between "your country" and the reigning monarch.

In claiming their position, the defendants are evoking a long history of traditional privilege: the withdrawal of allegiance. In the mid-thirteenth century, renouncing allegiance, which was called *diffidatio*, was held by barons as excusing later treasonable conduct. Feudal rules included the idea that one's retainer might change loyalties, and in what was called *diffication*, he could do so without penalty. By the end of the fourteenth century, there appeared a move to criminalize *diffidatio*, when Richard II made "compassing to renounce leige homage" into treason. The act was annulled two years later, however. In the late medieval period, disobedience or refusing a command were called "rebellion" but were not considered the equivalent of treason. By the 1530s, however, Thomas Cromwell declared to the Reformation Parliament that "rebellion is already treason," erasing the room for legitimate dissent.[25] And shortly before the Babington trials, Elizabethan treason legislation in 1581 again brought the issue forward. Attempting to "absolve, persuade or withdraw subjects from obedience to their queen" or from the established religion became treason, as did encouraging them to promise obedience to any foreign ruler.[26] Withdrawal of obedience was at the heart of the legislation, and though it had been of crucial importance, it had not been spelled out until the Elizabethan legislation. After that, allegiance was given pride of place in the formulaic beginning of indictments: the accused acted "contrary to your allegiance you owe to our sovereign lady the queen, her crown and dignity, and contrary to divers statutes in such case provided."[27]

The problem with allegiance, of course, is not only its withdrawal but its bestowal, and treasons trouble continuously over where displaced loyalty will go. In the Babington trials, although prosecutors evoke fears of foreign and papal powers, it is something much closer to home that claims the defendants' allegiance: male friendship. The trials present the accused as victims or perpetrators of misdirected loyalty; that loyalty is seen as specifically "wrongly" bestowed on male friends; and male friendship functions to distinguish among English men:

Then said Jones to the jury, I confess this, and put me to her majesty's mercy; my case was hard and lamentable, either to betray my dearest friend, whom I loved as my ownself; and to discover Thomas Salisbury, the best man in my country, of whom I only made choice; or else to break my allegiance to my sovereign and so undo myself and my posterity forever. And this was my case.[28]

Similarly, defendant Charnock testifies: "Babington was my good friend in divers respects, and therefore I thought it pertained to courtesy, to say I remained at his commandment. . . . For flying away with my friend, I fulfilled the part of a friend therein." Jones later laments: "I, desiring to be counted a faithful friend, am now condemned for a false traitor."[29] In the Babington treasons, male friendship signifies fidelity to personal companionship, and personal companionship signifies a challenge to political allegiance, that is, to claims of national loyalty. One of the most important unstated aspects of the trials is that they engage in a continual process of ordering a hierarchy of values within which such relationships are permitted to exist. They attend repeatedly to the notion that only traitors place personal above national fidelities. As prosecutor Hatton scornfully puts it, "To perform thy friendship, thou didst break thy allegiance to thy sovereign."[30]

Within these discourses of affiliation and differentiation, the contestants on both sides of the Babington treasons are continuously negotiating the social formation of masculinities. By adopting the language of service, representatives on both sides of the bench compete not only to define an abstract "realm" but also to designate what counts as manhood within it. They measure masculinity by the hazards it embraces. In one striking instance, the trial text expresses acute anxiety about the development of male selfhood, representing male adolescence as a treacherous, liminal period when a boy appropriates his mature identity as the prerequisite for entering the civil realm. As it recapitulates earlier themes, defendant Titchburne's scaffold speech lays out this teleology of errant masculinity:

Let me be a warning to all young gentlemen, especially *Generosis adolescentulis*. I had a friend, and a dear friend, of whom I made no small account, whose friendship hath brought me to this: he told me the whole matter, I cannot deny, as they had laid it down to be done; but I always thought it impious, and denyed to be a dealer in it; but the regard of my friend caused me to be a man in who the old proverb was verified, "I was silent, and so consented." Before this thing chanced, we lived together in the most flourishing estate: Of whom went report in the Strand, Fleet-street, and elsewhere about London, but of Babington and Titchbourne? No threshold was of force to brave our entry. Thus we lived, and wanted nothing we could wish for; and God knows, what less in my head than matters of State? Now give me leave to declare the miseries I sustained after I was acquainted with the action, wherein I may justly compare my estate to that of Adam's, who could not abstain "one thing forbidden," to enjoy all other things the world could afford; the terror of conscience awaited me. . . . I came to London, and there heard that all was bewrayed; whereupon, like Adam, we fled into the woods to hide ourselves, and there were apprehended.[31]

This is a provocative and dense passage, in which allusions to Adam clear Titchburne of responsibility by characterizing him as a sort of "first man," young, innocent, untainted by knowledge of the world. In what we might call a strategy of powerful victimization, the tale structures Titchburne's agency as contingent on the persuasive force of the unnamed other. It reduces Titchburne's culpability by reassigning it to that anonymous figure: although he had been a bold young man of "flourishing estate," who "wanted nothing [he] could wish for," at a threshold moment he fell prey to provocations that, paradoxically, both signify his initiation into manhood—he was no longer the brave, braggart boy—and color that initiation with guilty weakness of will. In this self-dramatizing morality play, the adolescent boy, who is interested more in "braving" it about town than in politics ("what less in my head than matters of State?"), and who "regard[s]" his friend enough to listen to him, is transformed into a pliant, weak youth.[32]

The popular theme of youthful ambition and its dire consequences, widely circulated in *de casibus* tragedies and tales of the falls of princes, underwrites this version of the young man's vulnerability and lends it persuasive force precisely because these tales are familiar modes of explanation.[33] Importing the biblical authority of Adam's fall and its status as a historical and spiritual truth, the story claims its credibility by displaying its identity with a predetermined, familiar type. Yet the threat evoked in these stories of powerful ambition is contained by a rhetoric that links that ambition not to power but to weakness, specifically to a weak mind. Defendant Savage, for example, is represented as having temporarily resisted allying himself with the accused. With a bit of urging, however, he relented: "At last Savage, overcome with their persuasions, gave his assent and oath."[34] What counted as weakmindedness in early modern culture was often conventionally associated with women. *The Homily on Marriage*, for example, which was read in church from 1562 onwards, states: "The woman is a weak creature not endued with like strength and constancy of mind; therefore, they be the sooner disquieted, and they be the more prone to all weak affections and dispositions of mind, more than men be; and lighter they be, and more vain in their fantasies and opinions."[35] Although they evoke comparisons with representations of the female mind, men's treason trials tend to reproduce weakmindedness less as a sign of natural female inferiority (Eve is notably absent from Titchburne's version of his fall) than as a sign of failed masculinity.

That masculinity is challenged to reveal a strong, virile, and disciplined mind in order to reveal the successful transit of boy to man. Such a mind, able to negotiate the conflicting claims of adolescence, resists being "overcome by persuasions" by ruling out thoughts of political reorganization. In this case, what counts as manhood is the capacity to suppress speculative thinking, to discipline the self not to imagine other worlds, and to align oneself with a dominant political view. In other words, to become an English man (as distinct from a youth) means to adopt the position of an intellectually obdurate political conservative.

By allying the defendants with ease, the Crown shows that the traitors are incapable of fidelity to the standards of chivalric courtiership. By allying them with male friendship, it shows them incapable of fidelity to the nation. And, in language inflected with contemporary anxieties about travel, by allying the defendants with promiscuous movement, the Crown shows them incapable of fidelity to "this realm." The government maps out loyalty and disloyalty relative to place: it presents the Babington conspirators traveling from city to city, from country to country, sending letters across the seas, sailing back to England. Defendant Savage "served in the camp of the prince of Parma, and from thence he departed towards Rhemes." Gifford and Morgan sent letters "from beyond the seas." Ballard traveled to meet with "Barnardino de Mendoza, a Spaniard, and Charles Paget, . . . at Paris, France." Babington sent "letters from friends in France and Scotland." Salisbury planned to "go into [his] country in the county of Denbigh, there to move and stir up sedition and rebellion."[36] All are described in dense repetitions as having traveled to "St. Giles . . . in the country of Middlesex, [there to] have speech and confer" with their fellows.[37]

By showing the accused expatriating themselves over and over again, the prosecution undermines the conspirators' position as men capable of fidelity to *any* nation. In these documents, the mobility of the accused is transformed into an evocation of fears associated with other contemporary travel discourses.[38] On the one hand, travel narratives help domesticate conceptions of the foreign and encourage the development of new markets. On the other hand, they discourage travel by representing places outside England as potentially threatening to its own Edenic tranquility. They ward off the kind of unauthorized exchanges "across seas" that color discourses of treason.[39]

Emphasizing these goings and comings, the Crown associates the accused with an undesirable multinationalism and with an equally undesirable rootlessness that calls into question their fidelity to "this realm." It develops a discursive link between the inner man and his travels, forming a rhetorical relationship among a man's disloyalty, intellectual promiscuity, and geographic mobility.[40] In this view, patriotic fidelity, like chivalric masculinity, is contingent for its meaning on the geography it occupies. The defendants, however, provide another way to think about the relationship between patriotism and place: they identify themselves with a conceptual nationhood, implicitly contesting the idea that "the country" is necessarily coextensive with particular land identification. Their homeland is not a place where geographical affiliation mystifies or obscures political affiliation, but a place that mutates with men's imaginations: "we shall have a new world shortly," Ballard promised his cohorts.[41]

More is at stake in these disputes than individual parries might suggest. Virtually every treason trial during the century circulates a larger social struggle over the form and cultural meanings of English law itself. The Babington trials take place amid heated debates comparing the value of received Roman law and native common law and amid debates about theories of legal authority, with Bacon striking blows for the queen (and later, king) against subjects, and Coke countering with hits for the lawyers against the monarch.[42] Both sides envision a nation of laws, but the right to interpret them is continuously asserted, challenged, and reasserted. Treason may or may not be a categorical choice between lawless and lawful actions, but a treason trial is certainly a competition between a ruler and (admittedly privileged) subjects to determine the category of the lawful itself. Defendant Savage, for example,

> sticked to do the fact, forasmuch as he, percase, was not resolved whether the killing of a prince were lawful or not. . . . He desired time to advise himself, and to ask opinion of others: and . . . having heard others affirm, that the murder was lawful, . . . at last . . . [he] answered that he was contented to do anything for his country's good.[43]

When it is activated by the resistance of these "traitors" in the courtroom, the meaning of "treason" shifts from a legal category within which a self-validating authority judges the acts of men, into a specific historical process in which men continuously renovate a notion of the lawful. Identifying or resisting specific legal precedents, the prosecution and defendants foreground a sustained historical awareness, marking off the present as different from or continuous with particular visions of the past. Tilney argues, for example, that he had done nothing wrong in making his confession to Ballard, since "it was not otherwise than all the subjects of the realm of England were confessed in the days of Henry 7." The Solicitor, Sir Thomas Egerton, however, quickly reorients him: "But now is the estate of this realm quite other than it was in the days of Henry 7."[44]

Abington made similar claims on the law. He defended himself by arguing

> Well then, Sir, to you my lords and the Judges I do now speak: There is a statute in the first and thirteenth of this queen made, That who shall conspire &c. it shall be Treason, & c. provided, that he shall have at least two lawful witnesses face to face to avow it, &c. Now may it please your honours to have two lawful witnesses to testify against me. As for Babington, what witness can he be, a condemned man, Savage, a condemned man likewise? So then there is no witness against me: but I stand not upon this point, I stand upon mine own not guiltiness.[45]

The two men who signed examinations against him, Savage and Ballard, cannot be found credible, argues Abington, because they are self-confessed condemned men. Their status as truth-tellers has been corroded by their status as conspirators. Thus, he concludes, there are no witnesses against him. But in a technical rebuttal, Anderson, the Lord Chief Justice of the Common Pleas, implies that the law is and ought to be beyond the ken of courtiers: "true it is, had you been indicted on the Statute of the 1st and 13th of this queen, two Witnesses ought to have been produced; but you stand indicted by the common law, and the Statute of 25 Edward 3, which is who shall *intend* the death of the king, &c, and in that statute is not contained any such proof" (emphasis added).[46] Before Abington can respond, Tilney remarkably makes a counter assertion by correcting the accuracy of Anderson's own pronouncement: "The statute of 25 Edw. 3 is, "who shall *compass or imagine*, &c" (emphasis added), Tilney tells him.[47] During his own testimony, Tilney becomes embroiled in a competition over intention. Accused of having confessed to supporting the "removing of the Lord-Treasurer and Mr. Secretary," he several times insisted on the right to explicate his own words during the proceedings:

TILNEY: I deny it, I never said so.
PUCKERING: Here is your own hand, and read it.
TILNEY: It is mine own hand, but what did I mean? When I said *concerning that matter*, I must interpret mine own meaning.

. . . .

TILNEY: I will tell you how I meant my words.[48]

Again, Puckering attempts to translate what Tilney had said—"Babington said yesterday at the bar, that Tilney would have had her majesty set upon in her coach"—and Tilney contradicts him:

> No, I said not so . . . I said it might be her majesty might be set upon in her coach, and I said no more. But that proves not that I did consent. . . . I tell you no, there is no such matter intended in my words.[49]

These are displays not only of legal knowledge but also of rhetorical prowess. They open to view the battle between men for a verbal superiority as each man competes to top the other. Contemporary theater audiences could call up comic versions of competitors like these in figures like Touchstone in Shakespeare's *As You Like It,* who finds that there is much virtue in "if" for deflecting disputes. In a trial, however, the fundamental contingency of legal precedent and its role in stabilizing histories is exposed: Tilney would have been justified in confessing to Ballard "if" this were King Henry VII's days; Abington would be right about witnesses "if" one statute instead of another were governing the proceedings.

What the documents also suggest is that the possession of legal knowledge and the willingness to use it by those outside the Court is becoming increasingly problematic, with the government assuming that unauthorized possession of that knowledge is itself evidence of suspicious intentions. Egerton uses the defendants' awareness of laws and challenges to interpretation to suggest their duplicity:

> See how they would acquit themselves for want of Witness; and if it should be as they would have it, then could never any Treason be sufficiently proved. The statute of 1 Eliz. is so, the Overt-Act must be proved by two Witnesses; but the statute of 25 Edw. 3 is, Who shall imagine: how then can that be proved by honest men, being a secret cogitation which lieth in the minds of traitors? And such traitors will never reveal their cogitations unto honest men, but unto such as themselves; so then they would have their treasons never revealed.[50]

Imputing to the accused a malicious misappropriation of law, Egerton implies that they are exploiting legal knowledge to disguise the truth. More than this, however, he exposes the contradictory meanings of legal knowledge in the courtroom: possessed by the government, it stands for a patriotic and objective application of procedure; possessed by the defendant, it stands for a self-serving interpretation of vulnerable texts. In this view, prosecutors *apply* the law to reveal the truth, defendants *manipulate* it to obscure the truth. More generally, legal knowledge (in the Crown's view) is positioned between approved authorities and an uneducated audience among whom they might dispense it.

Mediated by claims on legal precedent, this kind of jockeying for position represents an acting out of historical process. To know the law is to know a particular version of England, to possess an idea of the homeland that is historically constructed in what went before. References to particular laws pin down historical moments and aspects of English identity: *now*, this afternoon, this is English law and this the version of the loyal English man it comprehends. Most often, the recurrence to precedence is the recurrence to a vision of a univocal national past, one that gains definition and persuasiveness by being represented as a fact of memory. Yet what persists from trial to trial is not the authority of a particular precedent but the process of arguing about precedents, as legal practice continuously renovates mythic antecedents to bring forth what will count as a useable English past.

I have been arguing that traitors trouble the conventional meanings of words and the traditional stability of phrases. The disruption is particularly evident in the links forged among "country," "God," and "conscience" in the exchange among Clerk for the Crown Sandes, prosecutor Hatton, and defendant Abington:

SANDES: How wilt thou be tried?
ABINGTON: By God and my good country.
SANDES: Thou must say, by God and my country.
ABINGTON: Yea, Sir, by God and my country.
. . . . .
SANDES: How wilt thou be tried?
TILNEY: By God and honest men.
HATTON: What answers are these? Abington says, By God and my good country; and thou sayst, By God and honest men. Thou must say, By God and my country.[51]

According to Thomas A. Green, a verdict "of the country" was made by persons on oath before God to tell the truth according to their consciences. It was an inscrutable verdict during its height in the middle ages, when the jurors were presumed to know both the accused and something about the crime. It retains its inscrutability in positing the verdict as divinely inspired, and it allies that inspiration with the consciences of one's countrymen.[52] Here, in replacing the Crown's phrase with his own, Tilney makes Hatton both insist on and justify the ritual phrasing: "What answers are these? . . . Thou must say, By God and my country." Instead of participating in the sustained circulation of "what goes without saying," traitors compel others to talk, reducing the mystical effects of legal formulas by showing the need for additional explanations.

The formulaic language Hatton calls for functions as a means of solving a perceptual problem: it posits "God" as a divine judge with an essential virtue—he overcomes the problem of interiority, looking into the hearts of men and the recesses of their minds, where "imagined practices" take root. Sanctifying both the verdict and the countrymen who will make it with mystical percipience, the form lends the testimony an incantational quality and evokes a residual medieval system of justice in which God was perceived as the judge of man's actions.[53] However, when Tilney substitutes "honest men" for "my country," a gap between the Crown's country and Tilney's opens to view. A kind of cultural ventriloquism takes place, familiarly laid out in the advice of rhetoricians, who perceived a persuasive value in making the nation speak: "Some tymes," writes Wilson in the *Arte*, "it is good to make God, the Countrie, or some one towne to speake, and loke what we woulde say in our owne person, to frame the whole tale to them."[54]

What becomes visible in the documents is the self-consciousness involved in framing the tale so that God or the country speaks. These are arts of rhetoric, and as such, are vulnerable to another culturally-charged competition: neither "God" nor the "the country" is self-pronouncing, and their meanings are at the center of the trial's debates. Defendant Donn testifies:

DONN: When I was moved, and made privy to these Treasons, I always said that I prayed unto God, that that might be done, which was to his honor and glory.

HATTON: Then it was thus, that they said the queen should be killed, and thou saidst, God's will be done.

DONN: Yea, Sir.

Donn's spiritual turn does nothing to persuade prosecutor Hatton, who exclaims "O wretch, wretch! thy conscience and own confession shew that thou art Guilty."[55]

Evident in this exchange between Hatton and Donn is that unstated, prior interpretive acts condition the suasion and meanings of legal testimony. Inadvertently, Donn exposes Hatton's foregone conclusion about what characterizes "God's will" *as* foregone. In a classic case of question begging, Hatton appeals to the *authority* of the principles at issue as though there were no contemporary controversy over what constituted "God's will." Barbara Herrnstein Smith describes this sort of "epistemic self-privileging": it is "assuming that what one assumes is not an assumption but an established fact . . . ; assuming that one's terms are transparent and that the senses in which one uses them are nonproblematic; and assuming that no alternative conceptualizations or formulations are possible, or at least no 'adequate,' 'coherent,' or 'meaningful' ones."[56] Hatton's indictment of Donn's conscience depends less on the events of this case than on Hatton's prior, extra-legal interpretation of "God's will." In such moments, the trial text exposes the self-evident as a radically contingent thing, determined not by its transparency or stable referentiality, but by a range of personal, social, religious, and political contexts that precede a trial and color its outcome. Given the religious disputes shaking the nation, God's will could be no self-evident matter.

Donn has also unwittingly succeeded in calling attention to the politically-charged issue of conscience, whose own relativity becomes visible: referred to royal will, it is the sign of allegiance to the kingdom; referred to God, it is the sign of divine guidance and intervention; and referred to the self, it is the sign of autonomous subjectivity. Historically, conscience was becoming increasingly understood as more authoritative than government as a guide to behavior. William Perkins stated sharply:

> Now the courts of men and their authorities are under conscience. For God in the heart of every man hath erected a tribunal seat, and in his stead hee hath placed neither saint nor angel, nor any other creature whatsoever, but conscience itselfe. Who therefore is the highest judge that is or can be under God.[57]

Holinshed imagines the Babington conspirators' indicted by their consciences, which induce "them to the discovery of their intolerable treacheries": "And surely true it is, that the conscience of a malefactor is unto him in stead of an accuser, a witness, a judge, and a hangman: the scripture importing no less, in saying, that the wicked shall tremble at the fall of the leafe of a tree, and be as if their life hung by a thread."[58] In the trial documents, however, the prosecutors work to deny the defendants' claims to divine sanction by dividing up the discursive field into true and false consciences: as Hatton puts it, "Then wouldst thou have killed the queen for conscience. Fie on such a conscience!"[59] To Hatton, regicide and conscience are irreconcilable terms; to have a conscience is, by definition, not to kill the queen. Not orthodox morality nor personal conviction, but a decision in accord with a prior privileged value system is the term's referent. The defendants, however, are tailoring individual consciences outside the prosecution's jurisdiction. And when Barnewell confesses, "Forasmuch as I have offended against the law, I am contented to suffer punishment according to the law; howbeit, I here protest what I have done was only for my conscience-sake,"[60] he inserts into the proceedings a significant role for what might be done "for conscience-sake" by an individual subject against a government representative.

Traditional legal authority ultimately triumphs—all fourteen men are convicted—and it does so in part by officially repositioning the defendants, substituting criminal biographies for other speculations about their pasts. Who *had* the conspirators been? "A sort of brave youths otherwise endued with good gifts." What had become of them? They had been "brought to their utter destruction and confusion." How had this woeful transformation occurred? Babington explains: "Yea, I protest, before I met with this Ballard, I never meant nor intended for to kill the queen; but by his persuasions I was induced to believe that she was excommunicate, and therefore lawful to murder her."[61] Purifying Babington by tainting Ballard, the trial thematically repatriates the lost youth by expatriating the infuser of evil. It attributes the cause of the crime not to the individual man (though he will lose his head for it) but to an entire religious and national history: Hatton "declared, how priests continually had been the beginning of all the treasons committed against her majesty; he began at the rebellion in the north, and so proceeded till the Treasons of Throckmorton and Parry, and so ended."[62] Recapitulating themes circulating in a limitless supply of tracts, pamphlets, and fictions, Hatton presents anti-papal propaganda as historical truth and legal precedent.

As the Crown develops it, the discourse of treason conceives of limitless space and man's ability to traverse it with apprehension, as though it incited men to lawlessness. It resolves that apprehension by limiting the space treason is allowed to occupy. St. Giles Cripplegate had entered the accounts as an incidental fact, joining other work-a-day details. The accounts repeat "St. Giles" in indictments, in written confessions, and in the testimony of each of the accused, until the site accumulates meanings as a place where traitors meet. Because it is "the place where they used to meet," defendants are returned there for execution: on September 20, 1586, they "were drawn on hurdles from the Tower to their Execution at St. Giles's Fields, being the place where they used to meet; where was erected a scaffold and thereupon a gallows."[63] From its early designation as familiar local territory just outside the city walls, St. Giles is transformed into an extraordinary, ominous place desecrated by the activities of its occupants, whose treacherous imaginations range freely on the edges of a vulnerable city.[64] The account identifies the place with a traditional ethic of purgation and regeneration: it imposes narrative symmetry on the traitors' tale (where they began as traitors they will end as traitors), and it brings about a ritual cleansing of the tainted earth in their executions. Moreover, as the Crown contracts the discourse of treason from expansive images of travel to the relatively constricted image of St. Giles, it concomitantly contracts the idea that treason is a widespread threat by *locating* it in a particular spot: here treason germinated, here treason was eliminated.

In imagining a "new world," the conspirators had signified rebellion by estranging themselves from the conceptual contours of the land. In their scaffold speeches, they realign themselves with "this realm of England"; they recover themselves as "English men" by inserting themselves into a gendered discourse of patrilinearity. Like the archetypal stranger in the moot cases argued in the Inns of Court, whose foreignness is eased by his possession of English soil, the Babington conspirators recover their national identities by recovering their positions in land transmission. Jones pleads, "my good lords, the lands I have, which I held by descent from my father, at the marriage of a gentlewoman which is now my wife, were intailed unto me, and the heirs male of my body; I beseech you some consideration may be had of my posterity." Titchburne moralizes his fate: "My dear countrymen, my sorrows may be your joy, yet mix your smiles with tears, and pity my case; I am descended from an house, from 200 years before the conquest, never stained till this my misfortune."[65] In mentally moving back to the "realm," they raze the alternative nation by reclaiming a geographical homeland, as though to relegitimate themselves by inserting themselves into a gendered process of name and land distribution.

That renewed affiliation is curiously tenuous and arbitrary, however, for the language the accused adopt on the scaffold is not English. In their final acts of self-expression, the conspirators speak in a foreign language: they pray in Latin. Paradoxically, this is both an act of self-exile and an act of reclamation and resistance; in Latin, Ballard, Babington, and their friends demonstrate that they remain in possession of a selfhood that is not wholly expressed in government approved forms. Whatever the state of the defendants' souls, and despite the Crown's efforts to probe and define their consciences, the convicted make their ends in syllables authorized by something other than "this realm."

Like all trials, the Babington accounts are engaged in constructing what they also describe: in this case, the conceptual contours of something called "the country" and its lawful residents, those English men who mentally inhabit "this realm." In the old realm, momentarily stabilized by a verdict, codes of courtiership police forms of imagination, allegiance to the sovereign underlies male friendship, and royal authority announces its persistence in geographical terms. As they are progressively dissociated from the Crown's idea of England and from the official ideological associations that would identify them as "English men," Ballard, Babington, and their fellows are alienated not by birth but by imagination. Within this discourse, one man's treachery is another's patriotism. Or, put another way, in treason trials a "man" and his "country" are endless works in progress.

Christopher Marlowe is indebted to treason. Whether in the forms of his staged violence or in the political positions of his central figures—"infidels," "tyrants," and "traitors"—the discourse of treason figures prominently in Marlovian dramaturgy.[66] Marlowe had access to representations of treason from a range of literary and historical sources. He had been born in Canterbury with its rich history of political and religious intrigue; he had lived in London where he routinely passed the "grim row of traitors' heads" (in John Bakeless's image) that mark the passage across London Bridge; and he had become involved in personal and political legal activities, which eventually included his own arrest on possible charges of treason in the 1590s.[67] Throughout his career stories of traitors circulated widely throughout London, including tales associated with the Babington treasons. Holinshed reports "that the conspirators, . . . occupied their wits in dolorous divises, bemoaning their miseries." Titchburne's elegy "written with his own hand in the Tower before his execution, [was] printed by John Wolfe, 1586"; "The like elegies also did the rest (and namelie Babington) devise." Because they were "never yet authorized for print," Holinshed tells us, he chose not to publish them, though "copies are common."[68] The chronicler did, however, print his own commentary on the meanings of the conspiracy:

> But to the purpose, this execution being dispatched, and the testimonies thereof dispersed and visible in diverse places about the city, as at London bridge, where the traitors heads were ranged into their several classes: many rhymes, ballads, and pamphlets were set forth by sundry well affected people, wherein briefly were comprised the plot of their conspiracy, the names of the traitors, and their successive suffering, which growing common and familiar both in city and country, were chanted with no less alacrity and courage of the singer; than willingly and delightfully listened unto of the hearer. So that, what by one mean and what by another, all England was made acquainted with this horrible conspiracy.[69]

Marlowe's ties to the Babington treasons may have been even closer than local conversation, elegies, or commentaries. Charles Nicholl recently has argued that following the exposure of the Babington plot, Marlowe was among the spies commissioned by Walsingham to infiltrate the Catholics at Cambridge. His purpose, to spy on Cambridge's young radicals, would have come as a direct reaction to news of the Babington plot.[70] "Cambridge University had a long tradition of intellectual dissent," Nicholl writes, and although

Catholicism may have been a focus of government intelligence, it appears that what attracted youthful malcontents was the allure of a clandestine cause: "They were drawn to [Catholicism] more out of restlessness than religious conviction: it had that forbidden, atmospheric aura."[71] At the liminal stages of adulthood, men gathered at Cambridge, whose name had become synonymous with documentably treacherous anti-government thinking. Into their company, a young Marlowe entered.

The Babington conspirators had been executed in the fall of 1586; their elegies had circulated later that year. By summer of 1587, Marlowe had already been in Walsingham's service at Cambridge for some months, had moved to London, and was the subject of a letter from the queen's representatives to the heads of the university. As they had in the trials, formulaic allusions to Rheims in the letter evoke threatening images of men imagining an alternative nation. In the letter, however, the authors are at pains to interpret the meaning of the references for the readers:

> On 29 June 1587 the Privy Council sent a letter to the University authorities [Corpus] to scotch the rumor that "Christopher Morley" had entertained plans to quit the realm and to settle in Rheims, presumably at the English college for missionary priests. On the contrary, it was declared, he had behaved honourably in the service of his Queen and country; "in all his accions he had behaved him selfe orderlie and discreetelie, . . . and deserved to be rewarded for his faithfull dealinge." He was therefore to be admitted to the degree he was due to take at the next commencement—that is, his M.A. The Privy Councillors who authorized the letter were Burghley, Archbishop Whitgift, Lord Hunsdon, Sir James Croft and the new Lord Chancellor, Sir Christopher Hatton.[72]

Peter Roberts has argued that the letter can be read as a denial not of "the allegation that Marlowe 'was determined to have gone beyond the seas to Reames,' but of the report that he had contemplated settling there, and thereby defecting to the enemy camp."[73] Roberts attributes rumors of Marlowe's defection to a misperception of his full role: because Marlowe was acting as a government spy, his travel was to be seen in the service of, rather than in rebellion to the monarchy.

Like treason trials in general, and like the Babington trials in particular, Marlovian dramas stage conflicts over legitimate proprietorship in terms of disputed conceptions of "the country." The earliest of Marlowe's plays, *Tamburlaine I* (c. 1587–88), was possibly drafted while Marlowe was in secret service to the government at Cambridge. Amid repeated claims to shifting affiliations, it represents the relations among politically-charged ideas of "the country," male loyalty, and rootlessness as deeply volatile.

In discourses of treason, the Crown adopts a position as conservator of a clearly identifiable "country" with a sustainable, homogeneous past. As it strives to perpetuate this traditional view, the Crown speaks for "the country" or, to put it in early modern terms, makes the country speak. To do so, to align oneself imaginatively with the country and to make it speak, is to employ the best advice of contemporary rhetoricians to increase persuasiveness. Thomas Wilson writes:

> Again, amplificacion maie be used, when we make the law to speake, the dedde persone to make his complaint, the countrey to crie out of suche a deede. As if some worthie manne wer cast awaie, to make the countrie saie thus: if England could speake, would she not make suche, and suche complaints? if the walles of suche a citee or toune, had a tongue, would thei not talke thus and thus? And to bee shorte, all suche thynges should be used, to make the cause seme greate, whiche concerne God, the common weale, or the lawe of nature.[74]

Both legal and popular rhetorics take on the task of imagining the story the country would tell "if England could speake."

In the late sixteenth-century climate of increased treason prosecutions, it is striking that Marlowe begins his dramatic career skeptical of the idea that a country's identity is a permanent or self-evident thing. From the outset he deliberately disturbs the conceptual links between "the country" and its meanings; in *Tamburlaine I* no unified group or single figure speaks for the realm.[75] Unlike *Edward II*, which probes the contested relations between a beleaguered ruler and his nobles and which finally sides with a rehabilitated monarchy, *Tamburlaine I* dramatizes no sustained proprietorship of the nation; no privileged figure articulates its stability or instability.[76] The current ruler relies on an increasingly threatened hereditary right to speak for the nation; the ambitious pretender is possessed by his own mythic version of the country's former glory; and the treacherous challenger is intent on remolding the country into something new.

The initial possessor of the Crown, Mycetes, can assert no demonstrable possession of Persia either grammatically or imaginatively. From his earliest lines—"I find myself agrieved, / Yet insufficient to express the same" (1.1.1–2)—Marlowe positions him as a figure of deferral and displacement unsuited to act as a steadying ruler. His attempts to articulate a version of the nation are acts of ventriloquism in which Meander speaks; the country to which he throws his voice is characterized by rebellion; and the conditional language Marlowe assigns him—"might I not?" "I know I might" (1.1.24, 26)—indicts him. In contrast, Cosroe (and Bajazeth after him) positions himself as the salvation of a once-glorious nation in need of rebirth. He "see[s] the state of Persia droop / And languish in [his] brother's government" (1.1.155–56); he vows to wear the Crown "for [his] country's good" (1.1.157); and he rallies his troops "To save [their] king and country from decay" (2.6.34–35). Cosroe's Persia is the accumulation of its history, a seat of once-heroic conquerors: "Then, Cosroe, reign / And govern Persia in her former pomp" (2.4.18–19). The play's first "traitor," he sees himself as the custodian of a waning Persia, speaks for a return to a golden age, and memorializes this temporally distant homeland. What Cosroe does in the name of an imagined past, Tamburlaine does in the name of an imagined future: disrupt the idea of "the country." It is as though Marlowe has written a character whose very way of being Tamburlaine is to deny the referential certainty of "the countries" he conquers. He envisions each country not as something static nor self-defining, but as something volatile and continuously remade, its borders and identifying culture melded into his empire. For Tamburlaine, who means to "Measur[e] the limits of his empery / By east and west, as Phoebus doth his course" (1.2.9–10), expanding cosmography replaces self-defining geography.[77]

Throughout this play, Marlowe is systematically fragmenting the notions of what "the country" might mean. To Mycetes, the value of a homeland is largely a function of its materiality—it is dirt useful for hiding a crown: "Here will I hide it in this simple hole" (2.4.15). According to Marlowe, however, what is dirt to one man is sanctified ground to another. To Cosroe, Persia is the accumulation of its mythic past, the seat of legendary rulers. It is not that the Persia Cosroe imagines is more historically accurate than the one Mycetes sees; it is, in David Lowenthal's apt phrase, that "the past is another country," and Cosroe purges it of alien elements, homogenizes it, and fits it to his own aspirations.[78] Tamburlaine is Marlowe's challenge to Mycetes's reductive materialist view and to Cosroe's aggrandizing mystifying vision. Like that of all who are dubbed "traitors," his homeland is a conceptual space, sustained by imaginative and physical mobility.

Echoing discourses of treason, men in this play affiliate themselves with each other and obscure deep differences over ideas of "the country" by associating themselves with chivalric courtiership. As Harry Levin observed long ago in *The Overreacher*, Marlowe's play "is primarily a study in prowess" rather than in policy of the sort associated with Machiavelli.[79] And Wilson's rhetoric in 1560 gave men justification for linking the concepts of manhood, militarism, honor, and danger in the service of one's "Countrey": "In all ages the worthiest men have alwaies adventured their carcases for the savegarde of their countrie, thynking it better to dye with honor, than to live with shame."[80] Contemporary travel narratives, too, exhort men to glory by emphasizing putting the self at risk. Lopez de Gomara's *Pleasant Historie of the Conquest of West India* (1578), writes Thomas Nicholas, is as "a Mirrour and an excellent president, for all such as shall take in hande to gouern newe Discoueries; for here they shall behold, how Glorie, Renowne, and perfite Felicitie, is not gotten but with great paines, trauaile, perill and daunger of life."[81] In Marlowe's play, characters on all sides of battles align themselves with a traditional rhetoric of service: Techelles unites Tamburlaine's troops with Cosroe's—"With duty and with amity we yield / Our utmost service to the fair Cosroe" (2.3.33–34); and Meander defers to Cosroe after losing the battle—"I vow my service to your majesty, / With utmost virtue of my faith and duty" (2.5.16–17).[82] As it is in the culture generally, what counts as service is linked to martial displays: Cosroe acknowledges his soldiers' "discipline in arms" (1.1.173–75); Menaphon describes Tamburlaine "thirsting with sovereignty, with love of arms" (1.2.20); and Bajazeth foresees Tamburlaine's foolishness "if he be so mad to manage arms with me" (3.1.33–34). Binding men to each other, this common language of chivalric dedication becomes a means of evoking abstract affiliations and of consolidating what counts as shared masculinity within them.[83]

In what I take to be a deeply subversive move, however, Marlowe sets his complex discourse of male allegiance against the claims of courtiership. He awards friendship among men, which crosses national and class lines, a primacy unusual on the early modern stage. Although chivalric conventions direct the participants' loyalty to a ruler, what is especially striking in *Tamburlaine I* is that a counterdiscourse directs loyalty and service to male fellowship. Significantly, characters do not pledge "duty" or "service" to Tamburlaine; what they pledge is "friendship."

Marlowe sets friendship against other forms of male affiliations. As he does so, he develops a contest between traditional patriarchal bonds and alternative emerging loyalties. Put another way, Marlowe finds in certain forms of male friendship a counterdiscourse to traditional historically-privileged rhetorics of male authority. In *Tamburlaine I*, "patriarchy" stands not as a monological category but as a highly volatile grouping that describes one position—and a vulnerable one, as Marlowe presents it—among many afforded to early modern men. It is difficult for a postmodern reader to speak with certainty about the signs and meanings of early modern male friendship as it appears in the theater and to distinguish it from other same sex relationships.[84] In *Desire and Anxiety*, Valerie Traub argues that homoeroticism has no fixed social definition nor social discourse of its own, but rather makes its appearance in discourses that may seem other than specifically erotic.[85] Borrowing from Traub, I want to suggest that the related term homosociability is also unfixed, and though its meanings trouble perception, its implications form a key component of early modern male treasons. In *Tamburlaine I*, as in the discourses of treason to which it alludes, homosociability is referred to by those seeking to sustain authority as antisocial, seditious, and disastrous. Yet although authorities selectively position male friendship as the enemy of national stability, Marlowe positions it as the center of new national self-fashioning, revaluing it as the source of the social, patriotic, and miraculous. According to Marlowe's play, the Crown was right to fear friendship among unaccommodated men and to pit it against national allegiance. A group of "friends" who defy traditional rulers are the means by which a failing monarchy is reconstituted and secured. In *Tamburlaine I* loyalty to homosocial relationships is the central and productive form of fidelity out of which new nations might be made.

Scholars have noted that the play is structured as a series of battles, with new challengers emerging during the development of the play. What has escaped notice, however, is that although the play is punctuated with conflicts, the most prominent sustainable bond is that among male friends. "The country" is invaded, overthrown, and remade by a group of friends whose loyalty is first to that friendship. The effect is to stage a shift from such traditional authorized bases of affiliation as status to homosociability as the relevant category. The terms of this powerful affiliation are introduced initially following Techelles's and Usumcasane's imaginative reactions:

TECHELLES: Methinks I see kings kneeling at his feet. . . .
USUMCASANE: And making thee and me, Techelles, kings
That even to the death will follow Tamburlaine.
TAMBURLAINE: Nobly resolved, sweet friends and followers! (1.2.54–60)

The terms of alliance among Tamburlaine's retainers are "sweet friends and followers." This is not to suggest that Marlowe sees friendship as a bond among equals; to be a friend *of* Tamburlaine is not the same as to be a friend *to* Tamburlaine. He gathers "followers" and tributory kings, not competitors. What is significant, however, is the formal pattern of friendship as the chosen affiliation among men and the contemporary condemnation of that pattern in discourses of treason.[86]

Early theories of friendship (and I would include Marlowe's play among them) present intellectual likeness among men as one source of their attraction to each other. Federico in *The Courtier*, for example, places similarity at the center of desirability: "For to be sure it stands to reason that persons who are joined together in close amity and indissoluble companionship should also conform in their wishes, thoughts, opinions and aptitudes. . . . For it seems natural for like to attract like."[87] Based on this idea of mutual recognition, in Marlowe's play men do not pose each other a perceptual problem;

their characters are presented as readily legible to each other. Tamburlaine first sees Theridamas, and likes what he sees:

With what a majesty he rears his looks!
In thee, thou valiant man of Persia,
I see the folly of thy emperor.
Art thou but captain of a thousand horse,
That by characters graven in thy brows,
And by thy martial face and stout aspect,
Deserv'st to have the leading of an host? (1.2.164–70)

The scene is Marlowe's deft dramatization of Tamburlaine's ability to perceive the hearts of men and of Theridamas's valor. What typically escapes notice, however, is what attracts Tamburlaine: Theridamas is transparent to him. In contrast to the elusive Zenocrate, who remains partially inexplicable to Tamburlaine, Theridamas can be fully and instantly recognized and trusted, man to man: "Forsake thy king and do but join with me" (1.2.171).

This scene began with Tamburlaine's capture of Zenocrate, his assuring her that the victory need not "appal [her] thoughts," and her description of herself and her train as "poor friendless passengers" (1.2.1 and 70). One progress of the play is to persuade her to accept Tamburlaine, that is to hear him not, as Agydas does, "rattl[ing] forth his facts of war and blood" but sounding "sweeter than the Muses' song" (3.2.45,50). In contrast, the second half of the scene is devoted to Tamburlaine's meeting with Theridamas, and there is no mismatch between the men about the terms of affection. Moreover, the scene is more multivocal than is usually remarked in a way that sharpens the attractiveness of male-male affiliations. Between Tamburlaine's early invitations to Theridamas and Theridamas's assent, Techelles and Usumcasane interrupt. Marlowe triangulates the desire in the scene, heightening the allure of the friendship by reflecting its intensity in the vows of Techelles:

We are his friends, and if the Persian king
Should offer present dukedoms to our state,
We think it loss to make exchange for that
We are assured of by our friend's success. (1.2.213–16)

Techelles frames his expressions of fidelity between the scene's key terms: "friends" and "friend's."

Marlowe deftly glamorizes the friendship by extending it to more men and by mediating it among them: the "friendship" increases in value because other men desire and share it. If we look closely at the scene, we find that it is not only Tamburlaine's persuasiveness but also this loyalty oath that prompt

Theridamas to acknowledge: "What strong enchantments 'tice my yielding soul! / Ah, these resolved, noble Scythians!" (1.2.223–24). Not Tamburlaine alone (as is so often assumed) but the "noble Scythians," a group of men, elicit Theridamas's agreement to disavow Cosroe and join Tamburlaine's troops. When the two men then affirm the precise terms of their bond—"But shall I prove a traitor to my king?," Theridamas worries; "No, but the trusty friend of Tamburlaine," the hero claims (1.2.225–26)—it is as though Marlowe were satirically citing prosecutor Hatton's outrage during the Babington trial: "To perform thy friendship, thou didst break thy allegiance to thy sovereign."[88]

Valorizing male intimacy in a vow of fidelity, Marlowe again dramatizes the transparency of mutual recognition that accompanies male relationships. Here he associates that mutuality with the operations of nature:

Theridamas, my friend, take here my hand,
Which is as much as if I swore by heaven
And called the gods to witness of my vow.
Thus shall my heart be still combined with thine,
Until our bodies turn to elements,
And both our souls aspire celestial thrones. (1.2.231–36)

In a scene so devoted to relocations of personal and political fidelity (if such a distinction is possible) as this one, Marlowe is staging the homosocial in precise terms, for here (as Castiglione put it) men are "joined together in close amity and indissoluble companionship" and also "conform in their wishes, thoughts, opinions, and aptitudes." Perhaps one of the subversive things about the scene is that the same sex vow of fidelity is *not* readily distinguishable from the conventional heterosexed vow.[89]

Marlowe is deliberately debunking certain hereditary claims to kinship and authority, and he deepens his irony in the play's shadow plot about brotherhood. In contrast to the nonhereditary links forged among men, those that by convention "should" secure brotherhood are violently undone and replaced by other, provisional modes of affiliation. In the play's opening scene, Mycetes assumes the priority of traditional hierarchy, places kingship above kinship, and rebukes Cosroe, "What, shall I call thee brother? No, a foe, / Monster of nature, shame unto thy stock, / That dar'st presume thy sovereign for to mock" (1.1.103–105). Preparing for battle, he accurately describes Cosroe as "my traitorous brother" (2.2.4). But Cosroe positions Mycetes as brother rather than king; to Cosroe, he is no monarch but another mortal. Preparing to leave for Persepolis, Cosroe tells Tamburlaine, "Farewell, lord regent and his happy friends. / I long to sit upon my brother's throne" (2.5.46–47). (There is, of course, considerable irony in his referring to Tamburlaine and his "happy friends," which here is clearly a stronger bond than brotherhood.) Marlowe minimizes the importance of birth relations, robs the term "brother" of its mythic power to name a binding relationship, and transports that power to friendship. A brotherhood of blood, it appears, is less sustainable than a brotherhood of imagination.

The Babington treasons locate the threat to masculine adult identity in male friendship; the acute instance is Titchburne's allegory of homosocial identity, in which the transit from boy to man is represented as disrupted by the demands of friendship. The boy is vulnerable to persuasions that distort his progress to an acceptable masculinity, presumably a masculinity that would not imagine the death of the queen. Tamburlaine, however, positions the threat to male identity more conventionally. As Stephen Orgel explains, "for a man to associate with a woman was felt to be increasingly dangerous—not only for the woman, but even more for the man: lust effeminates, makes men incapable of manly pursuits; hence the pervasive antithesis of love and war."[90] Early in the play, Tamburlaine is in full possession of a specifically male authority. Responding to Zenocrate's claim to have letters guaranteeing her safe passage, Tamburlaine trumps: "But now you see these letters and commands / Are countermanded by a greater man" (1.2.21–22). His virility is signified by his seizing the word "man" at the center of "command" and "countermand" and turning them into stepping stones to reach himself, "the greater man." That Marlowe writes the scene as a competition among men, in which commands from one are not as powerful as those from another, places it firmly in the conventional triangulated patriarchal dynamic of the period, in which men compete for prowess with each other through the vehicle of women.[91]

However, what the discourses of treason make contingent on homosocial loyalties (that is, a perceived loss of masculinity) Marlowe makes contingent on formulaic heterosexual anxieties; women disrupt the foundation of masculine identity. In the complex and widely interpreted Beauty speech, Tamburlaine registers his awareness of jeopardy: his thoughts engage in "doubtful battle"; they are "tempted" by Zenocrate's emotions; and his soul is "beseiged" by her sorrows. "Troubled by conceit of foil," for the only time in the play, Tamburlaine acknowledges in violent imagery his awareness that defeat is possible. That acknowledgement precipitates his placing Zenocrate in a mythic rather than personal and historical realm: all the poets pens could not finally capture her and no amount of manly "virtue" could compress her powers into writing.[92] On the one hand, Zenocrate disturbs the discourse of masculine identity: "But how unseemly is it for my sex, / My discipline of arms and chivalry, / . . . / To harbor thoughts effeminate and faint!" (5.2.111–

14). On the other hand, she makes that same discourse of chivalry possible: "every warrior that is rapt with love / Of fame, of valor, and of victory, / Must needs have beauty beat on his conceits" (5.2.117–19). If this transit ended here, there would be a stalemate between conflicting gender claims. But in Tamburlaine's mind, the tensions are resolved. His speech continues, firmly placing Zenocrate in an abstract realm of Beauty's servants, and concluding with a reassertion of the priority of bonds of masculinity: "virtue solely is the sum of glory, / And fashions men with true nobility" (5.2.126–27).

What surfaces repeatedly in trials and plays is a culturally diffuse perspective on male friendship as troublesome. From the subject's point of view, friendship among men is personal and social; from the government's point of view, however, it is social and political. As a government problem, relationships among men justify the intervention and management of the Crown. In the Babington trials as well as in Marlowe's play, unauthorized male friendship (that is, men choosing where they bestow their loyalty) is as much an engine to new codes as a violation of the preexisting; it is *productive*; it produces differences, among them differences in what counts as manliness. Conventional authority positions male friendship as an obstacle and threat to the security of the country; Marlowe positions male friendship as the path to renewed empire. *Tamburlaine I* especially presents unauthorized affective homosocial bonds that cross national and class lines and that are valued over traditional affective bonds among historically privileged men as well as between men and women. Whether in the words of Tamburlaine or other figures, Marlowe stages the performance of friendship and establishes a pattern of befriending that underwrites the play. Contra the discourse of treason, which associates male friendships with "ease" and a corresponding military weakness, Marlowe's play images martial success as contingent on homosocial culture, and sets male friendship among rebels against masculine associations among those with hereditary claims to authority.

I have been suggesting that legal and fictive discourses of treason are engaged in constructing the conceptual contours of something called "the country" and its legitimate inhabitants, those who mentally occupy "this realm." The discourse of treason figures and expatriates the illegitimate subject by demonizing travel, by creating a conceptual link between geographic and political promiscuity. Mapping out fidelities relative to place, it assumes a continuity between the inner man, his birthplace, and his travels. In its negative form, it develops a rhetorical relationship among disloyalty, intellectual promiscuity, and rootlessness. Against this view, defendants identify themselves with a conceptual nationhood and a sustained loyalty for the new world they imagine. In *Tamburlaine I* Marlowe adopts the rhetoric of negative homelessness that characterizes treasons, but he reverses the value of that rhetoric, taking rootlessness as a productive form of a new and better nation.[93]

Certainly *Tamburlaine I* is infused with the energies of conquest and expansionism that ignited the late sixteenth century; its characters "in conceit bear empires on [their] spears" (1.2.64). Stephen Greenblatt associates this rootlessness with violence and a specifically Faustian interior life in Marlowe's plays, and finds an intimation:

> That man is homeless, that all places are alike, is linked to man's inner state, to the uncircumscribed hell he carries within him. And this insight returns us to the violence with which we began.[94]

More recently, John Gillies identifies geographical conquest as the "essence" of Tamburlaine's unique power, and describes Tamburlaine's speeches as "geographic wish-dreaming."[95] I want to suggest that we read Marlowe's work next to the contemporary discourses of treason. If we do, then points of view become sharper. From the point of view of the dominant culture, homelessness is "hellish," suspect, a violation. But from the point of view of the challengers, homelessness is potential, opportunity, a right rather than a violation.

In refocusing the terms of the discussion to a rhetoric of place, I want to return to the *Arte of Rhetorique*, in which Wilson makes it clear that theories of geographical place are significant modes of comprehension and explanation in late sixteenth-century culture. "The country," he writes, "declares [a man's] natural inclinations": "The house whereof a noble personage came, declares the state and nature of his auncestors, his alliaunce, and his kynsfolke." Wilson offers an especially useful version of the available meanings compressed into a theory of locale in 1560:

> The Realme, declares the nature of the people. So that some Countrey brengeth more honor with it, then an other doth. To be a Frenche manne, descendyng there of a noble house, is more honor then to be an Irishe manne: to bee an Englishe man borne, is much more honour, then to be a Scotte, because that by these men, worthy Prowesses have been dooen, and greater affaires by theim attempted, then have been doen by any other.
>
> The Shire or Toune helpeth somewhat, towardes the encrease of honour: As it is muche better, to bee borne in Paris, then in Picardie, in London, then in Lincolne. For that bothe the aire is better, the people more civill, and the wealth muche greater, and the menne for the most parte more wise.[96]

In this culture of masculine honor, although "place" understood as social status is significant, the geographic relationship also reveals the man. An origin is perceived as meaningful: it allows men to *predict* what one born in a particular place might think or do. Marlowe capitalizes on this idea when (in the passage I cited earlier) Tamburlaine meets Theridamas. He associates the country's value with the man's: in the "valiant man of Persia," Tamburlaine sees "the folly of [his] emperor," who has failed to comprehend the meaning of the warrior's "martial face" (1.2.164–70). A majestic and courageous version of the kind of man Persia breeds speaks through Theridamas; Mycetes's failure to read it marks him as an inferior man; and Tamburlaine's ability to interpret it signals their comraderie.

It is not that the land is monovocal, but that it mediates the work of differentiating and affiliating among men. In Marlowe's play, not only different places but also different conceptions of places allow the audience to make distinctions. Both Cosroe and later Bajazeth, two of the play's tradition-oriented voices, take personal identity as contingent on geographical identity, and geographical identity as the proof of a historically secured patrimony. Cosroe sees his homeland as the focal point of a particular history:

And in assurance of desired success,
We here do crown thee monarch of the East,
And Emperor of Asia and of Persia,
Great lord of Media and Armenia,
Duke of Africa and Albania,
Mesopotamia and of Parthia,
East India and the late discovered isles,
Chief lord of all the wide, vast Euxine Sea,
And of the ever-raging Caspian lake.
Long live Cosroe, mighty emperor! (1.1.160–69)[97]

Bajazeth makes his early challenge in similar terms, establishing his own identity by establishing a geography-saturated ancestry:

Tell him thy lord, the Turkish emperor,
Dread lord of Afric, Europe, and Asia,
Great king and conqueror of Graecia,
The ocean, Terrene, and the coal-black sea,
The high and highest monarch of the world,
Wills and commands—for say not I entreat—
Not once to set his foot in Africa. (3.1.22–28)

Both figures privilege particular versions of history to define their homelands and to legitimate themselves. In Thomas Wilson's formulation cited above, one's homeland ensures honorable paternity ("to be an English man borne is much more honor than to be a Scot") which in turn ensures masculinity ("because by these men worthie Prowesses have been done"). In treason trials, this kind of multinationalism is a sign of potential treachery and intellectual promiscuity. In Marlowe, it occupies the odd position of being instead the sign of a kind of stability based on one's links to a specifiable past.

Masculine identity is grounded in conceptions of place, and knowledge of a place allows one to predict what a man will do and what he might be—moral, patriotic, law-abiding. In this view, rootlessness is suspect.[98] Rather than shy away from the implications of such a representation, Marlowe extends and deepens it, breaking the links between emotional and spatial loyalty by associating his hero with homelessness: he is, in the Soldan's words, a "base usurping vagabond" (4.3.21). In Marlowe's day, there were a range of meanings for vagabondage and most were pejorative. Among the most prominent was "roaming or wandering from place to place, without settled habitation or home; leading a wandering life; nomadic." Citing an early usage from 1555—"owre men suppose them to bee a vagabonde and wandering nacion lyke unto the Scythians"—the *OED* finds a clear link between being a member of a "wandering nacion," which does not observe geographical distinctions as its primary mode of defining its identity, and being, like Tamburlaine, a Scythian.[99]

Vagabondage exists relative not only to immobility but also to specifiable borders as modes of positioning subjects. John Gillies identifies "the essentially moral character" of ancient boundary discourses, in which the primary role of the geography is to convey the moral.[100] The vagabond does not recognize traditional social or geographical boundaries, and there is much for a monarchy to fear in such a figure. If one is a "homeless wanderer," then a place of origin or upbringing cannot "predict" his character. Fidelity cannot be associated with a particular locale. Although discourses of treason rhetorically link place and rootlessness as modes of explanation, Marlowe breaks the link that binds a man to a place. As vagabond, Tamburlaine is positioned outside the mode of historically-privileged explanation preferred by Cosroe and Bajazeth. Representing the deliberate conqueror as an aimless tramp may be one means by which Tamburlaine's enemies reassure themselves; presenting him as outside the rules of place and predictability is certainly Marlowe's means of challenging easy equations between immobility and fidelity.

Given Marlowe's interest in the mobility of fidelity, his interest in the provisional, what are we to make of *Tamburlaine I*'s turn to the lawful at its conclusion? "Mount up your royal places of estate / . . . / And there make laws to rule your provinces" (5.2.461–63). The move might seem arbitrary from this triumphant warrior, but in fact Marlowe has been challenging and pushing aside the category of the lawful throughout. As I argued earlier, the jockeying for position regarding legal codes represents an acting out of historical process. To make a claim on the law is also to make a claim on a particular version of a country or a homeland that is constructed in what went before. What persists in trials is the process of arguing about precedents, through which legal practice cultivates mythic antecedents and produces a useable English past. As "traitor," Tamburlaine (like Cosroe before him) marks the boundaries of dying conceptions of the lawful. Meander tells Mycetes about Tamburlaine, who "robs your merchants of Persepolis, / . . . / And in your confines with his lawless train / Daily commits uncivil outrages" (1.1.37–40). At their first meeting, Zenocrate tells Tamburlaine, "seek not to enrich thy followers / By lawless rapine from a silly maid" (1.2.9–10). In phrases that echo each other, Zabina spits at Tamburlaine, "Unworthy king, that by thy cruelty / Unlawfully usurpest the Persian seat" (4.2.56–57). In these instances, characters refer to a range of meanings for the lawful, and as Tamburlaine violates, rejects, or ignores these laws, Marlowe makes the point that "the law" is always *somebody's* law whose authority holds only at *some time*. In this context, the play's conclusion is as provisional as any laws it has evoked and shouldered aside: the new laws Tamburlaine calls for are somebody's laws and will command obedience only some time.

In *Tamburlaine I*, Marlowe does away with two traditional forms of perceiving "the country": a reductive material form, in which the nation, comprehended as dirt, is significant only for the uses to which it might be put; and a mystifying aggrandizing form, in which the nation, comprehended as a cemetery of chivalric heroes (in a sort of dead warriors society), is significant only as a memorial to its past. Marlowe systematically refutes the idea, circulated widely in discourses of treason, that authentic loyalty can be seen in historically-secured geography. Instead, he replaces these ideas of the country with his staging of a triumphant "wandering nacion," transforming treasonous intellectual promiscuity into loyal mental affiliation. Marlowe is, I think, rewriting the key issue of the Babington treasons, the competitive relationship between loyalty to one's country and to one's friends. Here, male friendship is the productive force of a new nation, the path to a renewed empire, the means of achieving new lawful stability. And "the country" is the volatile result of men's material and imagined practices.

The Babington treasons and *Tamburlaine I* are among a vast array of treason literatures promulgated during the sixteenth century. At their centers is the basic issue of all treason: withdrawal and bestowal of allegiance. Each evokes the culturally diffuse codes of courtiership as a means of mediating conflicting loyalties. Within these traditional codes, which bring honor, hazard, and manhood into a relationship, masculine fidelity becomes a particularly prominent point of trouble. The trials and the play publicize an emergent theory of male friendship that is at odds with traditional views. The issue is not male homosociability itself; that had always been a founding value in patriarchal culture. The issue is the superior importance of male friendship over other values.

In his work on the meanings of "space," Yi-Fu Tuan theorizes the ways cultures frame the issue of "place": it is organized according to a perceived order which is socially-embedded, such as personal relations, a sense of spaciousness or crowding, or visible features that create markers; it can extend into perceptions of the mythical and legendary, and into the architectural and temporal; and it is made meaningful through experiences of intimacy and community, which produce what we call the "homeland" and attachments to it. "What gives a place its identity, its aura?" Tuan asks. "In what ways do people attach meaning to and organize space and place?"[101] As the Babington treasons, *Tamburlaine I*, and the trials and plays contemporary with them suggest, these discourses "give visibility to intimate experiences, including those of place."[102] These trials and plays contribute their voices to a developing discourse of competitive proprietorship that discovers its traitors not only among outsiders but among men who share similar status, background, and birthright. In these imaginative literatures, historical and fictive, the enemy to "this realm" is the enemy within.

4.
Secrecy and the Epistolary Self

On October 10, 1586, a special Commission of noblemen rode off from London to confront Mary, Queen of Scots, at Fotheringay Castle, the latest stop among the many she had made during the nearly twenty years she was held in custody. Pursued by her brother and a group of rebellious noblemen bent on deposing her, Mary had fled to England in 1568, seeking asylum and disturbing what historian J. E. Neale describes as England's hope of "peaceful insularity" from its neighbor's troubles.[1] She was a Catholic; she was, through her mother, a daughter of the House of Guise, proponents of Catholicism in France; and she was, by descent, perhaps the most authentic contender—"acquainted with blood"—for the throne of England after Elizabeth.[2] According to the Crown, Mary had plotted with Anthony Babington and his disaffected friends to assassinate Elizabeth and see herself enthroned.[3] Within just a few days of their arrival at Fotheringay, the queen's Commissioners completed their interrogation and rode away, claiming to possess the evidence of treason that would justify their finally ridding the realm of Elizabeth's perennial challenger.

Among the many widely-remarked cultural shifts during the sixteenth century was a decrease in the perceived authority of orality as a source of knowledge and site of truth and an increase in the perceived authority of writing.[4] In legal practice as in the culture more generally, written documents increasingly competed with persons as sites of creditable testimony. As writing came under scrutiny in trials as a means of structuring and revealing a person's thoughts, new theories of reading and writing made their way into (and were made in) legal practice. During the Babington prosecutions, defendant Tilney conceded having written that Elizabeth might be surprised in her own coach; he acknowledged that his comments were "in [his] own hand"; and he argued insistently that he, and not the prosecutor, "must interpret [his] own meaning."[5] What is especially striking about the Scots prosecution is the particular form of the evidence: a packet of cryptic letters. A pointed revelation of what writing can mean to a theory of interiority and its exposure, the Scots case is the exemplary epistolary treason. As the opposing figures battle it out in terms of documentary theory over the authenticity and authority of writing, they embed letters in larger social discourses on the meanings and metaphysics of writing, and they examine the roles letters play in structures of selfhood, gender, and status. What is a letter? For whom does it speak? And perhaps most relevant to a study of treason, how is it to be understood in a culture of betrayal?

Betrayal by letter, whether the document is authentic or forged, was hardly uncommon on Renaissance stages, and its prevalence in early modern culture more generally certainly contributed to a pervasive lack of trust among subjects that Lacey Baldwin Smith sees reflected in Elizabethan treason prosecutions.[6] Comic epistolary betrayal appears as early as *Ralph Roister Doister*, and occurs in Shakespeare in *Two Gentlemen of Verona*, *Love's Labor's Lost*, *Twelfth Night*, and *All's Well that Ends Well*, to name but a few instances. Betrayals by letter with more serious consequences appear in *King Lear*, *Hamlet*, and *1 Henry IV*.[7] Christopher Marlowe exploits their ambiguous potential prominently in *The Jew of Malta*, *Edward II*, and *The Massacre at Paris*, as does John Webster in *The Duchess of Malfi*. Letters were ideally suited to the stage: they were both props and concepts; their materiality forged a kind of mysterious presence; and even a scrap could attract the eye and provoke the imagination. They could promise visual accessibility with one hand, and take away certainty of interpretation with the other.

The unsettled principles of epistolary interpretation are also central in Thomas Kyd's *The Spanish Tragedy*, which may have been written soon after the Scots proceedings.[8] Kyd had a personal history of being immersed in the documentary practices of his day and a political history of being in trouble with the law in a case that itself turned on the status of the texts. Through Belimperia's letters, he brings into focus questions about the evidentiary force of writing. Probing the meanings of circulating, intercepting, and authenticating documents, Kyd ties those meanings to conceptions of secret interiority and mutating fidelity. Like the Scots trial, Kyd's play offers complex views of an unsettled competitive relationship between writing and selfhood, between letters and persons as sites of knowledge. In legal and theatrical practice, letters are a crucial means of forming alliances—of conveying and expanding the "truth"—among persons who come to "know" the same truth and who act to bring about their own ends. In both trial and play, we see a culture deeply conflicted about the elusive ways prior beliefs or disbeliefs condition the perceptions of writer and writings. And in both sites, the authorized proprietors of the "realm" attend to foreign alliances while the self-identified injured parties develop a local counterculture of letters.

Allowing legal proceedings against Mary was a long-deferred decision on Elizabeth's part. Elizabeth had continued to perceive of Mary as an anointed monarch, one of God's earthly lieutenants, and a figure above human judgment. When Mary was driven from the Scottish throne, Elizabeth had rebuked the Scottish nobles and tried to avoid acknowledging James's sovereignty. When it appeared Mary might have known about the Ridolfi plot, which involved a possible union between Thomas Howard, the Duke of Norfolk, and Mary and which may have strengthened Mary's claims to the throne, Elizabeth refused to let Parliament proceed against her. When Francis Throckmorton was arrested as a participant in a plot inspired by Mary, Elizabeth still chose not to act against the Scottish queen.[9] Only Francis Walsingham's evidence against the Babington group finally lead Elizabeth to agree to proceed officially.[10]

Although historians continue to debate whether Mary played an active role in plots against Elizabeth, it is clear that she played a powerful role ideologically and discursively as a theme of late sixteenth-century treasons well before she was formally accused.[11] When her prosecution finally did occur, it depended not only on evidence derived from the Babington convictions but also on a preceding documentary event unique in English legal history: the creation of a written Bond of Association in 1585 among Elizabeth's noblemen.

The Babington trials give us a glimpse of a culture for which allegiance among men had become a deeply and openly troublesome ideological category: what were its bases (birthright? origin?), what was its language (chivalric? courtly? legal?), what was its purpose (royal service?)? In short, what were the signs of male allegiance to a sovereign? Long-simmering fissures in the group identity of men had become obvious, and when the performance of friendship had conflicted with allegiance to the sovereign, friendship had won.[12] Shortly before those trials, however, another group of Englishmen had constructed a text in which the performance of friendship among men relied specifically and emphatically on allegiance to the sovereign. In this Bond of Association, a band of Elizabeth's noblemen vowed in writing "never [to] desist from all manner of forcible pursuit against such persons" as were perceived as jeopardizing the realm. As the originators develop their theme, formerly unspoken aspects of relationships among men of similar status (those things that went without saying) are converted into a written contract among signatories:

> Therefore we whose names are or shall be subscribed to this writing being natural-born subjects of this realm of England . . . do for these reasons and causes before alledged [sic], . . . acknowledge ourselves most justly bound with our lives and goods for [the sovereign's] defence, . . . to prosecute, suppress and withstand all such intenders, and all other enemies, of what nation, condition or degree soever they shall be. . . . [W]e do voluntarily and most willingly bind ourselves, every one of us to the other, jointly and severally in the band of one firm and loyal society.[13]

On the one hand, the Bond retrieves the rhetoric of proprietorship common to discourses of treason: it announces a "natural" affiliation with England among the Commissioners, identifying citizenship with a birthplace. Their "being natural-born subjects of this realm" produces, in this logic, an emotion of loyal defense and a predictable character (reiterating Thomas Wilson's link between birthplace and criminal or honorable acts in the *Arte of Rhetorique*). The signers beget an affiliation by subscribing to the same manuscript, and they make loyalty visible by presenting it in documentary form. On and in paper, an abstract England is formed into a shared, physical reality where faithful English men gather and unite in a dispersed yet communal identity. On the other hand, this document is self-conscious about its written status, and its reflexivity highlights its role in bringing about a second Eden. The written bond *as* document occupies an elusive position; it is partly a transparent conduit to thoughts, and it is partly a materialization in whose substance a transcendent notion of the land inheres and extends over place and time. The association struck herein, the document seems to say, is an effect not only of shared status and geography, but also—perhaps primarily—an effect of shared discourse, the solidarity it announces, an effect of shared documentary presence.[14]

Following the Babington prosecutions, Elizabeth authorized a Commission to question Mary: "To you, and the greater part of you we do give full and absolute power, faculty, and authority to examine all and singular matters compassed and imagined, tending to the hurt of our royal person" and, further, "to give Sentence or Judgement, as upon good proof matter shall appear unto you."[15] The Commissioners' authority derived from another unique legal event, a statute (27 Eliz. c.1) entitled "An act for the Security of the Queen's Royal Person, and continuance of the realm in peace" that affirmed the Bond of Association and specified that the queen could appoint commissioners to interrogate any persons the noblemen might believe to be traitors.[16]

Cloistered in the halls of Fotheringay, Elizabeth's Commissioners began their interrogation by recapitulating many of the themes that characterize discourses of treason throughout the century: a ruling group adopts a proprietary stance and speaks for "the realm" against a "traitor" who (from the authorities' perspective) threatens to destroy that country's "felicity" and to fill its lands with those who are foreigners by birth or by imagination. Before the trial Elizabeth's counselors insisted:

> Her Secretaries do write and print, that we be at our wit's end, world's end, if she overlive your majesty; meaning thereby, that the end of our world is the beginning of theirs. . . . [T]his enemy of our felicity seeks to undermine our religion, to supplant us, and plant strangers in the place.[17]

In the interrogations, however, instead of resisting this political "othering" as defendants generally do, Mary aligns herself with it: she rejects the modes of affiliation and discursive compasses by which defendants often fit themselves to the conceptual and geographical terrain of "our world." By her own acknowledgement, she is not one of them. To the Crown's claims of a natural loyalty that attaches them to a homeland, Mary responds with self-designated alienation: "The laws and statutes of England are to me most unknown," she argues, "I am destitute of countrymen, and who shall be my peers I am utterly ignorant."[18]

This self-alienation is not neutral, however, and in place of "the country," Mary identifies herself with the transcendent category of "majesty," which in her view supersedes legal, social, and geographical boundaries. "It seemeth strange to me," she claims, "that the queen should command me as a subject, to appear personally in judgment. I am an absolute queen, and will do nothing which may prejudice either mine own royal majesty, or other princes of my place and rank."[19] In Mary's view, she is proprietor not only (nor even primarily) of a specific realm, but of an immutable, transcendent royal dignity that does not change with shifts in her country or condition. She recognizes her place in an imaginary community based on birthright and status, and, more to the point, based on the mystification of royal blood: "Doth not your mistress know that I am a queen by birth? Or thinketh she that I will so far prejudice my rank and station, and blood whereof I am descended, the son who is to succeed me, and the majesty of other princes, as to yield obedience to her commands?"[20] In Ernst Kantorowicz's formulation, Mary identifies herself with and as the body politic and diminishes her role as the body natural, downplaying the categories of gender and country in favor of a powerful abstraction of royalty incorporate that resonated with Elizabeth's own status.[21] Inhabiting and inhabited by "majesty," this queen strives to adopt a position outside local habitations. Mary's efforts fail to prevent the trial from going forward—Commissioner Hatton counters, "You are accused (but not condemned) to have conspired the Destruction of our lady and queen anointed. You say you are a queen: be it so. But in such a crime the royal dignity is not exempted from answering, neither by the Civil nor Canon Law, nor by the Law of nations, nor of nature"[22]—but the theme of abstract identity registered in her resistance haunts the proceedings: in them, as in her claims to majesty, an abstracted "Mary" present in writing replaces the embodied woman accused of treason.

Initiating the proceedings, Commissioner Gawdy could assume what in the Babington prosecutions he had had to argue: the "facts" of the case. What had been a particular contest for conceptual proprietorship of the country in the earlier treasons had swiftly become a documentary record of historical and legal truth.

> [Gawdy] now opened the law from point to point, affirming that she [Mary] had offended against the same; and hereupon he made an historical discourse of Babington's Conspiracy, and concluded, That she knew of it, approved of it, and assented unto it, promised her assistance, and shewed the ways and means.[23]

"It was urged out of Babington's Confession, that there had been intercourse by Letters betwixt [Mary] and Babington, wherein the whole Conspiracy was set down."[24] In arranging and organizing the texts of the Scots trial, the prosecutors function as early modern editors, adding to and subtracting from their documents, nipping and tucking, guided by a teleology of national identity. Grouping the letters and written examinations in particular ways, the Crown creates a structure that implies what prosecutors can then avoid arguing: the potential relationships among the texts, such as homogeneity, filiation, and reciprocal explanation, by which Mary is subsumed into the documents of the case and the Babington history. The Crown's methods display the texts' historicity and (re)produce them as historical developments, as though they were representations of a progressive knowledge from an originary moment to the present.[25]

Gawdy's "historical discourse" notwithstanding, the status of the documents in the Scots trial is a vexed issue that forms the centerpiece of a sustained evidentiary struggle. What is at stake in that struggle is as much what Mary "is" (that is, her moral character) as what Mary might have done. To the earliest mention of letters in the questioning, Mary "confessed," with a passing reference to a potentially promiscuous epistolary life, "that there had passed Conference by Letters betwixt her and many men, yet could it not thereby be gathered that she was privy to all their wicked counsels."[26] "As for these Letters," she said, "it may be that Babington wrote them, but let it be proved that I received them: If Babington or any others affirm it, I say they lye openly; other men's crimes are not to be cast upon me."[27] The prosecutors attempt to secure letters as authentic revelations of their writer's mind and, more importantly, as uncomplicated vehicles of a direct transference of thought. In this structure, ideas pass uncensored and unresisted from a self-revealing writer to a receptive reader. The Commission's argument (which begs the question of Mary's prior inner assent) is lent credibility by its kinship with popular conceptions of female weakmindedness. Popular and religious texts and speeches helped keep a gendered notion of the fickle mind circulating.[28] And in the *Arte of Rhetorique*, Thomas Wilson insists that intellectual weakness is woman's lamentable birthright: "To be borne a woman, declares weakenes of spirite, neshenes of body, and siklinesse of mynde."[29] These contemporary commonplaces lend the idea of a woman's intellectual passivity the aura of common sense, subsuming selected "evidence" into a language of cultural norms.

Mary counterattacks, however, by arguing that receipt of a letter does not signify the exposure of its writer's mind, nor does written communication prove a recipient's agreement with what she reads. Granting that she had corresponded with many men, but refuting the idea that those men revealed inner or wicked thoughts, Mary challenges the gendered structure of unresistant cognition that her prosecutors presuppose. She resituates the letters in a context where the reader's will intervenes in her reception of a text. In this Marian structure, the reader's mind is neither passive nor pliant (nor, by cultural norms, female); it *works* on what it receives, guided by its inner constitution.

The competing theories in the Scots trial of the written transmission of ideas are complicated by a crucial issue: the authorship of the letters. The letter that draws the most scrutiny is also the only one insistently attributed *to* Mary. Purportedly an answer to a letter from Babington (July 12, 1586), the missive opens with comments on the suffering of Catholics in England, and continues to inquire about such strategies as "What forces, as well on foot as on horse, you may raise among you all"; "Which towns, ports, and havens you may assure yourselves, . . . to receive succours, as well from the Low-Countries, Spain, and France, as from other parts"; "By what means . . . the six gentlemen deliberate to proceed"; and "the manner of my getting forth of this hold."[30]

Unique in the density of its martial details, the letter is persuasive evidence indeed. But of what? And about whom? The problem is the result of two related questions: "who is its writer?" (that is, the one who inscribed the text), and "who is its author?" (that is, the one who thought the ideas inscribed in the text). Mary denies being either:

> Of this Letter she required a Copy, and affirmed, That it proceeded not from her, but haply from her Alphabet of Ciphers in France. . . . That it was an easy matter to counterfeit the Ciphers and Characters of others, as a yong man did very lately in France, which had vaunted himself to be her son's base brother. . . . That she feared also lest this were done now by Walsingham to bring her to her death.[31]

Walsingham, who had been Mary's relentless pursuer, hotly denied the imputations. Historians have documented, however, that he had been intercepting and withholding Mary's correspondence for nearly a year; that he had broken the code used in the letters or had come into possession of her "alphabet of ciphers"; and that he had hired a cipherer and forger, Thomas Phelippes, to insert statements and questions of his own into letters to and from Mary.[32] Presciently, Mary had claimed "That her adversaries might easily get the Cyphers, which she had used to others, and with the same write many things falsely."[33]

The questions are further complicated by a Tudor commonplace: whereas the discourse of monarchy explains ciphering one way, the discourse of treason explains it quite another. From the point of view of a royal figure with business of state to conduct, cipher is a legitimate form: state secrets had to be protected and prevented from falling into the wrong hands. From another point of view, however, that of the Commissioners who assumed that Mary could have no legitimate business of state to conduct in England, ciphering is evidence of her attempts to mask her seditious motives. What is called for is again the self-evident in two senses: evidence of a self so clear that it exposes her dishonest interior, and evidence so persuasive that it appears irrefutable. What we find, however, is an epistolary stalemate. While Mary's accusers would like her letters to mean one thing, she insists they mean something else altogether. What is the meaning, for example, of her words to Babington: "keep never a paper about you, that may in any sort do harm: for from like errors have come the condemnation of all such as have suffered heretofore against whom otherwise nothing could justly have been proved."[34] Is this, as the Crown would have it, proof of her guilt and a devious attempt to avoid prosecution for real acts? Or is it, as Mary suggests, a fearful reaction beginning to be shared in the culture more generally to the possibility of being unjustly attacked in the contemporary climate of espionage and counterespionage?

The answer to what Mary's caution means mutates with where one is standing, in the "new world" envisioned by the Babington defendants or in "this realm of England" claimed by Elizabeth's Commissioners. Annabel Patterson has shown that interception of writings was becoming a topic of explicit contention:

> Erasmus had noted Cicero's frequent fears that his letters might be intercepted, and commented on the hazard of committing such material to paper. In the seventeenth century the issue of confidentiality became central. Personal letters, the most private of all communication except whispers, carried no immunity against censorship. Letters *were* intercepted, and their authors might be dealt with as severely as if they had published a provocative pamphlet.[35]

It is not the interventions of Walsingham, however, which were not fully known at the time, but the hands of the secretaries—other figures who "wrote" the letters—that become prominent in the interrogations. Mary repeatedly presses the Commissioners to show her any letters "under her hand" or carrying "her own Subscription."[36] Like the logic Erasmus laid out—"A man's handwriting, like his voice, has a special individual quality"[37]—Mary implies that her signature functions as a guarantee of the authenticity of the document, a nontransferable sign of her inner thoughts. What the Crown produces, however, are copies of letters attributed to her, two of which are in the hands of her secretaries, Naw and Curle.

What is the relationship between the one who wields the pen and the one who authors the letter? On the one hand, a secretary was a trusted repository of his mistress's secrets, a recorder of her intimate thoughts, and a neutral conduit for her ideas. As such, he could easily be drawn into a circle of complicity. Jonathan Goldberg explains the position of the secretary in the 1599 edition of Angell Day's *The English Secretorie* (which first appeared in 1586): "The main office of the secretary, . . . lies in the '*trust* and *fidelitie*' of the relationship of the secretary to his lord and master, an office that can be read and understood in its very name, etymologically construed, secretary from secret; a secretary is 'as keeper or conserver of the secret unto him committed.'"[38] Positioned as the writers of their master's letters, "Secretaries were not only able to forge their master's hands—they were permitted and even expected to do so."[39] On the other hand, secretaries were mistrusted for the power they wielded over writing and the self-interest that might lead them to violate the intentions of the author in inscribing a letter. Erasmus, for example, has Leo impress upon Ursus the importance of writing *in one's own hand*:

> To be brief: a letter that is the product of someone else's fingers hardly deserves the name. For secretaries import a great deal of their own. If you dictate verbatim, then

it is goodbye to your privacy; and so you disguise some things and suppress others in order to avoid having an unwanted confidant.[40]

What if, as is the case in the Scots treason, the author did not "write" the letter? Given this threshold position at the borders of the author's written thoughts, the secretary's way of "being in the letter" is crucial to the Scots treason, and the trial returns again and again to a rudimentary, yet pressing contemporary question: what is a letter? For William Fulwood and Angell Day, as for Mary Stuart's prosecutors, a letter, including one written in a secretary's hand, is the unmediated exposure of the mind, a true record of thoughts, designed to make geographical and ideological distance collapse into mental proximity. In *The Enemy of Idleness*, which was published in 1568, Fulwood explained: "An Epistle . . . or letter is nothing else, but a declaration, by Writing of the mindes of such as bee absent, one of them to another, even as though they were present."[41] Anticipating the kind of authorship Michel Foucault calls "expressivist,"[42] in which a written document is taken as the sincere expression of the writer's thoughts, Angell Day's manual concludes also: "Letters are onely messengers of each mans intendments."[43]

As we saw in the Babington treasons, troubling over intentions is part of a wider cultural tension over the right to interpret meanings and to speak for a subject's inner life. With the technological, religious, and social shifts of the early sixteenth century, the individual had gained some new rights to interpreting texts. The conflict between Tilney and the Crown suggests the limitations of those new rights and the challenges to authority that make up discourses of treason. In epistolary treasons, such as Mary Stuart's, the interpretive challenges multiply, and what is at stake is authority over one's own speech: *who* speaks for the self, the accused or the Crown or the secretary? And what has the "self" spoken in speaking particular words?

Erasmus's counterclaims notwithstanding—that "Secretaries import a great deal of their own"—the Commissioners in the Scots trial erase the writer from the writing, tasking Mary with defining her relationship to letters she did not write but is charged with having thought; they become the revelation of her intentions. It is this enscripting power of the secretary that Mary rejects:

Then pressed they her with the Testimonies of her Secretaries Naw and Curle, out of Babington's Confession and the letters sent to and fro betwixt her and Babington, and the whole credit of their Proofs rested upon their Testimony [Naw's and Curle's]; . . . . Curle she acknowledged an honest man, but not a meet Witness to be against her. As for Naw, he had been sometimes a Secretary, said she, to the cardinal of Lorain, and commended unto her by the French king, and might easily be drawn either by reward, or hope, or fear, to bear false witness, as one that had sundry times bound himself by oath, and had Curle so pliable unto him, that at his beck he would write what he bade him. It might be that these two might insert into her Letters, such things as she had not dictated unto them. It might also be that such Letters came to their hands, which notwithstanding she never saw; and so she brake forth into such words as these: "The majesty and safety of all princes falleth to the ground, if they depend upon the Writings and Testimony of Secretaries."[44]

To make a distinction between writing and authoring, and to undermine the letter's claim to represent the truth about her thoughts, Mary activates contemporary anxieties about class stability and social mobility. Asserting her personal superiority—"Her integrity depended not upon the credit and memory of her Secretary"—Mary's testimony links crediting the socially inferior secretary with destroying the underlying bases of monarchy.

By crediting the secretaries against the mistress, she implies, the Commissioners violate hierarchical authority and empower the subordinate, who can topple the great by revealing *more truly* than the monarch herself the motives and thoughts that lie in her heart. As Mary sees it, at stake was not only her life or her legend but the structure of monarchy itself and the influence of servants within it: "Then enquiring what was become of Naw and Curle: she asked whether it were ever heard of before, that servants were suborned and accepted as Witnesses against their master's life?"[45] The Commissioners, in turn, substitute the agency of the author for the agency of the writers, assuming a hermeneutics of presence: from their vantage point, the authentic Mary is *more* present and more clearly defined in letters composed by secretaries than in her person.[46]

The Crown strives to have it both ways, sometimes describing the author revealing him or her self truly in letters, sometimes describing the author as a lying, feining interpreter of those letters. The Crown's mobility here points to a paradox: the belief that signs *reveal* hidden truths means that they must also be capable of *hiding* or concealing those truths. From both positions, the government places itself above the writer as the interpretive authority. Again, in both cases, the effect is to establish the written text as the authentic voice of the accused, and to transfer the site of evidence from the heart of the evidence-giver to the surface of the page. Put another way, the self is wholly identified with inscriptions authored elsewhere.

In his work on what he terms "the bibliographic ego" and Ben Jonson's contributions to literary marketing, Joseph Lowenstein comments in passing on "the way print stimulated a competitive relation between book and person, a competition for preeminence as the locus of intellectual summation."[47] Lowenstein traces the initiation of that competition to the advent of writing, registered in Plato's *Phaedras*, where Socrates fears that writing will erode the authority of human memory. The position granted letters in the Scots treason, where writing erodes the authority of the author, justifies Socrates' fear and places letters in a competitive relation with persons for ascendancy as the site of the authentic self.[48] As the trial develops, it is as though the self in letters is made to testify against the self in person, a kind of self-incrimination that might be comic were it not for threat of death hanging over the proceedings.

Like many treason trials in the sixteenth century, this one includes a final recantation that skews its stability and points toward problems of doubt. The anonymous recorder uses the last word to reintroduce questions of evidence:

> Concerning this sentence [of guilt], which depended wholly upon the credit of the Secretaries, and they not brought forth face to face . . . much talk there was, and divers Speeches ran abroad; while some thought them credible persons, and some unworthy to be credited. I have seen Naw's Apology to King James, written in the year 1605; wherein laboriously protesting, he excuseth himself, that he was neither author, nor persuader, nor the first revealer of the Plot that was undertaken, nor failed of his duty through negligence or want of foresight; yea, that this day he stoutly impugned the chief points of Accusation against his lady and mistress: which notwithstanding, appeareth not by Records.[49]

In attempting to shape the nation by shaping the transmission and interpretation of its letters, the Crown was unwittingly participating in razing the country it claimed to defend. Official interference with letters, including intercepting, interpreting, and censoring them, was beginning to elicit resistance by century's end. Typically, those who attended to interference with letters saw government intervention as a sign of the nation's decline from civility. And by the 1640s, James Howell would lament to his friends,

> Among many other Barbarisms which like impetuous Torrent have lately rush'd in upon us the interception and opening of Letters is none of the least. . . . 'tis a plundering of the very brain, as is spoken in another place. We are reduced here to that servile condition, or rather to such a height of slavery, that we have nothing left which may entitle us free Rationall creatures; the *thought* itself cannot say 'tis free, much less the *tongue* or *pen*.[50]

Envisioning Englishness as the undisrupted circulation of written ideas, and envisioning that free circulation as his birthright, Howell finds himself inhabiting a strangely barbaric land. As they resorted to textual manipulation and suppression to purge the land of Mary, and adopted the stance that they were thereby ensuring the nation's security, the Commissioners in the Scots trial were instead producing an unfamiliar England whose residents would come to redefine their lives in terms of slavery and servility. In the difficult matter of the Scots epistolary treason, letters had become weapons in a battle to limit the imaginative life of the nation's subjects and writing a means of replacing the self.

Two competing notions of the relationship between writing and characters emerge in the Scots treason. One notion, offered by the Crown, is that a person's "character" is an invisible, elusive composite of motives and moralities that precedes its verbalization yet is revealed and exposed in writing, even writing by "secretaries," whose special access to the author ensures their special access to the truth. A counternotion, offered by Mary during her defense, is that writing, especially writing by and from others, creates a "character" for a person that is not necessarily her own. She *ought* to be "her majesty." Instead, she implies, she comes to exist as "Mary the traitor" in and through inscriptions whose authorship and integrity are suspect.[51] The groundwork for those inscriptions, I want to suggest, which reintegrate the political with the natural body and taint Mary with the stigma of unchaste womanhood, had been laid decades earlier in the popular, published rumors that comprised her earlier biography as an erotic woman. Her reputation outside the treason trial conditions persuasion within it, making a discursive link between political and sexual treachery.[52]

By the time Mary was executed at Fotheringay Castle on February 8, 1587, it had been nearly two decades since she had appeared claiming political asylum.[53] Her arrival in England, which was charged with implications for the succession, was also preceded by well-known rumors that she had arranged the death of her second husband, Henry Darnley, prior to marrying his alleged murderer, the Earl of Bothwell.[54] As it would be in her trial, in this early episode of 1567 the evidence against Mary was a packet of letters: "a number of documents, chiefly letters allegedly written by Mary to Bothwell and found in a silver casket, and one supporting affidavit from the pen of a 'gentleman' of the Earl of Lennox, Darnley's father."[55]

Although the letters allegedly represent the thoughts of a woman in thrall to the demands of her own desire, their authenticity and authorship was and remains at the center of a lengthy debate. Many historians believe that they were devised by her brother, Moray, as his means of justifying dethroning his sister.[56] In June 1567, he and the members of his "secret council" had tried to arrest and depose Mary, claiming she was unfit to rule. In December of 1567, the secret council passed an Act

> declaring that "the cause and occasion of the taking of the Queen's person on the 15th June last was in the said Queen's own default, in as far as, by divers her Privy Letters,

written and *subscrivit* with her own hand, and sent by her to James Earl of Bothwell, Chief Executor of the horrible murder [of Darnley], and by her ungodly proceeding in a private marriage with him suddenly thereafter, it is most certain that she was privy, art and part, of the actual devise of the murder of the King."[57]

Historian Edward Parry points out, however, that the letters were not "'written and *subscrivit*' by the Queen's own hand. . . . [The conspirators] must have known that they were not *subscrivit*. The ultimate forgeries produced were unsigned."[58] Under the threat of action from England, Moray and his supporters arranged to defend their uprising before Elizabeth in January 1569. Until that date

the only documents mentioned by the Council as being found in the casket are private letters. We do not hear, as yet, of any love sonnets or of a marriage contract. These later documents are only found, or at all events are first referred to as coming out of the casket, in October 1568, when Moray, Morton, and Maitland are preparing their brief of evidence against the Queen to put before the English Commissioners.[59]

At the English inquiry "no comparison was ever made between the French letters produced by Moray and the letters acknowledged and proved to be in the queen's handwriting. Copies were made and collated with originals which were at once returned to Moray."[60] The consensus among historians is that in some instances Moray forged portions of the documents, and in other cases he collected letters and poems written by Mary for particular persons and situations, edited and collated them, and claimed they had been written to and for other situations.

The letters attributed to Mary fall into two groups: those which supposedly prove she conspired to murder her husband Darnley, and those which purport to show she was in love with Bothwell and staged her own abduction with him. Early in the longest of them, the "long Glasgow letter" allegedly written to Bothwell, the speaker details her isolation and loneliness: "Being gone from the place, where I had left my heart, it may be easily judged what my countenance was, considering what the body may without the heart, which was cause that till dinner I had used little talk, neither would anybody advance himself thereunto, thinking it was not good to do so."[61] Moving through conversational information about uneasy visitors, the diaristic notes give way to a description of a conversation between the estranged Mary and Darnley that reveals a hard-hearted woman denying her husband's pleas for reconciliation:

he told me his grief, and that he would make no testament, but leave all to me and that I was cause of his sickness for the sorrow he had, that I was so strange to him

"And, he said, you asked what I meant in my letter to speak of cruelty. It was of your cruelty who will not accept my offers and repentance. I avow that I have done amiss . . . and so have many other of your subjects and you have well pardoned them. . . . And I ask nothing but that we may be at bed and table together as husband and wife; and if you will not I will never rise from this bed. . . ." In the end he desired much that I should lodge in his lodging. I have refused it.[62]

Finally, near the letter's end, Darnley is replaced by another figure, and Mary emerges as a woman driven by desire, submissive to her lover, and regardless of morality:

Alas, I never deceived anybody; but I remit myself to your will. And send me word what I shall do, and whatsoever happens to me, I will obey you. . . . Now if to please you, my dear life, I spare neither honour, conscience, nor hasard, nor greatness, take it in good part, and not according to the interpretation of our false brother-in-law, to whom I pray you give no credit against the most faithful lover that ever you had or shall have.[63]

The Mary of this part of the letter adopts the gendered language of courtiership so prevalent in discourses of treason—"honour, conscience, . . . hasard, . . . greatness"—to express her conception of self-directed emotional and sexual fidelity as heroic risk. Yet to her accusers, the letter's lengthy transit through various relationships and emotions shows a Mary literally writing herself *out*, exposing in inscription the authentic unfaithful woman.

The Glasgow letter is engaged in crafting a sexual persona for Mary and in allying that persona with unlawful, illegitimate relationships. Similar sexual tainting occurs in the twelve sonnets also attributed to her.[64] In one (rumored at the time to allude to Bothwell's raping Mary when she was married to Darnley) the speaker vows, "Full many a tear have I wept because of him. / The first was shed when he took possession of my body, / Whose heart did not then belong to him."[65] In another, she laments:

For him since then I have despised honour,
Which alone can provide us with happiness.
For him I have risked dignity and conscience,
For him I have forsaken all my relatives and friends,
And all other considerations have been put aside. . . .
For his sake I would fain renounce the world,
I would gladly die that he might rise. . . .
For him alone I wish to be great,
And I shall so behave that he will recognize
That I have neither wellbeing nor luck nor contentment
Than in obeying and serving him loyally.

I hope for him nothing but good fortune.
For his sake I wish to retain health and life.[66]

All were interpreted by Moray's supporters as revealing a hidden, adulterous Mary.

This inscripted "Mary" was progressively publicized in the late 1560s and early 1570s. Defending his efforts to depose his sister, Moray had had all the "documents" against Mary read aloud at the Scottish Parliament in December 1567, circulating a popular version of a sexually driven woman.[67] Following the English inquiry in 1569, Moray consented to Elizabeth's request not to circulate the letters. Although they remained officially confidential, the letters continued to be topics of scandalous reports until 1572, when the Ridolfi treasons prompted Elizabeth to permit Moray's version of the Darnley affair, "together with the much-disputed Casket Letters, to be published for the first time."[68] One of the Ridolfi conspirators seized the opportunity of the publication to add to anti-Marian slanders:

> Thomas Wilson declared that the Queen his mistress was not fit for any husband; that he had been credibly informed that she had poisoned her first husband, the French king; that she had consented to the murder of her second; had matched with his murderer, the Earl of Bothwell, and had brought him to the field (at Carberry Hill) to be murdered.[69]

Rumors spread that Norfolk had seen the copies of the letters and "had expressed suitably shocked horror over the depth of moral turpitude they revealed," though they did not prevent him from considering a possible marriage to Mary. Later Norfolk reportedly told Elizabeth he would never marry "where he could not be sure of his pillow."[70]

It is not as evidence of matters of fact but evidence of matters of perception—in particular, of reputation—that these casket letters condition the discourses of treason. (Although she later changed her mind and allowed their publication, at the time of the Scottish inquiry Elizabeth announced that nothing was "produced nor shown by them against the Queen their sovereign, whereby the Queen of England should conceive or take any evil opinion of the Queen, her good sister, for anything yet seen."[71]) They become the history into which the later Mary is inserted, a revision of her from a body politic (in Kantorowicz's formulation) into a body natural, from a mythologized transcendent figure in whom "majesty" inheres to an earthly woman in whom illicit sexual desire inheres. In the interplay of the erotic and the political, the addition of sexuality to Mary's biography brings about a loss of majesty.

In publishing the casket letters, Mary's opponents had identified her from her earliest days in England not only as a political and religious threat, but also as a sexual threat.[72] When she emerges into visibility as an agent of her own thoughts in these letters, it is as a femme fatale, a stereotypical bewitching other whose erotic fatality was readily made identical with political fatality; she was "known" to be a violent woman whose extreme politics were merely reproductions of the extreme sexual passions that drove her. Her history had been crafted as a story not only of a sower of sedition, but also a notorious whore and murderess, both a "bonnie fetcher" and a "monstrous and hyge dragon."[73]

This, then, is the published past, and it becomes in the 1586 prosecution a paradigm of expectation against which the later woman is measured. Because of the casket letters, the treason prosecution could show her "again" leading men astray. (Holinshed decried "the scotish queen to be the principal comforter, director and embracer of these treasons, and imputint this error to their deceivable expectation of her future greatness in this land, the hope whereof joined with her allurements, hath . . . bred diverse rebellions within this kingdom.")[74] A known immoralist and unnatural woman, Mary "again" acts immorally and unnaturally, instigating Elizabeth's death and disinheriting her son. And just as she had hidden behind claims of forgery and counterfeiting in the Ridolfi plot, she "again" hid behind such claims in the Babington matter. The "again," that is, the sense of repetition constructed in these events, is significant here, for none of these things attributed to Mary had been proved. They had, however, been publicized, circulated in a story that in the later treason lent itself to the perception of a *pattern* of dangerous behavior. Presupposing a theory of the continuity of the self like that in the Howard prosecution, the proceedings of the 1580s revealed a Mary who continued to be the same seductive, violent, immoral figure who had in the 1560s murdered her husband, seduced a lover, and later disavowed her child. The "evidence" against her in the 1580s "corroborated" official rumors about her in the 1560s and became the means of consolidating her notorious identity.

What does the Scots treason know, and how does it know it? Among histories of trials, it recapitulates and sustains a nation's investment in demonstrating (or, according to some legal theories, eliciting) its own jeopardy as a self-justification for the use of governmental authority. Among evidentiary histories, it contributes to the considerable uncertainties of epistolary evidence, as documents in themselves and as reliable and authoritative "witnesses." Among studies of subjectivity, it pits competing theories of the mind, each linked to a theory of writing, against each other, resolving contemporary anxieties over hidden, sinister subjects not by warding off the idea of interiority, but by ensuring its exposure. No matter how many structures mediate and mask the sinister self, ultimately in writing it will "appear to the world."

Late in Thomas Kyd's *The Spanish Tragedy* Bel-imperia berates Hieronimo for failing to revenge his son's and her lover's death; why, she presses, would he "neglect the loss and life of him / Whom both my letters and thine own belief / Assures thee to be causeless slaughtered."[75] It is a small moment, but it marks a significant association among information in letters Bel-imperia wrote, beliefs Hieronimo held, and actions that might issue from either or both. It is to her, as to a generation of scholars, obvious who killed Horatio (she was there, audiences see the event, readers read it) and equally obvious that Hieronimo has been tardy in accomplishing revenge. What I mean to take up is a related question about the obvious in Kyd's play: the status of the letters. Like the Scots treason, Kyd's play offers a pointed revelation of what writing means to theories of interiority and its exposure, as it troubles over the unsettled relations between writing and truth. But in Kyd's work, letters also serve to form a confederacy of knowledge whose participants act to bring about their own ends. A neglectful "country," its attentions elsewhere, is brought down by the coincidental fatality of figures affiliated through letters.

Born in London in November 1558, Kyd was the son of a prosperous middle class family with ties to the profession of document-copying and the related field of law. His father, Francis, was a scrivener, successful enough to serve as Warden of the Company of Scriveners in 1580.[76] Thomas began attending Merchant Taylors' School in 1565, under the tutelage of Richard Mulcaster and among such fellows as Edmund Spenser and Thomas Lodge. Although we know little of his early years, we do know that by 1585 he was writing plays for the Queen's Company, none of which survive, and that during 1587–88, he entered the service of a lord who was also patron to an acting company.[77]

Knowledge of Kyd's later life comes almost entirely from writings connected with his arrest and possible torture for sedition at the hands of the Privy Council.[78] Kyd was arrested on May 11, 1593, by representatives of the Privy Council investigating certain "libels," probably writings against foreigners in London. Searching Kyd's papers, the Crown's officers reportedly discovered "vile heretical Concepts denying the deity of Jhesus Christe our Savior," and Kyd was imprisoned on suspicion of having written blasphemy. He saved himself by claiming that the writings were not his but Marlowe's. After Marlowe's death (May 30, 1593), Kyd wrote to Sir John Puckering asking for release from prison and explaining that Marlowe's papers came to be in his possession because the two authors were "wrytinge in one chamber twoe yeares synce" and their papers were shuffled together. In this letter and in another Kyd amplified the charges against Marlowe, whom he "accused of being blasphemous, disorderly, of treasonous opinions, an irreligious reprobate, 'intemp[er]ate & of a cruel hart.'" Although again we cannot know Kyd's motives in naming Marlowe, we do know that Kyd died just over a year after Marlowe, on August 15, 1594.[79]

Kyd's upbringing, his career as a writer, and his participation in literary circles all suggest that throughout his life the playwright contemplated issues having to do with documentation and authenticity in literary, legal and dramatic practices. The particular position of *The Spanish Tragedy* among his writings remains an object of conjecture.[80] It was probably written after 1582 because it alludes to materials from Thomas Watson's *Hekatompathia*, which was entered in the Stationers' Register during that year. (Kyd might have read Watson in manuscript, which would allow an even earlier date.) It was written before February 23, 1592, the day on which it was performed by Lord Strange's men. Conjecture tends to favor the later years.[81] If the play is written in the earlier years, then Kyd's interest in epistolary issues might be linked primarily to his upbringing, his work for court, and his London life with such fellows as Marlowe. If the play is written after the events of late 1586, however, then it might well be alluding to the culturally diffuse sense, evidenced in the Babington and Scots treasons and in Walsingham's forgery operation, of epistolary danger.[82]

Well before Mary Stuart's trial for treason, she was at the center of an episode with parallels to the murder of Horatio in Kyd's play. Rumored to be unhappy in her marriage to Henry Darnley, in 1565–66 Mary embraced the friendship and advice of her secretary, David Rizzio. Apparently envious of the secretary's role in Mary's life, Moray, Darnley and their supporters decided to rid themselves of Rizzio and to discipline Mary. They plotted Rizzio's death and lent it legitimacy by making Darnley, the titular king of Scotland, the protector of the conspiracy. The noblemen (and assassins) invaded Mary's apartment one evening and ambushed Rizzio, stabbing him to death while Darnley held her back and refused her pleas to prevent the murder.[83] While we do not know whether Kyd's version of Horatio's murder in *The Spanish Tragedy* is indebted to the Scots' episode, we do know that the play was written when anxiety ran high among the English about such things as reports of plots against powerful figures; that the spirit of treacherous betrayal is the spirit of the play; that a brother's murder of his sister's lover is one of its plots; and that epistolary intrigue is its constant.

From its frame story of Andrea's journey to the gods to its main plot of the political relations between Portugal and Spain, Kyd is dramatizing governments mesmerized by war and courtiers in the imaginative grip of battle's protocols. It is the promise and realization of "blissful chivalry" (1.2.21) that commands the energies of the King of Spain, the Viceroy of Portugal, the Duke of Castile. It is their love for Bellona (1.2.153) who "rageth here and there" that drives the main plot, with its representations of heroic battles, its stagings of political negotiations, and its renderings of self-congratulatory international reconciliations. These figures are compelled and inspired by the mythologies of heroic competition, drawn by the very gods who frame Kyd's play. Within that world of chivalric achievement, Bel-imperia is another tool for cementing political alliances, the aristocratic female whose marriage is one means of negotiating and securing political stability.[84]

Yet as Kyd writes it, those who speak for "the country" are speaking for fading codes of affiliation and courtiership. In the grip of obsolete and increasingly peripheral activities, the members of Kyd's ruling class misperceive where danger lies and so are unable to ensure domestic stability. In *The Spanish Tragedy*, as in *Hamlet*, the old code by which warriors navigated their relations to each other is fading, the ruling figures are vulnerable to death, and no clear dynasty survives. As the Spanish and Portuguese courtiers cross in and out of battle, however, Kyd suggests that their fascination blinds them to countercurrents in their own lands. In their homelands lie not only the roots of treason—the motives for killing the rulers' families—but a kind of justice to which Bellona also is blind. This is Kyd's epistolary underground, in which letters impel characters to deeds of their own, overlooked by political authorities. Put another way, in *The Spanish Tragedy* the circulation of letters forms a counterdiscourse to that of a government entranced by the trappings of battle.

The earliest mention of letters in Kyd's play comes as a response to Lorenzo's threats to Pedringano. Querying his sister's servant, Lorenzo seeks "to find the truth of all this question out" (2.1.40), to discover what Bel-imperia feels and for whom she feels it, and to govern her affections by any means necessary. "Truth" is what Lorenzo asks for, and Kyd repeats the term three times in four lines—"Tell truth and have me for thy lasting friend"; "My bounden duty bids me tell the truth, / If case it lie in me to tell the truth" (2.1.55–58). When Pedringano finally blurts out that "she loves Horatio" (2.1.78), Lorenzo questions his credibility—"Now say but how know'st thou he is her love" (2.1.81)—and Kyd delivers the answer to which he has been leading Lorenzo and his spectators: "She sent him letters which myself perused, / Full-fraught with lines and arguments of love" (2.1.84–85). Associations between sexual promiscuity and women's writing were common in the late sixteenth century. According to Giovanni Bruno in *The Education of a Young Gentlewoman*, writing is the slippery slope to female sexual indecency: "there is no lesse danger that they will sooner learne to be subtil & impudent lovers, than learnedly to write verses, poetrie, ballads and songs."[85] In his first mention of letters, Kyd evokes this public view, allying women's writing with illicit sexuality.

As they were in the Scots treason, however, in Kyd's deeply ironic play intercepted letters are understood according to conflicting standards of credibility. On the one hand, Pedringano's revelation about Bel-imperia's letters solves a problem. Both Lorenzo and Pedringano interpret them as repositories of truth about her inner self, the evidence of her emotional attachments. As he will again later in acknowledging Pedringano's letters—"Tell him I have his letters, know his mind" (3.4.57)—Lorenzo readily equates the letter with the writer, assuming that it reveals the "real" Bel-imperia, a woman secretly in love with Horatio. On the other hand, the revelation of the letters opens another problem shared by epistolary treasons: the position of the emissary conveying them.

In the little commonwealth of the family, as in the larger commonwealth of England, figures in authority displace onto servants motives and acts of disloyalty: to Mary's mind, Naw and Curle, motivated by desire for personal gain, betrayed their oath of fidelity to her; Naw "had sundry times bound himself by oath" to different patrons, only to now betray them, and Curle was "pliable" to Naw and "at his beck would write what he bade him."[86] By doing so, in Mary's view, these servants exposed their incapacity to be faithful to any oath and to tell the truth: "Men's minds, said she, are diversly carried about with affections, and they would never have confessed such matters against her, but for their own advantage and hope."[87] To the government's mind, Naw and Curle, recognizing their positions as subjects in England, told the truth about Mary's plans to depose. By doing so, they demonstrated their true loyalty to England and to the "majesty" for which its monarch stood. In Kyd's play, this dynamic of mutating loyalties and conflicting interpretations recurs inside the family in Pedringano's betrayals of Bel-imperia. In both cases, an ideology of the betraying servant is associated with men of lower status who reveal the secret contents of letters and import "much of their own."[88]

Like the position of secretaries, the position of servants in an early modern household is ambiguous, and Kyd presents his own exemplum of the untrue servant by calling attention to that ambiguity. As it was codified in late Tudor and early Stuart texts, the servant was akin to the apprentice: "the said apprentice his said master well and truly shall serve, his secrets keeping close; his commandments lawful and honest everywhere shall he willingly do: hurt nor damage to his said master he shall do none."[89] Bel-imperia believes that Pedringano is such a figure, and she reassures Horatio in the bower of the servant's loyalty: "make you doubt of Pedringano's faith?" (2.4.8); "No, he is as trusty as my second self" (2.4.9). But Lorenzo reveals that not stable fidelity but competing loyalties are the bases of this family structure: "Thou diest for more esteeming her than me" (2.1.70). As Kyd sees it, Pedringano's credibility with Lorenzo turns on his betraying Bel-imperia; not multiple but mutating loyalties characterize the servant.

That the "true" servant is also the betraying servant is the ideological point of the famous casket scene in *The Spanish Tragedy*; loyalty to one figure is defined as disloyalty to another. In the Scots treason, Mary emphasized the secretaries' way of being in the letter as a sign that the letters were not true: the secretaries were false, so the documents were too. In *The Spanish Tragedy*, Kyd also stages the servant's way of being in the matter he conveys. Lorenzo claims to send a written pardon to the jailed Pedringano—"Show him this box, tell him his pardon's in't, / But open't not" (3.4.72–73)—via a curious Page. Kyd turns the Page's violation of trust into a verification of something that does not exist:

> By my bare honesty, here's nothing but a bare empty box. Were it not a sin against secrecy, I would say it were a piece of gentleman-like knavery. I must go to Pedringano, and tell him his pardon is in this box; Nay, I would have sworn it, had I not seen the contrary. (3.5.5–10)[90]

The Page's would-be interception of the documents turns into a need for equivocation: no longer able to corroborate the truth of Lorenzo's message, that the pardon is in the casket, the Page is able now only to "tell" Pedringano what he "would have sworn." In place of the documents, Kyd suggests, stands the (false) testimony of the servant. For Kyd, a servant's true identity is inextricably linked with epistolary betrayal; he achieves his subjectivity by violating "the trust and fidelitie" granted him by a hierarchy of service. Moreover, Kyd links this slipping morality with a slipping gender identity: "for we men's-kind in our minority are like women in their uncertainty: that they are most forbidden, they will soonest attempt" (3.5.4–5). In this self-justification, the Page paradoxically clears himself by tainting himself: like women, who are the epitome of perverse instability, the young man cannot control himself.

In a reading of the casket that emphasizes Kyd's thematic irony, Frank Ardolino associates it with Pandora's box, in which only hope was left when all human qualities had escaped. Adopting a more philosophical context, Barbara Baines associates it with the Silenus box of Plato's *Symposium*, which Erasmus took as a symbol for a discrepancy between appearance and reality.[91]

I would add, however, that Kyd may also have been alluding skeptically to the infamous casket that reportedly contained letters evidencing Mary Stuart's involvement in murder. As we saw, late in 1567 Mary's brother Moray spread rumors that he had found a casket containing letters that proved Mary was party to her husband's death. The existence of any such writings, however, remains a subject of conjecture, as the only documents finally produced were "copies of copies." If Kyd is alluding to the Scots casket, it raises as many questions as it answers: to those who believed Moray, the casket itself would signify documentary evidence. To those who believed Mary, however, it would signify falsehood and fraud. In either case, prior belief would impinge on its interpretation. Offering only an empty casket, and positioning the Page to "tell" Pedringano it contains documents, Kyd sides with the skeptics and turns his casket into a material sign of falsehood.

Discourses of treason attempt to secure letters as authentic revelations of their writer's mind and, more importantly, as uncomplicated vehicles of direct transference of thought. In this structure, promulgated by the Crown, ideas pass uncensored and unresisted from a self-revealing writer to a receptive reader. But Kyd is troubled by this notion of undisturbed transmission, and he rejects it in Hieronimo's reaction to Bel-imperia's letter. Racked with pain at Horatio's death, Hieronimo pours forth his soul with words and challenges the gods to effect some vengeance:

Eyes, life, world, heavens, hell, night, and day,
See, search, show, send some man, some mean, that may—

A letter falleth

What's here? A letter? tush, it is not so!
A letter written to Hieronimo! (3.2.22–24)

The letter's arrival is mysterious, and the climate of concealment and surveillance establishes it as a potentially dangerous document. Nonetheless, its appearance ("like the catastrophe in an old play," to borrow Edmund's words from *King Lear*) risks laughter and requires interpretation. In his edition of *The Spanish Tragedy*, J. R. Mulryne speculates, "The pat arrival of the letter may be intended to emphasize how accident, under the direction of Revenge, favours the ultimate working out of vengeance."[92] In a production by the National Theatre of England, "the figure of Revenge manipulated every detail of the action by giving letters or weapons to the participants."[93] Whatever Kyd's intentions, when this letter appears in Hieronimo's path the audience already knows about other letters (Bel-imperia's) that were intercepted, subject to unauthorized reading and used for betrayal (by Pedringano), their contents exposed to a treacherous man (Lorenzo). The audience also knows that what was in those letters—"she loves Horatio"—has already produced one murder.

This is the situation into which Kyd inserts Bel-imperia's letter:

What's here? a letter? tush, it is not so!
A letter written to Hieronimo!
"For want of ink, receive this bloody writ.
Me hath my hapless brother hid from thee:
Revenge thyself on Balthazar and him,
For these were they that murdered thy son.
Hieronimo, revenge Horatio's death,
And better fare than Bel-imperia doth."
What means this unexpected miracle?
My son slain by Lorenzo and the prince!
What cause had they Horatio to malign?
Or what might move thee, Bel-imperia,
To accuse thy brother, had he been the mean?
Hieronimo, beware, thou art betrayed,
And to entrap thy life this train is laid.
Advise thee, therefore, be not credulous:
This is devised to endanger thee,
That thou by this Lorenzo should accuse,
And he, for thy dishonour done, should draw
Thy life in question, and they name in hate.
. . . . .
I therefore will by circumstances try
What I can gather to confirm this writ. (3.2.24–49)

Positioning Hieronimo as a fairly astute reader, Kyd displays considerable awareness of the complexities of documentary theory. Hieronimo queries the letter's meaning; he seeks motives for the putative murderers and the putative writers; he cautions himself to avoid being drawn by letter into a conspiracy (as treason defendants often were accused); and he determines to seek corroboration, in particular to "Close if [he] can with Bel-imperia, / To listen more, but nothing to bewray" (3.2.51–52).[94] In a brilliant display of verbal technique, Kyd adopts the passive voice in key lines to focus on the absence of the agent: by whom is this letter written? By whom is Hieronimo betrayed? By whom is this "train laid" or "this . . . devised"?

In the Scots treason, the authenticity of letters was a heated topic, and their vulnerability to falsification—and to being shared by an "unwanted confidant," in Erasmus's terms—became a central issue. "[I]t was an easy matter to counterfeit the Ciphers and Characters of others" in order to entrap them, Mary stated.[95] *The Spanish Tragedy* shares with the Scots trial the notion of a dispersed scribal identity, where secretaries were encouraged to imitate signatures or to write texts in place of their masters, and where members of the nobility who wrote were encouraged to adopt the same "hand" so as to be indistinguishable from one another.[96] But Kyd rejects what the authorities argued: that thoughts could be attributed to someone other than the writer of the letters. In discourses of treason, the Crown argues that the best interpreter of a letter is not its writer (recall Tilney's claim, "I must interpret mine own meaning"), but the legal authorities using the letter as documentary evidence. Kyd resists this notion that either the letter or the government's interpreters can replace the person, reversing that idea by sending Hieronimo to Bel-imperia to authenticate his document. Having set up the fear of forgery and falsification, Kyd solves the problem not by turning to legal authorities, but by returning the authority for interpretation to the writer. Put another way, to the scribal culture of dislocation, Kyd responds with the relocation of the writer in the text.

Like Hamlet, who, as Jonathan Goldberg has pointed out, "arrives in letters" when he returns to Denmark, Bel-imperia is delivered to Hieronimo for the first time as a speaking subject in this inscription.[97] Earlier in the play, the Bel-imperia revealed in letters had been associated with conventionally gendered practices of writing about love: women do so secretly, masking the wantonness that is both the topic of and evidenced by their writing. In this letter of revenge, however, Bel-imperia turns from self- to social-surveillance, producing herself as a figure with authentic knowledge of Horatio's death and with an active role in circulating that knowledge. What officials overlook, her letter reveals: Horatio's death at the hands of Lorenzo.

As he probes the circulation, interception, and interpretation of letters, Kyd brings into conjunction several versions of documentary theory. In one, evoked in Bel-imperia's love letters to Horatio, the palpable status of a letter disappears into its role as a transparent means of conveying thoughts and emotions and of replacing physical distance with intellectual proximity; to return to Fulwood, such a letter is "a declaration, by Writing of the mindes of such as bee absent." In another theory, however, evoked in the Senex's petition for justice for his son, the palpable status of a document is foregrounded and its materiality is identified as an inadequate representation of the bodily emotions it stands in place of. Hieronimo invites the Senex to "say, sir" what troubles him, and he resists:

> No sir, could my woes
> Give way unto my most distressful words,
> Then should I not in paper, as you see,
> With ink bewray what blood began in me. (3.8.74–77)

In this case, to write is to betray emotion, not to satisfy it, and paper is contrasted with blood as the site of genuine feeling. Yet neither "blood" nor "paper" can get at the emotional facts of the case. Like Hamlet, the Senex has "that within that passeth show" (1.2.85). Mediating between these theories is the more commonplace view that the relation between bodies and texts is predominantly metaphorical. Hieronimo, having torn up a petitioner's text, defends himself: "I gave it never a wound; / Show me one drop of blood fall from the same: / How is it possible I should slay it then?" (3.8.129–31). In this case, paper replaces the person as the object of violence, and its meaning is precisely that it is *not* a wounded body.[98]

These distinctions among documentary theories of presence in and presence of the text are obscured by Kyd's brilliant move to complicate these relationships: Bel-imperia's letter is written in blood—"For want of ink, receive this bloody writ."[99] The "blood" that to the Senex is the location of inexpressible emotion to Bel-imperia is the means of expression. In legal discourses throughout the century blood is asked to carry the weight of authenticating relationships: in mooting, distinctions between children of the "whole blood" and others privilege those children and validate their claims to a closer relationship to property than others have. In the Scots trial, a rhetorically crafted blood link between Elizabeth and England is designed to counter Mary's blood claim to the throne.[100] In widely dispersed texts and trials, blood is a means of authenticating expression, claiming particular identities, and asserting particular relationships. And in Kyd's play, blood is the means of returning a dispersed scribal identity to an individuated body.

Perhaps Kyd knew that many accused prisoners were deprived of a means to write during their imprisonments and trials.[101] Perhaps he was recalling Holinshed's account of the Babington treasons, in which the chronicler reviews the harsh penalties for treason in former ages. Although "the ancients had treason in mortal hatred," Holinshed writes, "they could not away with ingratitude, as may be observed by the laws of Draco (which were said to be written in blood, they were so sharp and peremptorie)."[102] Perhaps Kyd was thinking of Marlowe's Faustus, whose deed of soul could be inscribed only in his blood (*Doctor Faustus*, 2.1.48–71). Certainly he is using the stage to pose epistemological questions about the status of the documents that do not result in a monovocal answer; like Faustus's deed, Bel-imperia's document is not subsumed into either its referential or material role. Instead, employing blood as the ink of inscription, Kyd minimizes the gap between a letter's referentiality and materiality. On one hand, writing in blood seems to testify to the truth of what is written and to its proceeding from the soul of the writer; blood secures the authenticity of the letter in the body. On other hand, however, the bodily source of the blood remains stubbornly absent and inaccessible, unavailable as a means of corroboration.

I have been arguing that Kyd's play is deeply engaged in probing the meanings of circulating and authenticating documents, and in tying those meanings to conceptions of secret interiority and mutating fidelity. Whereas blood is one of Kyd's means of implying the truth of the text, multiplicity is another: getting at the truth through documents requires accumulating and affiliating more than one of them with others. This is the position of Pedringano's execution letter. It evokes again the specter of the betraying servant, this time turning against his second master to exact his own revenge, and it delivers both Pedringano-as-criminal and Lorenzo-as-criminal to Hieronimo:

My lord, I writ as mine extremes required,
That you would labour my delivery;
If you neglect, my life is desperate,
And in my death I shall reveal the troth.
You know, my lord, I slew him for your sake;
And as confederate with the prince and you,
Won by rewards and hopeful promises,
I holp to murder Don Horatio too. (3.7.32–39)

Pedringano's letter makes its truth claims by wearing the halo of a death bed document—"in my death I shall reveal the troth." Ironically positioned as a text intended for extortion (as blackmail to ensure Lorenzo's help) it instead becomes something unintended, the documentary evidence of a crime and its perpetrators. Moreover, it becomes the means of forcing into visibility what the ruling figures do not see: the "real" Lorenzo, who becomes more apparent to Hieronimo and more interpretable in this accidentally conveyed letter than in his person.

Kyd has been developing a pattern of accumulating and collating letters as vehicles for establishing a confederacy of knowledge that eludes the authorities, and it culminates in Hieronimo's reading of Pedringano's letter. Hieronimo can "compare" this with Bel-imperia's letter, and in comparing, find belief:

Now see I what I durst not then suspect,
That Bel-imperia's letter was not feigned.
Nor feigned she, though falsely they have wronged
Both her, myself, Horatio, and themselves.
Now may I make compare, 'twixt hers and this,
Of every accident; I ne'er could find

Till now, and now I feelingly perceive,
They did what heaven unpunished would not leave. (3.7.49–56)

Corroboration—"compare 'twixt hers and this"—and the belief it produces are shown to be effects of multiplicity; documentary certainty is a question of accretion. Bel-imperia's and Pedringano's letters are true because they match each other and because they both tell the same story about Horatio's death. With two documents to compare, Hieronimo can resolve the question of the letter's author and attribute it to her as a possession—"Bel-imperia's letter was not feigned"—and he can assure himself that the contents are true—"Nor feigned she." Although in the passages I cited earlier Bel-imperia implies that Hieronimo's prior "own belief" ought to have persuaded him to believe her letter, what Kyd shows is that a second letter (Pedringano's) establishes the "truth" of the first and a community of shared knowledge among the readers. Earlier Kyd established the writer as the best authenticator of her text: Hieronimo planned to seek verification of the "bloody writ" from Bel-imperia. With Pedringano dead, Kyd turns from the author to textual comparison as the mode of authentication.

Kyd has been offering a complex, shifting study of the challenges in authenticating documents and persons, in getting at the truth of writing and of characters. The relevant contrast to his emphasis on relations between writing and falsification, however, is his emphasis on the relation between eyewitnessing and falsification. The Alexandro-Villuppo subplot asks spectators to measure epistolary against visual evidence, and what Kyd shows is that witnessing in writing or in person may be not only wrong but more importantly easily counterfeited.

After the battle with Spain, the Viceroy of Portugal refuses to believe Alexandro's reassurance that the Viceroy's son, Balthazar, lives: "No doubt, my liege, but still the prince survives" (1.3.43). A pointedly astute Villuppo seizes the moment to replace Alexandro's version of events with his own: "Then hear the truth which these mine eyes have seen. /. . . / . . . Alexandro, that here counterfeits / Under the colour of a duteous friend, / Discharged his pistol at the prince's back" (1.3.59, 65–67). Basing his claim on the immediacy of being there, Villuppo succeeds in criminalizing Alexandro by offering the authority of eyewitnessing.

What Kyd perceives, however, long before postmodern scholars rediscovered it, is the extent to which prior belief conditions what will be taken as truth: Villuppo is believed by the Viceroy not only because of his empirical claim, but also because he tells a version of events that the Viceroy believed *before* Villuppo spoke. To Alexandro's repeated assurances that the prince had survived, the Viceroy also repeatedly refused to listen, concluding: "Tell me no more of news, for he is dead" (1.3.43–52). When Villuppo offers to tell his "ill news," however, the Viceroy greets it with readiness: "Speak on, I'll guerdon thee whate'er it be: / Mine ear is ready to receive ill news, / My heart grown hard 'gainst mischief's battery; / Stand up, I say, and tell thy tale at large" (1.3.55–58). Unlike Hieronimo, who skeptically greets Bel-imperia's letter and who seeks corroboration outside himself, the Viceroy corroborates Villuppo's tale by looking inside himself, acknowledging that *this* is the story he was prepared to hear: "Ay, ay, my nightly dreams have told me this" (1.3.76).

In this kind of corroboration, truth claims are organized to fit what a decision-maker has decided in advance is the truth. The structure of these scenes is too precise to be accidental; Kyd is clearly at work making prior belief the key to persuasion. Villuppo tells us that he is lying—"Thus have I with an envious, forged tale / Deceived the king, betrayed mine enemy, / And hope for guerdon of my villainy" (1.3.93–95). There is no suspense about who is telling the truth; instead, Kyd shifts the audience's attention from who is telling the truth to how the truth will be revealed—and it arrives in a letter. Villuppo stands ready to help burn Alexandro at the stake (3.1.55), when a messenger bearing letters from the Spanish king arrives just in the nick of time. Repeating the written news "Balthazar doth live" four times in nine lines, Kyd delivers the living son to his father in a moment that parallels and echoes the letter to Hieronimo describing Horatio's death. That letter is not only a vehicle for conveying knowledge of an event, but also the perpetual location of that knowledge, a locus of a particular memory in a particular form and a means of endlessly repeating the event.[103]

Kyd's representation of the unsettled relations between authenticating documents and exposing interiors culminates in the denouement of *The Spanish Tragedy*, where writing and its implements remain a final means of expression. Among the commonplaces of Kyd's culture, and surely one with which a scrivener's son would have been familiar, was an increasingly competitive view of the relations between the old courtier, committed to martial brilliance, and the new man, committed to rhetorical brilliance. In *The Courtier*, Lodovico argues that though both letters and arms are necessary skills, arms are more important in certain situations:

> And if you think the contrary, wait until you hear of a contest in which the man who defends the cause of arms is allowed to use them, just as those who defend the cause of letters make use of letters in their defense; for if each one uses his own weapons, you will see that the men of letters will lose.[104]

In the play-within-the-play, Kyd appears to share Lodovico's view. Hieronimo transforms the ink of a theatrical script he wrote long ago into the blood of revenge: Bel-imperia stabs Balthazar and herself, and Hieronimo stabs Lorenzo. Both "authenticate" Hieronimo's script as theatrical fiction by performing it and as truth by performing the murders only imagined in it. Initially blurting out explanations, Hieronimo abruptly silences himself ("Urge no more words, I have no more to say" [4.4.152]), and bites out his tongue.[105] The Duke of Castile, however, is unstoppable in his demands that Hieronimo again tell a story that would somehow legitimate these events: "Yet can he write" (4.4.195). Hieronimo pretends to agree and motions:

CASTILE: O, he would have a knife to mend his pen.
VICEROY: Here; and advise thee that thou write the troth.

The "troth" Hieronimo "writes," however, is another bloody scene: he stabs the Duke of Castile and himself.

We might understand Hieronimo's knife to be compensating metaphorically for what the pen could not do ("a knife to mend his pen"). But the integration of blood with writing has been a recurring pattern in Kyd's play, and in a play where blood is ink, we might also infer that the weapon is less knife than pen.[106] Kyd resists the simple logic of *The Courtier* and replaces it with a more complex view by turning the implement of writing into a weapon of revenge in a view closer to that of Juan Luis Vives's writing master. In the ninth dialogue, "Scripto," of *Linguae Latinae Exercitatio* (1538), the writing master asks his students, "But have you come here armed? . . . Ah, Ah! I don't speak of the arms of bloodshedding, but of writing-weapons, which are necessary for our purpose. Have you a quill-sheath together with quills in it?"[107] Like Vives, Kyd minimizes the difference between a pen and a sword as a weapon for particular kinds of action. Although convention has it that Hieronimo uses the knife to stab the Duke, I want to suggest that in light of Kyd's emphasis on the materiality of writing and the immediate provocations of the Duke's insistent "yet can he write," Hieronimo might have used the *pen* he had just sharpened, producing Kyd's final instance of that which is "bloody writ."

Both the Scots trial and *The Spanish Tragedy* investigate the conditions within which the authenticity of a document and its role in revealing character are shaped and positioned. Both contribute to a sustained interrogation (one that continues today) of the relative validity of epistolary evidence and of the status of documents in themselves and as reliable "witnesses." And in both, competing theories of character—one in which character precedes writing, one in which it is created in writing—complicate the process of revealing the potentially secret and authentic self. In those theories, the role of the emissary—his way of being in the letter—is to distort and betray. Both works make visible a culture of fear and uncertainty in which the confederacy of knowledge letters promise is also always precarious. In such worlds, fatal consequences might attend on even the simplest statements: "I found a letter written in your name."

Conclusion

If the cultural meanings of treason were exhausted by a legal verdict, or if vigorous, plentiful prosecutions were a sufficient deterrent to subjects' thinking unauthorized thoughts, the sixteenth century might have put an end to the crime in England. At least it might have put an end to the wrangling over certain forms of loyalty, those that were expressed in troublesome and unsettling notions of gender, affiliation, and homeland. The Henrician matrimonial treasons, the Babington prosecutions, and the Scots attainder, among many other proceedings, might have "solved" the pesky problems posed by getting at the "truth" of a subject's interior life and of "knowing" the loyal English man or woman. But the sixty-eight treason statutes enacted from 1485 to 1603 and the unparalleled number of prosecutions testify to something else: whatever its instrumental role, treason played a significant discursive role in the continual process of renovating "the realm."

Despite having served as the theme for many late sixteenth-century prosecutions, Mary Stuart's death did not result in an end to treason. Some of the century's more infamous prosecutions occurred after her execution in 1587. In the Lopez plot of late 1594, a possible influence on *The Jew of Malta* and *The Merchant of Venice*, a Jewish doctor allegedly assisted a Spanish conspiracy against Elizabeth and went to his death an apparent victim of political pursuit by Essex. In the Squyer Plot of 1598, a disgruntled Walpole reportedly planned to use a former scrivener of Greenwich to poison Essex and Elizabeth. In the Essex rebellion in 1601, the Earl rode through the city toward the queen's residence bearing arms. When he defended himself, Essex spoke in terms eerily reminiscent of Mary's: he claimed he sought only to ensure an audience with the queen because he believed she had been misled by his enemies among her counselors, and he swore that to entrap him "Letters had been Counterfeited both with his Hand and Seal."

The discourse of treason in trials and in plays was productive and helped shape the emerging English identity, an identity that both disciplines show to be provisional. Trials and plays produce "traitors" from the expressed and unexpressed values of the country, and those traitors in turn help to produce that most conditional of things, a nation. It emerges from a continuous, ad hoc negotiation among competitors who spring from sometimes unanticipated corners.

These early modern representations personal and political fidelity in law and theater did more than that. They also linked the act of imagining the realm with some of the most significant and sustained organizing principles of their culture: gender and sexuality, affiliations and alliances, notions of a homeland or homelessness. In so far as subjects shared their conception of these things with a prevalent, long-standing view, they might never come to be called traitor. But were one's relation to one of these to slip from the traditional—were a young man, for example, to feel his loyalty to male friends outweighed his loyalty to a government—even if he were a member of the dominant group in other ways, he could find himself facing charges of treason. One of the paradoxes of a study like this is the discovery that although the impulses and aims of the law as a code are exclusive—its end is to exclude the figure and the ideas he or she represents from the realm—the aims of the discourses of treason in legal and theatrical practice are inclusive: languages pick up and recirculate each other, rhetorics cross classes and national boundaries, shared codes and visions of a homeland cross geographical borders.

The epigraph with which I began this book is drawn from the play most often associated with early modern treason: Shakespeare's *Richard II*. It is typically cited in studies devoted to relationships between Shakespeare's work and the Essex rebellion of February 1601 or to the politics of its deposition scene.[1] These, however, are not what attracted me to the epigraph. It seems to me to be a representation of treasonous discourse aimed directly at contemporary practices. Exiled for his role in challenging Richard II, Bolingbroke listens to his father's advice. In a Boethian moment, Gaunt tries to console his son by advising him to reconceive the punishment, to recast his perspective on it so that it will seem tolerable; it will not be a punishment, but a quest. As he resists, Bolingbroke turns aside his father's call to intellectual mobility in words that suggest the limitations of his imagination:

GAUNT: Call it a travel that thou tak'st for pleasure.
BOLING: My heart will sigh when I miscall it so,
Which finds it an enforced pilgrimage.
GAUNT: The sullen passage of thy weary steps
Esteem as foil wherein thou art to set
The precious jewel of thy home return.
BOLING: Nay, rather, every tedious stride I make
Will but remember me what a deal of world
I wander from the jewels that I love. (1.3.269–77)

Bolingbroke is too much the materialist to leap the gap between the travel and the thought of what it means. In the midst of this long, stichomythic exchange, Gaunt suggests, "Think not the King did banish thee, / But thou the King" (1.3.286–87). Bolingbroke will bluntly end the exchange by insisting on a kind of palpability that would make these things impossible: "O, who can hold a fire in his hand / By thinking on the frosty Caucasus? / Or cloy the hungry edge of appetite / By bare imagination of a feast?" (1.3.294–97). But the words of the high counselor to the rebellious son speak the express language of the traitors and characters who make up this study. This is a call to treason: to imagine that the self is the agent of the events in one's life. Bolingbroke knows, with Gaunt, that this is an imposed exile. But to call it that is to acknowledge in oneself the power of the sovereign. To recast the banishment in the imagination, however, is to recast the structure of authority. It is in moments like these that the challenge posed by subjects' unauthorized imaginings makes itself apparent to popular audiences.

To restrict our understanding of legal practices only to statutes or to the political histories they generate is also to block off our view of the extent to which conflict characterizes these documents. In trials, we find not only challenges to a law but also conflicts within the law. We see the law's own continuous struggle to renew itself in order to encompass an apparently infinite range of "pasts" that might impinge on its present version of the country, and a similarly expansive range of thoughts that might be construed as threatening. In what they selected from the cultural materials as their focus, these trials and plays show the unpredictable scope and incoherence of what counted as treason: women engage in premarital sex, men befriend men, courtiers travel, women and men write. All these were represented as jeopardizing "this realm," and all illuminate the contentious ways categories of national and personal identity continuously come into being in our imaginary practices.

Notes

Introduction

1. See Lacey Baldwin Smith, *Treason in Tudor England: Politics and Paranoia* (Princeton, N.J.: Princeton University Press, 1986); and Stephen Rezneck, "The Trial of Treason in Tudor England," *Essays in Honor of C. H. McIlwain* (Cambridge, Mass.: Harvard University Press, 1936), 258–88. Lacey Baldwin Smith has pointed out that neither the truth of the testimony nor the question of guilt was as important as publicity: truth "had already been settled by royal will"; "the prisoners were considered guilty until proven otherwise"; and the role of adjudicators was not to judge facts, but "to achieve complete publicity" of an official version of events and their perpetrators; see *A Tudor Tragedy: The Life and Times of Catherine Howard* (New York: Pantheon, 1961), 196–97.

2. Pierre Bourdieu, "The Force of Law: Toward a Sociology of the Juridical Field," trans. Richard Terdiman, *Hastings Law Journal* 38 (July 1987): 837.

3. By referring throughout to the Crown as a single body, I mean to imply a ruler and those associated with him or her who generally shared the same political views. My usage is not intended to obscure differences among members of the group.

4. Among those who have argued either that a conception of personal interiority hardly existed in early modern England, or that the language of inwardness refers primarily to external factors, see Stephen Greenblatt, *Renaissance Self-Fashioning: From More to Shakespeare* (Chicago: University of Chicago Press, 1980); Francis Barker, *The Tremulous Private Body: Essays on Subjection* (New York: Methuen, 1984); Jonathan Dollimore, *Radical Tragedy: Religion, Ideology and Power in the Drama of Shakespeare and His Contemporaries* (Brighton: Harvester Press, 1984); Catherine Belsey, *The Subject of Tragedy: Identity and Difference in Renaissance Drama* (New York: Methuen, 1985); Jonathan Goldberg, *James I and the Politics of Literature* (Baltimore: Johns Hopkins University Press, 1983); and Patricia Fumerton, *Cultural Aesthetics: Renaissance Literature and the Practice of Social Ornament* (Chicago: University of Chicago Press, 1991). An especially useful counter to these views is Katharine Eisaman Maus's *Inwardness and Theater in the English Renaissance* (Chicago: University of Chicago Press, 1995). For an argument that multiple selves and a sense of internal otherness developed in response to market relations, see Jean-Christophe Agnew, *Worlds Apart: The Market and the Theater in Anglo-American Thought, 1550–1750* (Cambridge: Cambridge University Press, 1986).

5. As scholars have begun to explore relationships between early modern legal events and drama, they have emphasized the ways these disciplines theatricalize legal performance, represent justice on their respective scaffolds, and criminalize members

of a particular class or gender. For examples of the growing bibliography in early modern legal studies, see Marie Axton, *The Queen's Two Bodies: Drama and the Elizabethan Succession* (London: Royal Historical Society, 1977); Terry Eagleton, *William Shakespeare* (New York: Blackwell, 1986); Annabel Patterson, *Censorship and Interpretation: The Conditions of Writing and Reading in Early Modern England* (Madison: University of Wisconsin Press, 1984); and *Reading Holinshed's "Chronicles"* (Chicago: University of Chicago Press, 1994); Richard Helgerson, *Forms of Nationhood: The Elizabethan Writing of England* (Chicago: University of Chicago Press, 1992); Constance Jordan, *Shakespeare's Monarchies: Ruler and Subject in the Romances* (Ithaca, N.Y.: Cornell University Press, 1997); and *Renaissance Drama and the Law*, ed. Frances E. Dolan, special issue of *Renaissance Drama* n.s. 25 (1994).

6. Among studies of Shakespeare and the law with a strong biographical component, see, for example, W. Nicholas Knight, *Shakespeare's Hidden Life: Shakespeare at the Law, 1585–1595* (New York: Mason & Lipscomb, 1973); John Lord Campbell, *Shakespeare's Legal Acquirements Considered* (1859; rpt. New York: Appleton, 1972); and William C. Devecmon, *"In Re" Shakespeare's Legal Acquirements* (New York: Shakespeare Press, 1899; rpt. AMS Press, 1971). On Marston and the law, see Philip J. Finkelpearl, *John Marston of the Middle Temple* (Cambridge, Mass.: Harvard University Press, 1969). On Sackville and Norton, see Albert C. Baugh et al. eds., *A Literary History of England* (New York: Appleton-Century-Crofts, 1948), 461.

7. Cynthia B. Herrup, *The Common Peace: Participation and the Criminal Law in Seventeenth Century England* (Cambridge: Cambridge University Press, 1987), 1. See also J. A. Sharpe, *Crime in Early Modern England, 1550–1750* (London: Longman, 1984).

8. For an argument that "Legal case-history is not just a record of past 'applications' of the law, but a tradition of continuous reinterpretation of it which bears forcibly on any current act of legal judgement," see Eagleton, 36.

9. On the theatrical potential of executions in evoking and containing anxiety, see Stephen Greenblatt, *Shakespearean Negotiations: The Circulation of Social Energy in Renaissance England* (Berkeley: University of California Press, 1988), 136. On executions as elements in a discourse of treason, see Curt Breight, "'Treason doth never prosper': *The Tempest* and the Discourses of Treason," *Shakespeare Quarterly* 41,1 (Spring 1990): 1–28. On relations between early modern executions and stage violence, see James Shapiro, "'Tragedies Naturally Performed': Kyd's Representation of Violence," in *Staging the Renaissance: Reinterpretations of Elizabethan and Jacobean Drama*, ed. David Kastan and Peter Stallybrass (New York: Routledge, 1991), 99–113; and Karen Cunningham, "Renaissance Execution and Marlovian Elocution: The Drama of Death," *PMLA* 105,2 (March 1990): 209–22. The seminal work on the scaffold-theater link is Michel Foucault, *Discipline and Punish: The Birth of the Prison*, trans. Alan Sheridan (New York: Vintage, 1979).

10. Helgerson, 4. On the tendency of new historicism to emphasize monarchical power and to imply that Elizabeth and James "author" England, and on competing literary voices, see Helgerson 9–10; and Claire McEachern, *The Poetics of English Nationhood, 1590–1612* (Cambridge: Cambridge University Press, 1996).

11. My idea of the dialogic and of multivocal discourses is indebted to Mikhail Bakhtin, *The Dialogic Imagination*, ed. Michael Holquist, trans. Michael Holquist and Caryl Emerson (Austin: University of Texas Press, 1981). In this view, a main compo-

nent in the constitution of a culture in general and literature in particular is a plurality of contending, mutually qualifying voices.

12. Philip Sidney, "An Apology for Poetry" (1583; 1595), in *Critical Theory Since Plato*, rev. ed., ed. Hazard Adams (New York: Harcourt, 1992), 155.

13. Sidney, 145. Sidney comments further on lawyers: their goal is to prevent one from doing bad to others, not to implant goodness in the heart (148), and their adoption of fictive names in order to bring a legal suit is not an instance of "lying" (155).

14. Sidney, 145.

15. Thomas Wilson, *Arte of Rhetorique*, ed. Thomas J. Derrick (New York: Garland, 1982), 387–88.

16. On forensic rhetoric, see for example *Aristotle's Treatise on Rhetoric*, ed. Theodore Buckley (London: Bell and Sons, 1894), 24–25. On the persuasive force of similitudes and images, see Sidney, 150–51.

17. Horace, "Art of Poetry," in *Critical Theory Since Plato*, rev. ed., ed. Hazard Adams (New York: Harcourt, 1992), 72.

18. Sidney, 146, 151.

19. Patricia Parker, *Shakespeare From the Margins: Language, Culture, Context* (Chicago: University of Chicago Press, 1996), 259. Relatively few scholars have focused on the rhetorical and narrative strategies in these texts. In addition to Parker's, two studies that attend to the forms of persuasion are Stephen Greenblatt's *Sir Walter Ralegh: The Renaissance Man and His Roles* (New Haven, Conn.: Yale University Press, 1973); and Maus, *Inwardness*.

20. Patricia Parker, *Literary Fat Ladies: Rhetoric, Gender, Property* (London: Methuen, 1987), 97. See also Victoria Kahn, *Rhetoric, Prudence, and Skepticism in the Renaissance* (Ithaca, N.Y.: Cornell University Press, 1985).

21. John Ponet, "A Short Treatise of Politic Power," *John Ponet (1516?-1566): Advocate of Limited Monarchy*, ed. Winthrop S. Hudson (Chicago: University of Chicago Press, 1942).

22. My reading of legal narratives as cultural texts is informed by Clifford Geertz, *The Interpretation of Cultures* (New York: Basic Books, 1973); and *Local Knowledge: Further Essays in Interpretive Anthropology* (New York: Basic Books, 1983).

23. Mary Douglas, *Cultural Bias* (London: Royal Anthropological Institute of Great Britain and Ireland, 1978). On bias in legal practice generally, see Stanley Fish, *Doing What Comes Naturally: Change, Rhetoric, and the Practice of Theory in Literary and Legal Studies* (Durham, N.C.: Duke University Press, 1989); Ronald Dworkin, *Law's Empire* (Cambridge, Mass.: Belknap Press, 1986); and Richard Posner, *Law and Literature: A Misunderstood Relation* (Cambridge, Mass.: Harvard University Press, 1998). See also Brook Thomas, "Reflections on the Law and Literature Revival," *Critical Inquiry* 17,3 (Spring 1991): 510–39.

24. John Bellamy, *The Tudor Law of Treason* (London: Routledge and Kegan Paul, 1979), 216. Like definitions of treason, specifications of forfeiture tended to contract and expand during the sixteenth century; see 54–63 for an overview of some of these changes.

25. Margaret Atwood Judson, *The Crisis of the Constitution* (New Brunswick, N.J.: Rutgers University Press, 1949), 19–20. See also, G. R. Elton, "The Rule of Law in Sixteenth-Century England," in *Tudor Men and Institutions*, ed. Arthur J. Slavin

(Baton Rouge: Louisiana State University Press, 1972), 265–94, and *The Tudor Constitution* (Cambridge: Cambridge University Press, 1960); and J. E. Neale, *Elizabeth I and Her Parliaments, 1584–1601* (London: Jonathan Cape, 1957). The word "constitution" acquired its present meaning comparatively recently. For an overview of earlier terms and meanings, especially with reference to the relations between Roman continental thought and English views, see Charles Henry McIlwain, *Constitutionalism Ancient and Modern*, rev. ed. (Ithaca, N.Y.: Cornell University Press, 1947).

26. J. P. Sommerville, *Royalists and Patriots: Politics and Ideology in England, 1603–1640*, 2nd ed. (London: Longman, 1999), 79. As Sommerville characterizes this relationship, "the king and his subjects were in fact bound together by mutual dependencies. It was to this idea of mutual dependency that the doctrines of mixed and limited government gave formal expression" (55).

27. References to treason statutes throughout this book are to *Statutes of the Realm* and are specified in the text.

28. Bellamy, *Tudor Law*, 9. For a historical overview of reasons for the redefinitions, see esp. 9–13. According to Bellamy, "it is clear that Edward III's treason act was founded on crimes that were customarily held as treason under common law" (9). For a useful study of the multiple ways the king was perceived as embodied, see Ernst Kantorowicz, *The King's Two Bodies: A Study in Mediaeval Political Theology* (Princeton, N.J.: Princeton University Press, 1957).

29. Bellamy, *Tudor Law*, 10–11.

30. Bellamy, *Tudor Law*, 9–13, 29. The Reformation Parliament of 1530–34, particularly with the Henrician statute of 1534 (26 Hen. VIII c. 13), continued the Edwardian trend, extending the statutes by making wishing and words the centerpiece of treason. See Bellamy, *Tudor Law*, 29; and G. R. Elton, *Policy and Police: The Enforcement of the Reformation in the Age of Thomas Cromwell* (Cambridge: Cambridge University Press, 1992), 286–87.

31. Bellamy, *Tudor Law*, 11.

32. There were at least two significant pieces of treason legislation before the Reformation Parliament. In 1495 a "de facto act" extended imagining the king's death to include *intending* to levy war against him, and in 1517 a judicial conference interpreted an act from the third year of the reign of Henry V as including riots in London directed against foreigners among treasons; "the insurrection in it selfe was high treason as a thing practiced against the regal honor of our soveryn lord the king" (Bellamy, *Tudor Law*, 19).

33. Overall, the Henrician acts were designed to defend Henry's matrimonial arrangements, his anti-papal policy, and his attack on the liberties of the church: three were the result of the king's matrimonial ventures, and two supported his marriages with sanctions of treason (Bellamy, *Tudor Law*, 62).

34. Bellamy, *Tudor Law*, 12. Although treason legislation tends to contract and expand with changes in the monarchy, the Edwardian statute of 1352 was continuously evoked throughout the sixteenth century (62).

35. Bellamy, *Tudor Law*, 56, 48. Bellamy argues that Stanford was on shaky ground himself: every type of treason had been included in the 1352 act except one, failure to reveal a knowledge of intended treason.

36. See Jean E. Howard, *The Stage and Social Struggle in Early Modern England* (New York: Routledge, 1994), 34; and "Scripts and/versus Playhouses: Ideological Pro-

duction and the Renaissance Public Stage," in *The Matter of Difference: Materialist Feminist Criticism of Shakespeare*, ed. Valerie Wayne (Ithaca, N.Y.: Cornell University Press, 1991), 226. See also Louis Althusser, "Ideology and Ideological State Apparatuses (Notes towards an investigation)," in *Lenin and Philosophy and Other Essays*, trans. Ben Brewster (New York: Monthly Review Press, 1971), 162; and Raymond Williams, *Marxism and Literature* (Oxford: Oxford University Press, 1977), 175.

37. William Shakespeare, *Hamlet, Prince of Denmark*, in *The Complete Works of Shakespeare*, 3rd ed., ed. David Bevington (Glenview, Ill.: Scott, Foresman, 1980), 3.4.150–51. All subsequent references to the plays of Shakespeare are to the Bevington edition and are identified in the text.

38. See, respectively, Karin S. Coddon, "'Suche Strange Desygns': Madness, Subjectivity, and Treason in *Hamlet* and Elizabethan Culture," in *Hamlet*, ed. Susanne L. Wofford (New York: Bedford, 1994), 380–402; Elizabeth Hanson, *Discovering the Subject in Renaissance England* (Cambridge: Cambridge University Press, 1998); and Maus, *Inwardness*. Coddon argues that the discourse of treason "disintegrates the identity so precariously fashioned by notions of inward control and self-vigilance" (381–82).

39. Quoted in John Bellamy, *The Law of Treason in England in the Later Middle Ages* (Cambridge: Cambridge University Press, 1970), 123. In *A Crisis of Truth: Literature and Law in Ricardian England* (Philadelphia: University of Pennsylvania Press, 1999), Richard Firth Green points out that the common law first begins to consider intention in the context of institutional treason, but its appearance in other legal areas, such as private obligation, is less clear (119). On judges refusing to entertain a felon's thoughts, see William Holdsworth, *A History of English Law*, 5th ed. (London: Methuen, 1942), 3:373–74.

States of mind did come under consideration in English common law of contract, and it may be that the common law had silently imported the issue of intention from continental law and the civil law in England that derived from it. On relations between English common and civil law, see Brian P. Levack, *The Civil Lawyers in England, 1603–1641* (Oxford: Clarendon Press, 1973); and Barbara J. Shapiro, *A Culture of Fact: England, 1550–1720* (Ithaca, N.Y.: Cornell University Press, 2000).

40. Bellamy, *Tudor Law*, 32.

41. Thomas Stapleton, *The Life and Illustrious Martyrdom of Sir Thomas More*, Part 3 of "Tres Thomae," printed at Douai, 1588, trans. Philip E. Hallett (London: Burns, Oates, and Washburn, 1928), 192.

42. Raphael Holinshed, *Holinshed's Chronicles of England, Scotland, and Ireland*, vol. 4 (London, 1587; rpt. 1808), 920. The text I refer to as "Holinshed" includes the work of many writers. It was conceived by a printer named Reyner Wolfe; the first edition included William Harrison's descriptions of Britain, England, and Scotland and Richard Stanyhurst's description and history of Ireland, as well as Holinshed's histories of England and Scotland, themselves compiled from a variety of sources. The second edition, published after Holinshed's death, expanded the text with additions by John Hooker (Vowell), Francis Thynne, Abraham Fleming, and others. See Phyllis Rackin, *Stages Of History: Shakespeare's English Chronicles* (Ithaca, N.Y.: Cornell University Press, 1990), 23.

43. H. L. Stephen, ed., *State Trials: Political and Social*, 2 vols. (London: Duckworth, 1899), 1:53.

44. Bellamy, *Tudor Law*, 77. Other legal complications impinged on the issue of witnesses. In an early act of Philip and Mary (1 & 2 Ph. & M. c. 10), one clause demanded witnesses-accusers when anyone was accused under it, yet another clause said treason trials were to be by the "common law," which did not allow such accusers. A meeting of judges and law officers of the crown in October 1556 decided that in cases of treason under statute (by which Bellamy infers they appear to have meant under a sixteenth-century statute, since the 1352 statute in their view was only a declaration of common law treason), two accusers or *testes* should always be at the indictment. If the offense was within the act of 1352, this was unnecessary because the common law operated, they said, by jury and witness and not by accusers. They noted that if the offense came under the act 1 & 2 Ph. & M. c. 10, then witness-accusers were required at the arraignment as well as the indictment (Bellamy, *Tudor Law*, 77).

After 1580, two earlier acts (the Edwardian act of 1352 and 13 Eliz. c. 1 in 1571) were often allied in indictments, which were phrased in such a way that they could have been based on the 1352 act, the general treason statute of 1571, or both. When Edward Abington was arraigned during the Babington trials, he was told by one of the justices that he stood indicted "by the common law and the statute of 25 Edward 3," not by the statutes "of the 1st and 13th of this queen," Elizabeth. However, the indictment followed the form of the 1571 Elizabethan act (Bellamy, *Tudor Law*, 76).

45. Bellamy, *Tudor Law*, 31.

46. Bellamy, *Tudor Law*, 32.

47. Writing under the Stuarts, Coke provided a revisionist history, insisting that the Tudors had required a concrete "overt act":

> Divers latter acts of parliament have ordained, that compassing by bare words or sayings should be high treason; but all they are either repealed or expired. And it is commonly said, that bare words may make an heretick, but not a traytor without an overt act. And the wisdome of the makers of this law would not make words only to be treason, seeing such variety amongst the witnesses are about the same, as few of them agree together.

Coke, *The Third Part of the Institutes of the Laws of England* (1797: Buffalo, N.Y.: Hein, 1986), 14. Coke pointed to 25 Eliz. st. 3 as requiring an overt deed.

48. Holinshed, 911.

49. The rhetorical strategies themselves are familiar, the legacy of classical rhetoricians to every English school boy or girl: Cicero and Quintilian would have recognized the focus on the verbal construction of guilt as the main concern of rhetoric, whose proper aim was "artistic arguments," verbal constructions that did not rely on material evidence for their persuasiveness. In *De Inventione*, Cicero codifies the rhetorical topics to be used in the lawcourt, noting that "every inference . . . is based on arguments from the cause of the action [by which he means motive], from the character of the person involved, and from the nature of the act"; Cicero, *Works: English and Latin* (London: W. Heinemann; Cambridge, Mass.: Harvard University Press, 1913–77), vol. 2, *De Inventione. De optimo genere oratorum Topica*, 5–16. See also Quintilian, *The Institutio Oratoria of Quintilian*, trans. H. E. Butler (Cambridge, Mass.: Harvard University Press, 1959–63), 2: 8–12.

50. Proof tended to develop on a case-by-case basis. See Bellamy, *Tudor Law*, 9–82; and John H. Langbein, *Torture and the Law of Proof* (Chicago: University of Chi-

cago Press, 1977), esp. 3–17. For recent studies of the idea that proof is constructed, see the series of essays on "questions of evidence" in three consecutive issues of *Critical Inquiry*—17,4 (Summer 1991); 18,1 (Autumn 1991); 18,2 (Winter 1992). The question of providing trustworthy evidence was also bound up with a broad historical shift that gradually differentiated "evidence" from "fact": understood as interpretable signs from the natural and supernatural realms, prodigies and miracles competed for authority during an extended process in which reliable evidence came to be incompatible with human intention. See Lorraine Daston, "Marvelous Facts and Miraculous Evidence in Early Modern Europe," *Critical Inquiry* 18,1 (Autumn 1991): 93–124; and Barbara J. Shapiro, *A Culture of Fact*.

51. Martin Luther, *The Babylonian Captivity of the Church* (1520), in *Martin Luther: Selections from His Writings*, ed. John Dillenberger (New York: Doubleday, 1961), 341. Similarly William Whitaker draws on Calvin to conclude, "although there is much obscurity in many words and passages [of Scripture], yet all the articles of faith are plain"; *A Disputation on Holy Scripture* (1588), ed. William Fitzgerald, Parker Society 45 (Cambridge: Cambridge University Press, 1849), 362. In *The Performance of Conviction: Plainness and Rhetoric in the Early English Renaissance* (Ithaca, N.Y.: Cornell University Press, 1994), Kenneth J. E. Graham writes that this plainness is "not a quality of the *words*, which are an external, intellectual manifestation of scriptural truth, but rather of the heart moved by the Spirit" (7).

52. Graham, *Performance*, 18. My summary of this issue is indebted to Graham, 1–24. On the idea that "one man's plain is another man's distortion," see Stanley Fish, "Epilogue: The Plain Style Question," in *Self-Consuming Artifacts: The Experience of Seventeenth-Century Literature* (Berkeley: University of California Press, 1972), 383.

53. Thomas B. Howell, ed., *Cobbett's Complete Collection of State Trials* (London: R. Bagshaw, 1809–26), 1:1145.

54. Stephen, *State Trials*, 1:38.

55. Susan Amussen, *An Ordered Society: Gender and Class in Early Modern England* (Oxford: Blackwell, 1988), 154.

56. Amussen, 155.

57. Amussen, 154. On the difficulties of defining and ascribing literacy in the period, see also for example David Cressy, *Literacy and the Social Order: Reading and Writing in Tudor and Stuart England* (Cambridge: Cambridge University Press, 1980). Keith Thomas argues that Cressy seriously underestimates the numbers of reading women; see "The Meaning of Literacy in Early Modern England," in *The Written Word: Literacy in Transition*, ed. Gerd Baumann (Oxford: Clarendon Press, 1986). H. S. Bennett concludes that the ability to read was widespread; see *English Books and Readers: 1475–1557* (Cambridge: Cambridge University Press, 1970).

58. Herrup, 148–49.

59. Quoted in Lacey Baldwin Smith, *Treason in*, 278, n. 3.

60. Michel Foucault, "Discourse on Language," Appendix, *The Archeology of Knowledge*, trans. A. M. Sheridan Smith (New York: Pantheon, 1972), 215–37.

61. Thomas Hobbes, *Leviathan*, ed. C. B. Macpherson (Harmondsworth: Penguin, 1968), 105.

62. On the forceful use of strategic language to construe and produce authoritative interpretations in legal and rhetorical studies, see Fish, *Doing*, 9.

63. On the diversity of audiences for the theater, see Ann Jenalie Cook, *The*

Privileged Playgoer of Shakespeare's London, 1576–1642 (Princeton, N.J.: Princeton University Press, 1981); Margot Heinemann, "Shakespearean Contradictions and Social Change," *Science and Society* 41 (1977): 7–16; and Andrew Gurr, *Playgoing in Shakespeare's London* (Cambridge: Cambridge University Press, 1987).

64. L. W. Abbott, *Law Reporting in England 1485–1585*, 96, 112. My summary of law reporting throughout this section relies on Abbott's work. Among historians, G. R. Elton and H. S. Bennett, respectively, have documented the printing and reprinting of various treason statutes in the late sixteenth and early seventeenth centuries. See G. R. Elton, "The Sessional Printing of Statutes, 1484–1547," in *Wealth and Power in Tudor England*, ed. E. W. Ives, R. J. Knecht, and J. J. Scarisbrick (London: Althone, 1978), 68–76; and H. S. Bennett, *English Books and Readers, 1603–1640*, (Cambridge: Cambridge University Press, 1970), 119–21.

65. "Coke on Littleton," in *Institutes of the Laws of England*, Part 1, 15th ed., 3 vols. (1794), 293a.

66. Plowden's *Commentaries* is regarded as the most accurate collection of its kind in the sixteenth and seventeenth centuries. It is unusual among contemporary legal works for being the only set of reports prepared for publication by an author in his own lifetime, and Plowden's own cases were being cited within a year of their being printed. Most unusual in the context of legal publishing, the first volume came out within a few months of the adjudication of the last case. Plowden explained this swift transition from notes to print in his Preface, saying that after he lent his notes to colleagues, some unscrupulous persons gained access to them and hastily prepared copies of cases for printing. The threat of inaccurate transcription and inferior printing prompted Plowden to put forth an edition of his own. The first book came out in October 1571; Part I of a second collection came out in 1578, and Part II came out in 1579. (There were editions in 1578, 1579, 1584, 1588, 1594, 1599.) Legal reports were typically written in law-French with interjections in Latin and English, depending on the disposition of the author. The first English edition of Plowden's *Commentaries* did not appear until 1761 (Abbott, 199–207).

The Yearbooks, which disappear in the sixteenth century as the standard vehicles of reporting, are anonymous. Extant at the same time are the compilations of the first generation of "private" reporters, many of whom remain anonymous. Some of the early private reports can be attributed to students and practitioners at the Inns of Court. The second generation of reporters, those of the post-Yearbook period, include such identifiable authors as William Bendlowes, William Dalison, Richard Harper, James Dyer, Edmund Plowden, and Edward Coke. Only Plowden and Coke oversaw publication of volumes of their reports during their lifetimes (Abbott, 7).

67. Abbott, 240.

68. Abbott, 5.

69. Abbott, 5.

70. Abbott, 184–95. "Table cases" of this sort arose from the practice of mooting which was carried on at the Inns of Court and Chancery. Points of law were frequently cited from lectures and moots in reports. "The reports of the sixteenth century demonstrate how essential extra-judicial proceedings, formal and informal, were to decision-making. In the final analysis the success of such a system, like that of Tudor government on a wider scale, rested on the skill and leadership of a small, but powerful, group of men drawn mainly from the same social class" (Abbott, 194–96).

71. Plowden, *The Commentaries or Reports*, 2 parts (London: S. Brooke, 1816), Part 1, Preface 4.

72. Abbott, 207, 144.

73. Coke, *The Reports of Sir Edward Coke*, 2nd ed. (London, 1680), vol. 3, Pref. xviiia; "Dedication to Lord Buckhurst," *Reports*, vol. 1.

74. Coke, "Coke on Littleton," 293b.

75. Coke, "Calvin's Case," *Reports*, vol. 7, 4a.

76. See Holinshed, 914–23, for commentaries on the Babington conspiracy and the Scots trial.

77. Patterson, *Reading*, 182.

78. "Coke on Littleton," Pref. xxix–xxx. Differences in the concept of sovereignty behind absolutist and limited monarchies corresponded to differences in the assumptions of civil and common lawyers about the proper reach and execution of the law. In general, civilian lawyers were closer in theory to absolutists; they adopted the view that the English king's authority over public matters was "sovereign" or "absolute," and was expressed in the written law derived from Justinian. Common lawyers, in contrast, were in theory on the side of limited or constitutional monarchy; they recognized the royal dignity and authority of the monarch over matters of state, but that authority was seen as depending on relations with the subject, and was expressed in the case-law derived from English practice from time immemorial. See Levack, 95–96.

79. Generally we do not know who produced the trial records or how they were acquired by those who printed them. In the chapters that follow, I discuss the trials as though the texts in which they are available had been arrived at by the compromise method suggested by Annabel Patterson in her reading of the Nicholas Throckmorton trial of 1554: they might be "either very extensive notes made at the time, by another interested party or parties . . . ; subsequent *fabrication* by someone with a great ear for dialogue and a lively political imagination . . . ; or some combination of the two" (*Reading*, 161).

80. In a general way, the trials I discuss trace an arc from the "high point for Parliament in the law—the Reformation Parliaments and Thomas Cromwell's activities in them regarding Catherine Howard"—to the late Elizabethan prosecution of Mary in 1586 that entangles Elizabeth in justifying the execution of a monarch; see Elton, *Tudor Constitution*, 234.

81. McIlwain, 61

82. See for example Peter Fitzpatrick and Alan Hunt, eds., *Critical Legal Studies* (Oxford: Blackwell, 1987).

83. For an argument that "we never really confront a text immediately, in all its freshness as a thing-in-itself," see Fredric Jameson, *The Political Unconscious: Narrative as a Socially Symbolic Act* (Ithaca, N.Y.: Cornell University Press, 1981), 9. Among discussions of the position of the late twentieth-century critic, comments I have found most useful include those by Phyllis Rackin, "Historical Difference/Sexual Difference," in *Privileging Gender in Early Modern England*, ed. Jean R. Brink, *Sixteenth Century Essays and Studies* 23 (1993): 37; and *Stages*, ix–xi; Jean E. Howard, "The New Historicism in Renaissance Studies," *English Literary Renaissance* 16 (1986): 13–43; and "Scholarship, Theory, and More New Readings: Shakespeare for the 1990's," in *Shakespeare Study Today*, ed. Georgianna Ziegler (New York: AMS Press, 1986), 127–

31; Jonathan Dollimore, "Introduction: Shakespeare, Cultural Materialism and the New Historicism," in *Political Shakespeare: New Essays in Cultural Materialism*, ed. Jonathan Dollimore and Alan Sinfield (Ithaca, N.Y.: Cornell University Press, 1985), 2–17; and Belsey, *The Subject*.

Chapter 1: Fugitive Forms

1. Foucault, *Discipline*, 106. For one of his most extensive definitions of "power," which he perceives as dispersed and disunified, see 26–27. On court-centered power, see, for example, Goldberg, *James I*; Greenblatt, *Shakespearean Negotiations*; Greenblatt, ed., *The Forms of Power and the Power of Forms in the Renaissance* (Norman: University of Oklahoma Press, 1982); and Leonard Tennenhouse, *Power on Display: The Politics of Shakespeare's Genres* (New York: Methuen, 1986).

2. Throughout this chapter I use the more general term "mooting" to include the related specific practice of "reading." "Mooting" describes all instances of speculative, theoretical study; "reading" describes a particular form of "mooting." Differences between these have primarily to do with the barrister's stage in legal education. See the descriptions in J. H. Baker and Samuel Thorne, eds., *Readings and Moots at the Inns of Court in the Fifteenth Century*, vol. 2, *Moots and Readers' Cases* (London: Seldon Society, 1990); and Philip Smith, *A History of Education for the English Bar* (London: Butterworths, 1860), 21–40.

3. J. H. Baker, "The Inns of Court and Legal Doctrine," in *Lawyers and Laymen*, ed. T. M. Charles-Edwards et al. (Cardiff: University of Wales Press, 1986), 283. Although they did not make law in the sense of establishing statutes, readers of moots did contribute to consolidation and explanation of unwritten principles, establishing a tradition as to what was received learning and what was dubious. The influence of the law schools, though unofficial, was deep: "It must have been far harder to overturn a proposition which had been constantly laid down in the inns of court than a chance remark of a serjeant at the bar. Indeed, Littleton himself offered to 'prove' a proposition in the *Tenures* by saying that he had often heard it in the readings on Westminster II, c. 3. It will be noted that the reference is not to a specific reader, but to a repeated assertion" (Baker, "The Inns," 278).

4. Baker, *Readings*, xvi.

5. Baker, "The Inns," 278. According to J. P. Sommerville, "the main elements of common law political thinking . . . were the ideas of custom, of the rationality of English laws, and of the sacrosanctity of private property"; *Royalists*, 84. Liberty "depended on property in the literal sense that to deprive a man of property in his goods was to reduce him to villeinage" (137). Although property dominated moots, topics did sometimes also extend to the criminal law: Baker lists a series of questions about homicide, for example, that formed part of the "readings." Although readers could not lecture on the common law as such, there were pretexts for doing so under the guise of statutory interpretation (Baker, "The Inns," 279–80).

6. Baker, *Readings*, xv; Baker, "The Inns," 280. See also Philip Smith, 21–22.

7. Quoted in Philip Smith, 31–32.

8. Sommerville, 81.

9. Mooting emerges as a practice at the same time as the earliest known refer-

ence to any of the Inns of Court by name as legal societies—1388, when the names Inner Temple, Gray's Inn, and Middle Temple began to appear. Lincoln's Inn, absent from the early references, may have developed early in the fifteenth century. The early Inns of Chancery grew up around the same time as the Inns of Court. Two of the earliest references are to Clifford's Inn and Thavies Inn. Writing in the 1460s, Fortescue refers to the Inns of Chancery during his earlier days (Baker, *Readings*, xxviii–xxxii).

As mooting lost its authority, "a few classic readings and various moots retained their vitality and circulated widely in MS., transmitting unprinted learning both old and new." Baker speculates that there are three main reasons readings lost authority as transmitters of "common erudition": 1) the increasing independence of the four main houses (the three inns and the house of Chancery), which reduced cross-influences in the transmission of "common learning"; 2) the advent of printing, which was seen as a means of circulating truer "common learning" than lecture notes by anonymous students; and 3) (the chief reason) the increasing authority of judges as repositories and makers of law (Baker, "The Inns," 281–83). See also Baker, *Readings*, lxxv–lxxvi.

10. Baker, "The Inns," 281.

11. Baker, *Readings*, lxxvi. Later readings began to depart more often from the case law, and MSS. in the hands of successive owners would be marked, annotated, and etched with refutations: the student notebooks contain unattributed notes and queries, Biblical quotations, self-exhorting markings that say *Stude*, *Vide*, "Look up"; the names of some people; the self-directive "Argue," which may suggest participation in some formal presentation; and many moot cases ending with the phrase "Ceux que droit," the hallmark of the moot (Baker, *Readings*, xxxv). Also appearing on the ms. pages are references to Christmas revels and marginal names of cases such as "Jacob and Esau"; "Le Verge"; "Hobbe et John"; and "Cat in Pan." The marginalia signifying familiar moots served as mnemonic names, and were sometimes accompanied by drawings (Baker, *Readings*, xli–xlii).

12. Ben Jonson, *Volpone, or the Fox*, ed. Jonas Barish (Arlington Heights, Ill.: AHM Press, 1958), 4.2.122–27. For the historical process of paid attorneys distinguishing themselves from benchers, see Wilfrid R. Prest, *The Inns of Court under Elizabeth I and the Early Stuarts, 1590–1640* (London: Longman, 1972).

13. Baker, *Readings*, xvii. The form derives from the typical classroom structure of rhetorical training documented by Joel Altman, who identifies its use in explorative comedy: "the form reflects the rhetorical structure and aim or argument *in utramque partem*. The play is fashioned around a central question or questions, and the plot constitutes proof and counter-proof in a progressive movement toward a solution"; *The Tudor Play of Mind: Rhetorical Inquiry and the Development of Elizabethan Drama* (Berkeley: University of California Press, 1978), 229. For moral and social implications of the rhetorical tradition of *in utramque partem*, see also Victoria Kahn, *Rhetoric*. For an argument that rhetorical training was also training in the "paranoia" that precipitated or discovered treason everywhere, see Lacey Baldwin Smith, *Treason in*, 72–117.

14. Baker, *Readings*, 9, 7, 5 respectively.

15. Baker, "The Inns," 276.

16. Mary Douglas, *Purity and Danger: An Analysis of Concepts of Pollution and Taboo* (New York: Frederick Praeger, 1966).

17. Mary Douglas, *Cultural Bias*.

18. Baker, *Readings*, 17–18.

19. Clark, "The 'Strange' Geographies of *Cymbeline*," in *Playing the Globe: Genre and Geography in English Renaissance Drama*, ed. John Gillies and Virginia Mason Vaughan (Madison, N.J.: Fairleigh Dickinson University Press, 1998), 234.

20. See Genesis 25:21–34, 27.

21. Steven H. Gifis, *Law Dictionary*, 3rd ed. (Hauppauge, N.Y.: Barron's Educational Series, 1991), 187. Subsequent definitions of legal terms are from this edition and cited in the text. A villein was a tenant who was required to perform all the services demanded by the lord of the manor (520).

22. Michel Foucault, *The History of Sexuality*, trans. Robert Hurley (New York: Vintage, 1980), 4.

23. See Rackin, *Stages*, 158–60. Legal history here shares the ideological work of chronicle histories in positioning women in such a way that succession is formally accounted for.

24. Baker, *Readings*, lxxii.

25. Baker, *Readings*, 16–17. On blood and kinship relations, see Mary Douglas, *Purity*.

26. Baker, *Readings*, 16–17. The full text of the moot reads:

> A man has two carucates of land by inheritance, one in fee simple and the other in fee tail; he marries a wife, they have issue two daughters, and die; the two daughters enter as two daughters and one heir, and make partition so that the carucate of land in fee tail is allocated to the elder and the other carucate in fee simple to the younger; the elder marries; she and her husband have issue a son and a daughter; the husband dies; she marries another husband and they have issue a son and die; the issue by the first marriage leases the same land to a woman for life upon condition that if he grants the reversion to anyone else she shall have fee; he then grants the reversion to a stranger; the tenant for life by his lease recovers; the person to whom the reversion was granted enters upon the woman; she brings an assize and recovers; the son of the whole blood purchases a carucate of land unto him and his heirs, and dies seized; the son of the second issue enters into his carucate of land and brings writ of a formedon against the woman who holds for life and against her husband, and they plead that he has assets by descent, which is true, and so he is barred; the daughter by the first marriage brings an assize of mort d'ancestor in respect of the death of her brother of the whole blood and recovers; the brother of the half blood brings a writ of formedon in the descender against, etc. Discuss.

27. Baker, *Readings*, 14.

28. Quoted in Keith Thomas, *Puritans and Revolutionaries: Essays in Seventeenth-Century History Presented to Christopher Hill*, ed. Donald Pennington and Keith Thomas (Oxford: Clarendon Press, 1978), 262.

29. For a convenient overview of critical positions regarding representations of "self-Other," see R. S. Khare, "The Other's Double—The Anthropologist's Bracketed Self: Notes on Cultural Representation and Privileged Discourse," *New Literary History* 23,1 (Winter 1992): 1–23; Edward Said, *Orientalism: Western Concepts of the Orient* (New York: Vintage, 1978); and Clifford Geertz, *Local Knowledge*.

30. For a perceptive discussion of this issue as it relates to drama, see Jonathan Dollimore, "Transgression and Surveillance in *Measure for Measure*," in *Political Shakespeare*, 72–87.

31. Mary Douglas, *Purity*, 1.

32. Baker, "The Inns," 280. See also Philip Smith, 21–22.

33. Francis Bacon, *Essays*, intro. Michael J. Hawkins (London: Dent, 1972), 119.

34. Quoted in Baker, *Readings*, lxi. An elder barrister introduces and interprets a statute, and the utter barristers "by all ways of learning and reason that can be invented do impugn his opinion; and sometimes some of them do impugn it and others do approve it; and all the rest of the house give ear unto their disputations; and at last the reader doth confute all their sayings and confirmeth his opinion" (lxx). See also Philip Smith, 14–41.

35. All quotations from M. L. J. Abercrombie, "Face to Face—Proximity and Distance," in *Rules and Meanings: The Anthropology of Everyday Knowledge*, ed. Mary Douglas (Baltimore: Penguin, 1973), 92. The replication of traditional, fixed ideas of spatial order inside the Inns was increasingly at odds with the challenges to that order outside their walls; see Amussen, *An Ordered Society*, 138–40.

36. For ideas on disciplinary gestures that shape this paragraph, see Foucault, *Discipline*, 156, 170, 175.

37. Philip Smith, 29.

38. According to Baker, one case uses the names of the actual serjeants involved, but the case could be real or fictional, and the serjeants' names may merely stand for positions: "One case has the names Herle, Claver and Pass[ley], who were all serjeants before the reign of Edward II; and this raises the confusing possibility that actual cases might sometimes have been abridged into disputation form" (*Readings*, xxi).

39. Baker, "The Inns," 278.

40. Finkelpearl, *John Marston*, 41. My debt to Finkelpearl's excellent work is apparent throughout this chapter.

41. Sir John Fortescue, *On the Laws and Governance of England*, ed. Shelley Lockwood (Cambridge: Cambridge University Press, 1997), 67–68. Fortescue's work was first printed around 1545. For a history of the Inns, see also Philip Smith; Louis A. Knafla, "The Matriculation Revolution and Education in the Inns of Court in Renaissance England," in *Tudor Men and Institutions*, ed. Arthur J. Slavin (Baton Rouge: Louisiana State University Press, 1972), 232–64; and the Appendix by Sir George Buck, "The Third University of England," in John Stow, *Chronicle of England* (London, 1615).

42. Fortescue, 69.

43. Finkelpearl, 4–5. By the Restoration, William Dugdale observes that the students "are so unquieted by Clyents and servants of Clyents, . . . that the Students may as quietly study in the open streets, as in their Studies"; *Origines Juridiciales* (1666; 3rd ed. 1680); quoted in Finkelpearl, 10.

44. Records of the Inner Temple, MS, Micellanea 31, 24; quoted in Prest, 16.

45. John Earle, *Micro-Cosmographie* (London, 1628), 13; quoted in Prest, 92.

46. Records of the Middle Temple, MS, Minutes C, f. 204; quoted in Prest, 13.

47. William Harrison, *The Description of England* (London, 1577), ed. Georges Edelen (Ithaca, N.Y.: Cornell University Press, 1968), 76. See also Philip Smith, 15–19.

48. Gray's Inn had a high percentage (twenty-three percent) of students from the northern counties; Middle Temple had a high percentage (forty-seven percent) of students from counties in the south and southwest, and Warwickshire; Finkelpearl, 7.

49. Fortescue, 68–69. On expenses incurred by members of the inns and their economic status, see also Philip Smith, 27–34.

50. Finkelpearl, 6.

51. Finkelpearl, 7.

52. Finkelpearl, 5. By the end of the century, there were 1,040 men in residence at the four Inns of Court; the total of admissions for the last five years of the century was 1,096 men.

53. Thomas Smith, *De Republica Anglorum* (1583); quoted in Peter Roberts, "'The Studious Artizan': Christopher Marlowe, Canterbury and Cambridge," in *Christopher Marlowe and English Renaissance Culture*, ed. Darryll Grantley and Peter Roberts (Hants: Scolar Press, 1996), 36, n.37.

54. Philip Smith, 30–31.

55. Fortescue, 69. Dugdale recorded that the Inns had "wont to be entertained with *Post Revels*, performed by the better sort of young Gentlemen of the Society with Galliards, Corantocs, and other Dances; or else with Stageplayes" (203–5). Early in the seventeenth century, Buck defended the revels against accusations of triviality by suggesting that their apparent frivolity masked their real value as links to higher knowledge: the "Art of Revels," Buck wrote, "requireth knowledge in Grammar, Rhetorike, Logicke, Philosophie, Historie, Musick, Mathematikes, and in other Arts" (988). Reprints and discussions of Gray's Inn and Middle Temple revels are in Finkelpearl, 32–61.

56. See Mikhail Bakhtin, *Rabelais and His World*, trans. Helene Iswolsky (Bloomington: Indiana University Press, 1984).

57. Finkelpearl, 33.

58. Finkelpearl, 36. Finkelpearl bases this summary of the Christmas Prince revel on a variety of documents, including: Dugdale's account of the Inner Temple's revels (*Origines*, 153–57); the texts of the revels at Gray's Inn in 1594–95 and 1617–18 (*Gesta Grayorum, 1688*, ed. W. W. Greg, Malone Society Reprints [Oxford: Clarendon Press, 1914], 2–10); and the Middle Temple's "Prince d'Amour" revels of 1597–98 (*Middle Temple Records*, ed. Charles H. Hopwood [London: Butterworths, 1904], 1:303–4).

59. Abbott, *Law Reporting*, 31.

60. Finkelpearl, 19. According to Finkelpearl,

> Passing through Middle Temple at the end of the sixteenth century were such figures as William Lower, the astronomer; Peter Maunsell, Greshman Professor of Physics from 1607 to 1615; and Bartholomew Gosnell, the explorer. Among such, Herbert Croft is a notable example. After years of orthodox pursuits (M.P., 1588; admitted to the Middle Temple, 1594; knighted, 1603), he became a Catholic convert at the age of fifty-two and died at Douay, having written some Catholic apologetics. On the other hand, the learned anti-Catholic Puritan, Humfrey Lynd, was also a member, admitted in 1601. For a more bizarre deviation from the law we may note the lives of Robert and Thomas Winter. Both at the Middle Temple from 1590–1592, they devoted their lives almost wholly to Catholic plotting, and both were executed in 1606 for their deep complicity in the Gunpowder plot. (10–11)

For a discussion of the literary movement in the Inns at this time, see 20–31. And for mention of the diversity of the members, see also James Nichols, ed., *The Church History of Britain* (London, 1840), 3:128.

61. Sidney, "An Apology," 155.

62. John Gassner, ed. *Medieval and Tudor Drama* (New York: Applause, 1987), 404.

63. Finkelpearl, 22.

64. Jonson, Dedication to *Every Man Out of His Humour*, ed. F. P. Wilson (London: Oxford University Press, 1920).

Chapter 2: Female Fidelities on Trial

1. Bellamy, *Tudor Law*, 37–38. For a study of the language in "the fictions that Henry VIII had published to discourage resistance to his divorce" from Catherine of Aragon (1529–35), see J. Christopher Warner, *Henry VIII's Divorce: Literature and the Politics of the Printing Press* (Woodbridge: Boydell Press, 1998).

2. Boleyn was accused of having procured several of the king's servants, including her own brother, to become her adulterers and concubines. This behavior was called traitorous when it was described in the indictment, and then in summary all of those named were said to have imagined the king's death at Westminster on October 31, 1536 and at several times before and since. This might have been inferred from the adultery, or it might have been connected to another charge: Anne was accused of promising to marry one of her suitors when the king should die, and had said she would never love the king in her heart. According to Bellamy, there had been nothing in the history of treason to suggest that adultery on the part of the queen was treasonous (Bellamy, *Tudor Law*, 40–41).

3. Charles Wriothesley, *A Chronicle of England during the Reigns of the Tudors, From A. D. 1485 to 1559*, ed. William Douglas Hamilton (1875; rpt. New York: Johnson Reprint Corp., 1965), 1:130–31.

4. Employed when the Crown preferred to avoid bringing a defendant to trial at common law, attainders allowed prosecution when evidence against the accused might be doubtful, when the Crown preferred that it not be made public, or when the offense did not seem to fall within existing treason laws. For additional reasons rulers and Parliaments might use attainder acts, see Bellamy, *Tudor Law*, 211–14. Both Bellamy (*Tudor Law*, 41) and Lacey Baldwin Smith (*A Tudor Tragedy*, 201–2) speculate that there was opposition to the Howard attainder in Parliament because there was a delay of about two weeks between its introduction and its passage and there were two second readings.

What I am calling "the Howard attainder" is a compilation of documents. The full text of the formal charges appears in Walter Jerrold's biography (*Henry VIII and His Wives* [New York: Doran, n.d.]), 273–74, reprinted from *Letters and Papers of the Reign of Henry VIII*, vols. 15, 16; and in Howell, *Cobbett's*, vol. 1, which relies also on *Lord Herbert's Life of Henry VIII*. Other commentary is drawn from Wriothesley's chronicle; *Hall's Chronicle; Containing the History of England* (London: 1809; rpt. New York: AMS Press, 1965); and Martin Hume's *The Wives of Henry the Eighth* (New York: Brentano's, n.d.), which agrees with the *Letters and Papers*, vols. 15, 16. I cite in this essay only those elements of Howard's biography and attainder that appear in two or more of the sources here identified. The notable exception is the second scaffold speech (see p. 50 of this chapter), which appears in Hume and about which he says: "The accounts of Chapuys, Hall, and Ottewell Johnson say simply that she confessed her faults and made a Christian end. The *Spanish Chronicle of Henry VIII* gives an account of her speech, of which the above is a summary" (395, n. 1).

5. *Letters and Papers of the Reign of Henry VIII*, vol. 14, part 2, 286, 572; quoted

in Stanford E. Lehmberg, "Sir Thomas Audley: A Soul as Black as Marble?" in *Tudor Men and Institutions*, ed. Arthur J. Slavin (Baton Rouge: Louisiana State University Press, 1972), 8–9.

6. Thomas Cromwell, architect of Henry's protestant policy and supporter of the Cleves marriage, was beheaded on Tower Hill on July 28, 1540, the same day Henry married Katherine Howard at Oatlands. Howard's uncle, the Duke of Norfolk, was Cromwell's arch rival and "the likely agent of a strong Catholic papal dominion which for ten years Cromwell had striven to make impossible" (Jerrold, 256). On the idea that Cromwell was an early constitutionalist, see G. R. Elton, "The Rule of Law," 281–90.

7. Indictment of Katherine Howard, quoted in Hume, 384. In the indictments against Dereham and Culpeper, both the pre-marital and post-marital offences of the queen are summarized; these are printed in Jerrold, 273–74.

8. Attainder of Katherine Howard, printed in Jerrold, 278–79.

9. Donald Thomas, ed., *State Trials: Treason and Libel* (London: Routledge and Kegan Paul, 1972), 43. For a useful study of the Boleyn treason and the rhetoric of slander, see M. Lindsay Kaplan and Katherine Eggert, "'Good queen, my lord, good queen': Sexual Slander and the Trials of Female Authority in *The Winter's Tale*," in *Renaissance Drama and the Law*, ed. Frances E. Dolan, special issue of *Renaissance Drama* n.s. 25 (1994): 89–118.

10. Donald Thomas, 46.

11. Hume, 369.

12. Jerrold, 256. See also Hume, who states that Howard "was known to have been a giddy, neglected girl before her marriage, having been brought up by her grandmother . . . without the slightest regard for her welfare or the high rank of her family" (368).

13. *Hall's Chronicle*, 842.

14. Aristotle, *Metaphysics*, trans. W. D. Ross, in *Introduction to Aristotle*, ed. Richard McKeon (New York: Modern Library, 1947), 247. On the emotional and speculative effects of rhetorical strategies, see also Aristotle's *Poetics*, trans. Ingram Bywater, in the same edition, 637.

15. Donald Thomas, 46.

16. *Wimbish v. Willoughby*, T. 6 Edw. VI, Edmund Plowden, *Commentaries*, Part 1, 73–76.

17. Abbott, *Law Reporting*, 213.

18. Stephen, *State Trials*, 1:18. Ralegh resisted the charges against him by attacking the authority of the oral testimony as evidence and demanding a more material form of proof.

19. Angell Day, "Of the partes, place and Office of a Secretary," in *The English Secretary*, ed. Robert O. Evans (Gainesville, Fla.: Scholars' Facsimiles and Reprints, 1967), facsimile of the 1599 edition, 130.

20. Before the case concludes, evidence against Katherine will include Mary Lassells Hall's gossip with her brother; her brother's recounting of that gossip to Cranmer and inclusion of himself in the story; Cranmer's first written version, which includes Lassells as both participant in the original conversation and as informant and good citizen, and includes Cranmer as the loyal servant of the king reporting distasteful information in writing; the individual interrogators' written fragments of testimony

from the various witnesses each questioned independently; the initial written version presented to Parliament with the recommendation that Howard be invited to testify; and the second written version presented to Parliament that conflated the multiple statements of witnesses into generalizations about all agreeing to the tale.

On the reciprocal shaping of legal and fictional texts, see Natalie Zemon Davis, *Fiction in the Archives* (Stanford, Calif.: Stanford University Press, 1987).

21. Lacey Baldwin Smith asserts that Lassells was motivated by protestant hatred and zeal and that the "discharge of his duty" and the "welfare of his soul" demanded that he expose Howard (*A Tudor Tragedy*, 158).

22. On the priority of having a purpose before one can bring the meaning of a statute to light, see Stanley Fish, "Normal circumstances, Literal Language, Direct Speech Acts, the Ordinary, the Everyday, the Obvious, What goes Without Saying, and Other Special Cases" (1978), in *Critical Theory Since Plato*," rev. ed., ed. Hazard Adams (New York: Harcourt, 1992), 1204.

23. Howell, 418.

24. Jerrold, 270.

25. Hume, 380. Lord Chancellor Audley, Cranmer's ally, presided over the trials of Culpeper, Dereham, and several of Howard's relatives. According to Eustace Chapuys, Audley inveighed against Howard in his speech opening Parliament in 1542, "aggravating and exaggerating her misdeeds" (*Letters and Papers of Henry VIII*, vol. 17, App. B.; quoted in Lehmberg, 9).

26. Fish, *Doing*, 94.

27. Howell, 447.

28. See Fish, *Doing*, 77–78.

29. Coke, *The Third Part*, 14.

30. On the classical and grotesque bodies, see Bakhtin, *Rabelais and His World*, 24–28.

31. Hume, 355–56.

32. Among the paradoxical elements in the Cleves-Howard history is a rumor about Anne: "there was other loose talk also going on to the effect that on one of the visits of Anne of Cleves to Hampton Court after Henry's marriage with Katherine, the King and his repudiated wife had made up their differences, with the consequence that Anne was pregnant by him" (Hume, 368). Though the rumor proved false, it took Anne's reported pregnancy as evidence of her spousal legitimacy, despite Henry's having another wife.

33. The officials were Archbishop Cranmer, the Lord Chancellor, the Duke of Norfolk, the Lord Great Chamberlain and the Bishop of Winchester.

34. Donald Thomas, 48.

35. For an argument that the Crown had suppressed its finding that Howard had been secretly engaged to Dereham, which would have made her marriage to the king voidable and her crime the lesser one of concealment rather than treason, see Hume, 374–76. For a counterargument, that Howard refused to acknowledge any such contract, see Lacey Baldwin Smith, *A Tudor Tragedy*, 185. Smith argues also that Culpeper and Dereham were prosecuted on the basis of intent rather than physical act: Culpeper had not "carnally known the Queen," though he confessed his intention to do so; and Dereham was retained by the queen "to the intent" that they might continue their wicked activities (191–92).

36. Donald Thomas, 48.

37. Hume, 395.

38. *Letters and Papers of the Reign of Henry VIII*, vol. 16; quoted in Hume, 394.

39. Quoted in Hume, 395.

40. Quoted in Hume, 394–95.

41. Pye, *The Regal Phantasm*, (London: Routledge, 1990), 115. Compare Elaine Scarry, who identifies the condemned as one made "to understand [her] confession . . . as an act of self-betrayal . . . in which the one annihilated shifts to being the agent of [her] own annihilation" (*The Body in Pain: The Making and Unmaking of the World* [Oxford: Oxford University Press, 1985], 47). On the formulaic and normative aspects of scaffold speeches, see also J. A. Sharpe, "'Last Dying Speeches': Religion, Ideology and Public Execution in Seventeenth-Century England," *Past and Present* 107 (May 1985): 144–67; and Lacey Baldwin Smith, "English Treason Trials and Confessions in the Sixteenth Century," *Journal of the History of Ideas* 15 (1954): 471–98. For a focus on women on the scaffold, see Frances E. Dolan, "'Gentlemen, I have one thing more to say': Women on Scaffolds in England, 1563–1680," *Modern Philology* 92,4 (November 1994): 157–78; Karen Newman, *Fashioning Femininity and English Renaissance Drama* (Chicago: University of Chicago Press, 1991), 69; and Belsey, *The Subject*, 190–91.

42. Jerrold, 259. The translation and social meanings of Howard's motto remain in dispute, varying with conflicting assumptions about her role. The motto appears in a letter from a French ambassador: "Non autre volonte que la sienne" (*Letters and Papers of Henry VIII*, vol. 16, 12; quoted in Hume, 386). "Volonte" is feminine; "la sienne" has been variously translated "hers" or "his." Jerrold finds the feminine translation consistent with his view of Howard's character as an independent woman; in contrast, Lacey Baldwin Smith offers the masculine translation ("No other wish than his" [*A Tudor Tragedy*, 150]), which he finds consistent with his idea of Howard's submissiveness to Henry.

43. Donald Thomas, 45.

44. Jerrold, 273.

45. Rackin, *Stages*, 160.

46. Hume, 377. On the idea that "women were important instruments of social control, often to their own detriment, since they were the primary target," see Nicole Castan, "The Public and the Private," in *A History of Private Life*, ed. Roger Chartier, trans. Arthur Goldhammer, vol. 3, *Passions of the Renaissance* (Cambridge, Mass.: Harvard University Press, 1989), 418.

47. Hume, 379. According to Catherine Tylney, she and another servant, Margery Morton, had tried to accompany Howard to Lady Rochford's rooms but had been sent back. Morton, however, crept back up the stairs to Lady Rochford's rooms and waited until about 2 o'clock in the morning, when she saw Howard leave Lady Rochford's rooms and return to her own; Morton did the same, spreading the gossip among the maids (Hume, 377–78).

48. Hume, 279.

49. Lena Cowen Orlin, *Private Matters and Public Culture in Post-Reformation England* (Ithaca, N.Y.: Cornell University Press, 1994), 8. On the significance of the mouth, chastity, and the threshold as borders of property, see Orlin, 82–83; and Peter Stallybrass, "Patriarchal Territories: The Body Enclosed," in *Rewriting the Renais-*

sance, ed. Margaret W. Ferguson, Maureen Quilligan, and Nancy J. Vickers (Chicago: University of Chicago Press, 1986), 123–42.

50. Hume, 373. According to several historians, she had grown up "uncared for in the house of her grandmother" (Hume, 273). Jerrold comments that in the Dowager's "household [Katherine] became, it would appear, an unimportant, and more or less neglected and uneducated inmate" (254).

51. Ranum, "The Refuges of Intimacy," in *A History of Private Life*, ed. Roger Chartier, trans. Arthur Goldhammer, vol. 3, *Passions of the Renaissance* (Cambridge, Mass.: Harvard University Press, 1989), 207–9.

52. Hume, 373.

53. Quoted in Jerrold, 271.

54. Hume, 373.

55. Howell, 448. Quoted from *Lord Herbert's Life of Henry VIII.* Mannock later deposed: "Young Bulmer's wife, who was [Katherine's] bedfellow and also entertained by Dereham, Dorothy Dawby, then chamberer with the Duchess, Catherine Tylney, now chamberer with the Queen, Edward Walgrave, servant to my lord Prince (Edward), Mary Lassells and Malyn Tylney, widow, can speak of the misrule between Dereham and Mistress Catherine" (Jerrold, 272).

56. Orlin, 185. See also Alain Collomp, "Families: Habitations and Cohabitations," in *A History of Private Life*, ed. Roger Chartier, trans. Arthur Goldhammer, vol. 3, *Passions of the Renaissance* (Cambridge, Mass.: Harvard University Press, 1989), 493–529.

57. Orlin, 185. See also Ranum, who argues that social activities dominated in the great hall, but secretly pleasurable activities dominated in the chamber (218–25).

58. Howell, 448.

59. Glenn Clark, "The 'Strange' Geographies," 242.

60. Christopher Marlowe, *Doctor Faustus*, in *The Complete Plays of Christopher Marlowe*, ed. Irving Ribner (New York: Odyssey Press, 1963). Subsequent references to plays by Marlowe are to this edition and are cited in the text.

61. Ranum, 212. A person's "level of privacy" was elusive and could not be assimilated to nor assessed by its dependency on space (212). A useful overview of the concept of "divided spheres" and of the ways the private/public division encodes and disguises women's positions is in Dorothy O. Helly and Susan M. Reverby, eds., *Gendered Domains: Rethinking Public and Private in Women's History* (Ithaca, N.Y.: Cornell University Press, 1992), 1–24.

62. "The Schoolhouse of Women," in Katherine Henderson and Barbara McManus, *Half Humankind: Contexts and Texts of the Controversy about Women in England, 1540–1640* (Urbana: University of Illinois Press, 1985), 141. See also Constance Jordan, *Renaissance Feminism: Literary Texts and Political Models* (Ithaca, N.Y.: Cornell University Press, 1990), 127. For a discussion of "the gossips' meeting," see Linda Woodbridge, *Women and the English Renaissance: Literature and the Nature of Womankind, 1540–1620* (Urbana: University of Illinois Press, 1984), 224–43.

63. Jerrold, 272.

64. Hume, 374.

65. Orlin, 3.

66. On the status of widows, see Barbara J. Todd, "The Remarrying Widow:

A Stereotype Reconsidered," in *Women in English Society 1500–1800*, ed. Mary Prior (London: Methuen, 1985), 54–92.

67. Woodbridge, 177–79, 255–61.

68. Hume, 384.

69. Jerrold, 278. Everyone implicated in the scandals was imprisoned, most in the Tower; several members of the Howard family were put under guard; and the Duke of Norfolk, who had supported the Howard marriage, suddenly denounced Katherine Howard (Hume, 381). The attainder act against Katherine Howard that extended treason to issues of women's premarital chastity was repealed in 1547 under Edward VI (1 Edw. VI c. 12).

70. An implicit part of my larger argument is that repetition bestows familiarity on modes of thinking, and familiarity conditions persuasiveness; see Joel Altman, "'Preposterous Conclusions': Eros, *Enargeia*, and the Composition of *Othello*," *Representations* 18 (1987): 129–57.

71. Baugh, *A Literary History*, 449. A useful overview of sixteenth- and early seventeenth-century writings about the Henrician marriages and divorces relative to issues of domestic order is Chilton Latham Powell, *English Domestic Relations, 1487–1653* (New York: Columbia University Press, 1917).

72. Norman Sanders et al., *The Revels History of Drama in English*, vol. 2, *1500–1576* (London: Methuen, 1980), 137–38. For studies of classical influence in *Ralph Roister Doister* and the "Englishing" and "rationalizing" of drama, see Glynne Wickham, *Early English Stages 1300–1600*, vol. 3, *Plays and Their Makers to 1576* (London: Routledge and Kegan Paul, 1981), 200–207; and E. K. Chambers, *The Mediaeval Stage*, vol. 2 (Oxford: Oxford University Press, 1903), 451–52. On the debt of the play to classical precedents, see Norman Sanders, 216–21.

73. Gassner, *Medieval and Tudor Drama*, 264. The play is variously classified as medieval, Tudor, or Elizabethan.

74. Norman Sanders, 216. On conflicting representations of the widow in early modern drama and society, see Todd, 54–92.

75. Norman Sanders, 220.

76. Mark Breitenberg, *Anxious Masculinity in Early Modern England* (Cambridge: Cambridge University Press, 1996), 188–89. See also Katharine Eisaman Maus's discussion of the "voyeuristic satisfaction" experienced by an audience, "Horns of a Dilemma: Jealousy, Gender, and Spectatorship in English Renaissance Drama," *English Literary History* 54 (1987).

77. Nicholas Udall, *Ralph Roister Doister*, in *Medieval and Tudor Drama*, ed. John Gassner (New York: Applause, 1987), 263–345. Subsequent references are to this edition.

78. Similarly, a servant in the Howard household, Margery Morton testified that she had seen "her Majesty look out of the window to Mr. Culpeper in such sort that she thought there was love between them," which then caused Morton to "mistrust" Howard's loyalty to Henry (Hume, 378). Such scenes in the attainder and the play emphasize a social concern with the reading and misreading of what observers "see," especially regarding women's actions.

79. "Of Virginity," Juan Luis Vives, *Instruction of a Christian Woman* (1529); printed in Joan Larsen Klein, ed. *Daughters, Wives, and Widows: Writings by Men About Women and Marriage in England, 1500–1640* (Urbana: University of Illinois

Press, 1992), 103. Vives's *A Very Frutefull and Pleasant Boke called the Instruction of a Christian Woman*, written in Latin in 1523, was translated into English by Richard Hyrde in 1540.

80. Hume, 374, 381.

81. Vives, *Instruction*; quoted in Orlin, 176. On the relationship between a growing social idea of intimacy and exchanges of objects among lovers, see Ranum, 207, 232, 246–48.

82. Suresby again expresses this compulsion to tell his story in the play's conclusion: "If ye be honest, my words can hurt you nothing; / But what I heard and saw, I might not but report" (5.2.20–21). Two essential studies of ways male-male relations employ women as mediating figures are Gayle Rubin's "The Traffic in Women: Notes on the 'Political Economy' of Sex," in *Toward an Anthropology of Women*, ed. Rayna R. Reiter (New York: Monthly Review Press, 1975) 157–210; and Eve K. Sedgwick's *Between Men: English Literature and Male Homosocial Desire* (New York: Columbia University Press, 1985).

83. Donald Thomas, 52. The act was later repealed (1 Edward VI c. 12).

84. Thomas Wilson, *Arte*, 247.

85. For a discussion of observation as a means of social control among women, see Castan, who argues that women's conversations in doorways provided them with considerable knowledge of local events; they were important instruments of social control, often provoking scandal when norms were violated. "Not even thefts or secret births could remain unknown in this panoptic society, in which anonymity was so hard to come by" (417–18).

86. See Jean E. Howard, "Renaissance Antitheatricality and the Politics of Gender and Rank in *Much Ado About Nothing*," in *Shakespeare Reproduced*, ed. Jean E. Howard and Marion F. O'Connor (New York: Methuen, 1987), 176.

87. Hume, 381.

88. See Orlin: "A second clue [to the original power of the 'house'] can be located in . . . [a] synecdoche for house and correlative of wife, that is the door, signifying ownership, exclusion, and the enclosure and protection of possessions, principally including the wife" (192). Writing about European conventions, Castan finds that "In the country it was considered immoral for a man to enter another man's house when only women were home. When the door was closed at the end of the day, visits normally ceased" (412).

89. Castan, 414

90. Ranum, 232.

91. On female go-betweens, see Castan, 412.

92. Gassner, 264.

93. The Henrician acts were repealed 1 Edward VI c. 12 and 1 Mary I. The dissolution of matrimonial high treason may have had to do with the fact that after Henry VIII, no adult male served as monarch again until 1603. Succession passed from Henry in 1547 to the young Edward VI (son of Henry VIII and Jane Seymour); in 1553 to Lady Jane Grey for nine days; in 1553 to Mary I (daughter of Henry VIII and Catherine of Aragon); in 1558 to Elizabeth I (daughter of Henry VIII and Anne Boleyn); and in 1603 to James I.

Although incidents of actual petty treason may or may not have risen during the Jacobean era, popular representations increase significantly; see Frances E. Dolan,

Dangerous Familiars: Representations of Domestic Crime in England, 1550–1700 (Ithaca, N.Y.: Cornell University Press, 1994). On the links among historical and civil order, rhetorical order, and household order, see Parker, *Literary*, 125.

94. The most familiar text in such studies is *Othello*. For diverse readings, see Parker, *Shakespeare*, 227–72; Greenblatt, *Renaissance*, 222–54; Maus, *Inwardness*, 104–27; and Valerie Wayne, "Historical Differences: Misogyny and *Othello*," in *The Matter of Difference: Materialist Feminist Criticism of Shakespeare*, ed. Valerie Wayne (Ithaca, N.Y.: Cornell University Press, 1991), 153–79.

95. Gail Kern Paster, *The Body Embarrassed: Drama and the Disciplines of Shame in Early Modern England* (Ithaca, N.Y.: Cornell University Press, 1993), 244.

96. Agnew, *Worlds Apart*, 97–98.

97. Perceptive readings of *Cymbeline* in general and Posthumus's character in particular are by Douglas Peterson, (*Time, Tide, and Tempest* [San Marino, Calif.: Huntington Library, 1973]), who identifies the conventional humanist problem of "the inability to discern between truth and seeming" (119); Joan Hartwig, (*Shakespeare's Tragicomic Vision* [Baton Rouge: Louisiana State University Press, 1972]), who asserts that "to a certain extent, reality depends upon the person who perceives it, and habitual attitudes tend to narrow the individual's vision" (86); and James E. Siemon, ("Noble Virtue in *Cymbeline*," *Shakespeare Survey* 29 [1976]: 51–61), who makes the argument for Posthumus's nobility. For a reading of the play in terms of contract law and the binding power of conscience, see Jordan, "*Cymbeline*," in *Shakespeare's Monarchies*, 69–106.

For an overview of wager plots, in which a husband bets on his wife's fidelity, see J. M. Nosworthy's introduction to the Arden edition of *Cymbeline* (Cambridge, Mass.: Harvard University Press, 1955), esp. xx–xxv; and Homer Swander's "*Cymbeline* and the 'Blameless Hero,'" *English Literary History* 30 (1964): 259–70.

98. See Leah Marcus ("*Cymbeline* and the Unease of Topicality," in *The Historical Renaissance*, ed. Heather Dubrow and Richard Strier, [Chicago: University of Chicago Press, 1988]) on Cloten's use of legalisms and legal themes (144–46) and her discussion of conflicts between Roman and common law in James's efforts to establish the union with Scotland (152).

99. On the nationalism theme, see G. Wilson Knight, *The Crown of Life: Essays in Interpretation of Shakespeare's Final Plays* (1947; rpt. New York: Barnes & Noble, 1966); and Marcus, who comments that the "ruptured, then revitalized marriage of Imogen and Posthumus in *Cymbeline*, like the actual marriages engineered by James, can be linked to his higher policy of creating a united Britain out of nations and discord" (142). Allying *Cymbeline* with James's interest in "the geopolitical restructuring of Britain and in altering the mentalities of its inhabitants," Glenn Clark develops a powerful reading of the ways the play "dissects and dramatically highlights the relation between geography and a subjective sense of identity and of otherness" (230).

100. Howell, 1145.

101. On the sexually violent images of Tarquin and Tereus, see Robert S. Miola, "*Cymbeline*: Shakespeare's Valediction to Rome," in *Roman Images*, ed. Annabel Patterson (Baltimore: Johns Hopkins University Press, 1984), 51–63.

102. Georgianna Ziegler asserts that "the woman's room signifies her 'self,' and the man's forced or stealthy entry of this room constitutes a rape of her private space,"

in "'My Lady's Chamber': Female Space, Female Chastity in Shakespeare," *Textual Practice* 4,1 (Spring 1990): 71–90.

103. Baldesar Castiglione, *The Book of the Courtier*, trans. George Bull, rev. ed. (New York: Penguin, 1976), 71.

104. Barbara Herrnstein Smith, "Belief and Resistance: A Symmetrical Account," *Critical Inquiry* 18,1 (Autumn 1991): 126–27.

105. In their recent work on twentieth-century evidence, Elizabeth Loftus and Katherine Ketchum argue: "Implicit in the acceptance of this [eyewitness] testimony as solid evidence is the assumption that the human mind is a precise recorder and storer of events" (*Witness for the Defense* [New York: St. Martin's Press, 1991]), 16. According to this assumption, memories are preserved intact.

106. See Scarry: "when one encounters an object in a legal proceeding, one will be encountering it only in it aberrant condition" (296).

107. For an analysis of how Shakespeare imitates and differs from his sources in his use of the evidence, see Swander, 261–64.

108. Parker, *Shakespeare*, 238. Parker has shown that *blazon* and inventory are intended to invoke plenitude, wealth, and increase; *Literary*, 131–35. Writing about the role of Petrarchism in the history of interpretation, Nancy J. Vickers situates the *blazon* in the context of male empowerment: "bodies fetishized by a poetic voice logically do not have a voice of their own; the world of making words, of making texts, is not theirs" (265); "Diana Described: Scattered Woman and Scattered Rhyme," *Critical Inquiry* 8 (1981). Rhonda Lemke Sanford reads Iachimo's representations of Imogen in terms of the iconography of Elizabeth, gendered cartography, and the travel tale, the latter of which privileges having *seen* the territory it describes; "A Room Not One's Own: Feminine Geography in *Cymbeline*," in *Playing the Globe: Genre and Geography in English Renaissance Drama*, ed. John Gillies and Virginia Mason Vaughan (Madison, N.J.: Fairleigh Dickinson University Press, 1998), 63–85.

On rape as a form of male-male competition and its relationship to women's honor, see: Coppélia Kahn, "The Rape in Shakespeare's *Lucrece*," *Shakespeare Studies* 9 (1976); Katharine Eisaman Maus, "Taking Tropes Seriously: Language and Violence in Shakespeare's 'Rape of Lucrece,'" *Shakespeare Quarterly* 37 (1986); and Catherine Stimpson, "Shakespeare and the Soil of Rape," in *The Woman's Part: Feminist Criticism of Shakespeare*, ed. Carolyn Ruth Swift-Lenz, Gayle Greene and Carol Thomas Neely (Urbana: University of Illinois Press, 1980).

109. Christina Larner, *Witchcraft and Religion: The Politics of Popular Belief* (Oxford: Blackwell, 1984), 30.

110. Paster, 244, 253, 244–45. This emphasis on the evidentiary force of a privy mark has a distinctly national identity: "a major difference between English and virtually all other forms of witchcraft prosecutions was the almost obsessive attention authorities paid to the presence on the witch's body of a 'bigge' or mark. . ." (Paster, 247). On the interpretation of bodily marks as signs of witchcraft, see also Newman, ch. 4; and Alan Macfarlane, ed., *Witchcraft in Tudor and Stuart England* (London: Routledge and Kegan Paul, 1970).

111. Donald Thomas, 48.

112. Foucault, "Discourse," 224.

113. Howard's year of birth is variously identified between 1515 and 1523. For a

detailed overview of the question, see Lacey Baldwin Smith, *A Tudor Tragedy*, "Appendix: Catherine Howard's Birth," 209–11.

Chapter 3: Masculinity, Affiliation, and Rootlessness

1. Howell, *Cobbett's*, 1132–33. The accusation is from the indictment of the Babington conspirators.

2. Helgerson, *Forms*.

3. On the stereotype as a function of discourse, see Said, *Orientalism*, 60–63.

4. Barbara Correll, "Malleable Material, Models of Power: Women in Erasmus's 'Marriage Group' and *Civility in Boys*," *English Literary Renaissance* 57 (1990): 241. See, for example, Louis Adrian Montrose, "'Shaping Fantasies': Figurations of Gender and Power in Elizabethan Culture," in *Representing the English Renaissance* (Berkeley: University of California Press, 1988). On the wider imaginative possibilities of exemplary females in Tudor culture, see Mary Bowman, "'she there as Princess rained': Spenser's Figure of Elizabeth," *Renaissance Quarterly* 43,3 (Autumn 1990): 509–28; and Stephen Orgel, "Making Greatness Familiar," in *The Forms of Power and the Power of Forms in the Renaissance*, ed. Stephen Greenblatt (Norman: University of Oklahoma Press, 1982), 41–48.

5. Correll, 241–42.

6. John Hungerford Pollen, *Mary Queen of Scots and the Babington Plot*, Publications of the Scottish History Society 3rd ser. 3 (Edinburgh: University Press, 1922), xvii–xx. See also Wallace MacCaffrey, *Elizabeth I* (London: Edward Arnold, 1993), 342. For arguments and counterarguments that the clergy, acting independently of the king, could exercise temporal power to a spiritual end, see Sommerville, *Royalists*, 176–205. A brief sketch of the many religious groups is in Lawrence Stone, *The Crisis of the Aristocracy, 1558–1641* (Oxford: Clarendon Press, 1965), 725.

7. Pollen, civ–cvii.

8. MacCaffrey, 346.

9. MacCaffrey, 169. Among Walsingham's allies was Christopher Hatton, who in 1577 was appointed Vice Chamberlain and who presided over the Babington trials.

10. Letter from Walsingham to Elizabeth, August 5, 1586, *Calendar of Scottish Papers*, ed. William Boyd, vol. 8: 589–90; quoted in Alan Gordon Smith, *The Babington Plot* (London: Macmillan, 1936), 189. Alan G. Smith argues that the Babington plot, which was ineffectual and "harmless," was instigated by Walsingham and Burghley in order to develop a case against Mary of Scotland. Holinshed insists the accused were not tortured (909).

11. Full texts of the indictments are printed in Howell, 1141–42; and in Roger Lockyer, *Tudor and Stuart Britain, 1471–1714* (New York: St. Martin's Press, 1985), 179. Summaries appear also in Holinshed, 913–14. There were fourteen conspirators in all: John Ballard, Anthony Babington, John Savage, Robert Barnewell, Chidiock Titchburne, Thomas Salisbury, Henry Donn, Edward Abington, Charles Tilney, Edward Jones, John Travers, John Charnock, Jerome Bellamy, and Robert Gage.

12. One of the trial's great ironies is that the Babington group adopted conventions so thoroughly that they decided to have their portraits painted. Commemorating one's service had become a popular pastime. Like poets, playwrights, and players,

who were themselves copying successful merchants and theologians in signifying their "arrival" in their professions, "so too with the [Babington] adventurers, the impulse to project a contrived image of themselves for posterity could be compelling. It was not unknown for those engaged in 'underground' activities at this time to have portraits painted as memento of their endeavour. In 1586 Anthony Babington and his fellow conspirators commissioned portraits which were intended to serve as a record of their sacrificial service to Mary Queen of Scots and the Catholic cause. After the plot was exposed by Walsingham's 'intelligencers'. . . prints of these portraits were reproduced to accompany a proclamation to apprehend them on their flight—perhaps the first 'Wanted' posters in English history"; Roberts, "The 'Studious Artizan,'" 29.

13. Howell, 1138.

14. Howell, 1131. The indictment also includes sedition and insurrection, and subversion of "the true and Christian religion."

15. Howell, 1130.

16. Yi-Fu Tuan employs these lines to explain, "In *Richard II*, Shakespeare succeeds in evoking a sense of patriotic fervor partly though the insistent use of 'this,' which is identified with 'we the English. . . .' 'This happy breed of men, this little world, this precious stone. . . .' A distinction that all people recognize is between 'us' and 'them.' We are *here*; we are *this* happy breed of men. They are *there*; they are not fully human and they live in *that* place"; *Space and Place: The Perspective of Experience* (Minneapolis: University of Minnesota Press, 1977), 49–50.

17. Howell 1130, 1137, 1175. The same kind of language characterized those working for the Crown. Nicholas Berden, a spy *for* Walsingham, vowed "Whensoever any occasion shall be offered wherein I may adventure some rare and desperate exploit such as may be for the honour of my country and my own credit, you shall always find me resolute and ready to perform the same"; quoted in Alison Plowden, *The Elizabethan Secret Service* (New York: St. Martin's Press, 1991), 106.

18. Castiglione, *The Book*, 57. Originally published in Venice in 1528, Castiglione's work was translated into English in 1561 by Thomas Hoby. The roles of the courtier expressed by Castiglione for his Italian audience and translated into English by Hoby are made more complex when we focus on the idea of the counselor in England. In Thomas More's *Utopia*, for example, Hythloday equates royal service with slavery and scorns the fawning that accompanies being a counselor; see Thomas More, *Utopia*, trans. Paul Turner (Harmondsworth: Penguin, 1961), Book 1, 41–42.

19. Thomas Wilson, *Arte*, 247. On the early modern linking of martial courage with manliness, see also Woodbridge, *Women*, 159–68.

20. Cicero, *Works*, 46.135.

21. Howell, 1130, 1144. Historically, Leicester proved a poor military leader. Appointed supreme commander of an expeditionary force to the Netherlands in 1585, he "could not resist the opportunity to enact the role of chivalric hero in earnest. Unfortunately, the Netherlands expedition only exposed his inadequacies in that role"; see Richard C. McCoy, *The Rites of Knighthood: The Literature and Politics of Elizabethan Chivalry* (Berkeley: University of California Press, 1989), 46–47.

22. Holinshed, 924.

23. See also Anthony Miller, who shows that imputations of ease were part of a militant Protestant rhetoric that found Elizabeth's policy of defense without conquest unacceptable; "Domains of Victory: Staging and Contesting the Roman Triumph in

Renaissance England," in *Playing the Globe: Genre and Geography in English Renaissance Drama*, ed. John Gillies and Virginia Mason Vaughan (Madison, N.J.: Fairleigh Dickinson University Press, 1998), 260–87. Links between authentic service and loyal English manhood are also suggested by the form of *Holinshed's Chronicles*. Holinshed places the report of the Babington group's capture just before a detailed report about "sir Francis Drake knight," who is returning "after manie feats of good service accomplished in forren countries" and whose "valor did induce us into this remembrance" (905–906). Later, immediately following the report of the Babington indictments and pleadings, Holinshed turns to the heroic military death of national hero Sir Philip Sidney (926).

24. Helgerson, *Forms*, 51–52. See also McCoy, *The Rites*, 2–3.

25. Bellamy, *Tudor Law*, 25.

26. Bellamy, *Tudor Law* 70, 26–27.

27. Howell, 1135, 1140.

28. Howell, 1152.

29. Howell, 1153, 1155.

30. Howell, 1153.

31. Howell, 1136. Holinshed takes Titchburne's scaffold speech as the cue to reiterate the greatness of the queen: "In this man's confession thus much is to be observed, that in comparing his offence to Adam's, was implied a resembling of her highness to the pleasant and glorious fruit, so precious in God's eyes, as he forbade Adam and all others to lay violent hands upon. And thus by the mouth of her enemies, God causeth her sacred excellencie to be blazed" (917).

32. Similar representations of youthful males' victimization punctuate prosecutor Hatton's diatribes on priests: "The inventors and beginners [of these treasons] were these devilish priests and seminaries, . . . who, now-a-days, do not go about to seduce the antient and discreet men, for they (as the priests say) be too cold; but they assail, with their persuasions, the younger sort, and of those, the most ripe wits, whose high hearts and ambitious minds do carry them headlong to all wickedness" (Howell, 1140–41). On the "Romish theme" as the cause of all treasons, see also Holinshed, 903, for example. Wallace MacCaffrey (353–54) argues that the events of the Babington treasons "marked a division within English Roman Catholic ranks," which involved resident Catholic gentry who were not disposed to revolt against the queen and who were seeking an accommodation. An overview of the meanings of "atheism" in the period is in David Riggs, "Marlowe's Quarrel with God," in *Marlowe, History, and Sexuality*, ed. Paul Whitfield White (New York: AMS Press, 1998), 15–37. For a reading of treason as a mystified category that overcomes the victim's volition, see Steven Mullaney, *The Place of the Stage: License, Play and Power in Renaissance England* (Chicago: University of Chicago Press, 1988), 116–34.

33. See Altman, "Preposterous," 130.

34. Howell, 1130.

35. "The Homily on Marriage," quoted in Henderson and McManus, *Half Humankind*, 78.

36. Howell, 1129–30, 1131, 1132, 1134, 1133.

37. Howell, 1132 and passim.

38. For an argument that trade and travel narratives typically expressed a widespread discomfort and ambiguity about the island's relationship to other countries,

see Richmond Barbour, "Britain and the Great Beyond: *The Masque of Blackness* at Whitehall," in *Playing the Globe: Genre and Geography in English Renaissance Drama*, ed. John Gillies and Virginia Mason Vaughan (Madison, N.J.: Fairleigh Dickinson University Press, 1998), 129–53. In the *Arte of Rhetorique*, Thomas Wilson takes the position that travel to foreign countries is good for developing a healthy English person (78).

39. Although the government claimed it was prosecuting "traitors" whose national loyalty was suspect, dissident writers claimed it was often prosecuting itinerant Catholic missionaries under the guise of treason; itinerancy itself was cause for suspicion; Arnold Pritchard, *Catholic Loyalism in Elizabethan England* (Chapel Hill: University of North Carolina Press, 1979), 8–9.

40. Compare John Wheeler in *A Treatise of Commerce* (1601), who described mercantile exchange between England and Barbary as a "promiscuous, straggling, and dispersed trade"; quoted in Barbara Sebek, "'Strange Outlandish Wealth': Transglobal Commerce in *The Merchant's Mappe of Commerce* and *The Fair Maid of the West, Parts I and II*," in *Playing the Globe: Genre and Geography in English Renaissance Drama*, ed. John Gillies and Virginia Mason Vaughan (Madison, N.J.: Fairleigh Dickinson University Press, 1998), 177.

41. Howell, 1149.

42. The dispute reiterates some of the themes present in constitutionalist arguments and illuminates a contest between civil and common lawyers. Bacon, like civil lawyers, tended to prefer Roman theories of law. Under the influence of continental values and humanist criticisms of English common law as "barbaric" and uncertain, civil lawyers argued that the monarch was superior to the law; their model was Justinian's *Institutes*, written laws that stood for a certain formal order and a certain conception of authority. The governing ideas were that law should be written (so as to be certain), should deal with private law, and should avoid taking up public law, which was the rightful jurisdiction of the monarch. Common lawyers like Coke preferred homegrown English case law. Defining and defending English law against the Romanists, common lawyers argued that the historical practices in common law cases and the decisions of judges were authoritative; that even monarchs were subject to law; that writing the law was merely setting down what judges had already determined; and that law in England rightfully took up both private and public law. On the English reception of Roman law, see McIlwain, *Constitutionalism*, 41–66. See also J. H. Baker, *An Introduction To English Legal History* (London: Butterworths, 1990); and Helgerson, esp. ch. 2, "Writing the Law."

43. Howell, 1130. The argument about the "lawful" has an immediate relevance to the contemporary religious tensions and the growing body of interrogation of the rights of subjects to respond to monarchs. In early modern papalist theory, an act of deposition, like the bull issued against Elizabeth in 1570, "absolved subjects from their civil allegiance. A king who continued to exercise power after deposition was nothing more than a usurping tyrant, and could be assassinated by anyone" (Sommerville, 185). Protestant theorists like Calvin also viewed resistance to monarchs as lawful: "earthly princes when they rise up against God abdicate their authority, nay even become unworthy of being reckoned in the number of men" (John Calvin, Commentary on the Book of Daniel, *Works*, 5:91; cited in McIlwain, 96).

44. Howell, 1149.

45. Howell, 1147.

46. Howell, 1147. According to John Bellamy, "a meeting of judges and law officers of the crown in 1556 decided that in cases of treason under statute (which meant under sixteenth-century statute, since in their eyes the 1352 statute was only a declaration of common law treason), two accusers should always be at the indictment. But if the offense was within the act of 1352, the appearance of witness-accusers was unnecessary since the common law operated by jury and witness [that is, written document], not by accusers"; *Tudor Law*, 77.

47. Howell, 1147.

48. Howell, 1145, 1151.

49. Howell, 1150. According to Alan Gordon Smith, both Abington and Tilney were opposed to the assassination of Elizabeth and proposed instead that she be carried off to some safe place and there advised "to grant toleration in religion, if not reformation." The plan would accomplish the main goals: preserving the queen's health and life, removing her from a circle of undesirable counselors, and replacing them with other advisors (23).

50. Howell, 1148.

51. Howell, 1143.

52. Thomas Andrew Green, *Verdict According to Conscience* (Chicago: University of Chicago Press, 1985), 27–28. On the view that religion was primarily an issue of political policy, and that only a few cared about it as an aspect of salvation, see Stone, 726–27.

53. On the decline of belief in providentialist historiography, see Dollimore, *Radical Tragedy*; Greenblatt, *Sir Walter Ralegh*, esp. ch. 5; and Rackin, *Stages*.

54. Thomas Wilson, 358. Wilson often makes an imaginative link between the forms of judicial oration and the example of treason. Here is Wilson's example of the judicial category "Of the state Legall":

> Assertion.
> Thou has committed treason in this facte.
> Aunswere.
> I denye it to be treason.
> State or issue.
> Whether his offence done maye be called treason or no. Here is denied that any suche thing is in the dede done, as is by word reported, and saide to bee. (191–92)

55. Howell, 1136.

56. Barbara Herrnstein Smith, "Belief and Resistance," 128.

57. William Perkins, *Christian Oeconomie* (1618), *Works*, vol. 3, trans. Thomas Pickering; quoted in Belsey, *The Subject*, 110. On the idea of personal conscience as a "space in which to know the will of God and from which to disobey the will of the sovereign," see also David Little, *Religion, Order, and Law: A Study in Pre-Revolutionary England* (Oxford: Blackwell, 1970), 87. An overview of the main lines of development in the function of conscience is in *The New Bible Dictionary*, ed. J. D. Douglas (Grand Rapids, Mich.: Eerdmans, 1962), 250.

58. Holinshed, 909.

59. Howell, 1139.

60. Howell, 1139.

61. Howell, 1138.

62. Howell, 1139.

63. Howell, 1156. The second group was executed the next day.

64. On the background of St. Giles, with its mix of noble and unsavory activities, see William Denton, *Records of St. Giles' Cripplegate* (London: George Bell, 1883); and Rowland Dobie, *History of the United Parishes of St. Giles-in-the-Fields and St. George, Bloomsbury* (London: Henry Bickers Press, 1834).

65. Howell, 1155, 1157.

66. See Cunningham, "Renaissance Execution," 209–22.

67. John Bakeless, *The Tragicall History of Christopher Marlowe*, 2 vols. (Cambridge, Mass.: Harvard University Press, 1942), 27. On Marlowe's legal entanglements, see Frederick S. Boas, *Christopher Marlowe: A Biographical and Critical Study*, rev. ed. (Oxford: Clarendon Press, 1953); and Charles Nicholl, "'Faithful Dealing': Marlowe and the Elizabethan Intelligence Service," in *Marlowe, History, and Sexuality: New Critical Essays on Christopher Marlowe*, ed. Paul Whitfield White (New York: AMS Press, 1998), 1–13; and *The Reckoning: The Murder of Christopher Marlowe* (Chicago: University of Chicago Press, 1992). "The Baines note" contains claims by Richard Baines against Marlowe for sexual, religious, and political deviance; see C. F. Tucker Brooke, *The Life of Marlowe and the Tragedy of Dido Queen of Carthage* (London: Methuen, 1930), 98–100.

68. Holinshed, 911.

69. Holinshed, 922–23.

70. Nicholl, *The Reckoning*, 8. See also Conyers Read, *Mr. Secretary Walsingham and the Policy of Queen Elizabeth*, 3 vols. (Oxford: Clarendon Press, 1925).

71. Nicholl, "Faithful," 6. Nicholl points out that among the men who went from Cambridge to Rheims was John Ballard, who was ordained in Rheims in the early 1580s and who became the prime-mover of the Babington plot (7–8). Tracing a charge of treason against Marlowe for coining in the Netherlands in 1592, Nicholl argues for Marlowe's status as double agent and provocateur; see "'At Middleborough': Some Reflections on Marlowe's Visit to the Low Countries in 1592," in *Christopher Marlowe and English Renaissance Culture*, ed. Darryll Grantley and Peter Roberts (Hants: Scolar Press, 1996), 38–50.

For a brief consideration of the ways traditional authorities sought to control what they perceived as threatening gatherings of young men, see Dollimore, "Transgression," 72–87.

Summary discussions of the legal status of Catholics are in David Jardine, ed., *Criminal Trials . . . During the Reigns of Queen Elizabeth and James I* (London: M. A. Nattali, 1947), 2:7–8; and Pritchard.

72. Roberts, 24–25. Nicholl, in "Faithful" (4), prints a copy of the letter.

73. Roberts, 35, n.28. See also Nicholl, "Faithful," 5–9; and Millar MacLure, *Marlowe: The Critical Heritage, 1588–1896* (London: Routledge and Kegan Paul, 1979).

74. Thomas Wilson, 239.

75. For a study of the play as a "drama of empire, played 'out there' in the infinite regions of the East," see Emily Bartels, *Spectacles of Strangeness: Imperialism, Alienation, and Marlowe* (Philadelphia: University of Pennsylvania Press, 1993), 53–81.

76. Marlowe's most explicit articulation of the terms of treason, especially imag-

ining the death of the king, is in *Edward II*. Like Tamburlaine, who encourages Cosroe, "Think thee invested now as royally. . ." (2.5.2), Gaveston resists the attacking noblemen, "No, threaten not, my lord, but pay them home! / Were I a king— " (1.4.25–27). Edward repeatedly refers to his own status in conditional terms: "If I be king, not one of them shall live" (1.4.105); "If I be England's king. . ." (3.2.135). Spenser exhorts Edward to resist Gaveston's murder, "Were I King Edward, England's sovereign, / Son to the lovely Eleanor of Spain, / Great Edward Longshanks' issue." (3.2.10–12).

77. Tamburlaine's character is read most often as ambiguous and composed of extremes. See, for example, David Bevington, *From "Mankind" to Marlowe: Growth of Structure in the Popular Drama of Tudor England* (Cambridge, Mass.: Harvard University Press, 1962); William Godshalk, *The Marlovian World Picture* (The Hague: Mouton, 1974); and Simon Shepherd, *Marlowe and the Politics of Elizabethan Theatre* (London: Harvester Press, 1986), esp. 151–52. For speculation that Marlowe takes Sir Walter Ralegh as a prototype for Tamburlaine, see Eleanor Grace Clark, *Ralegh and Marlowe: A Study in Elizabethan Fustian* (New York: Russell & Russell, 1965), 396–413.

78. David Lowenthal, *The Past Is a Foreign Country* (Cambridge: Cambridge University Press, 1986).

79. Harry Levin, *The Overreacher: A Study of Christopher Marlowe* (Cambridge, Mass.: Harvard University Press, 1952), 38. Levin contrasts the prowess-driven *Tamburlaine* with the policy-driven *Jew of Malta* and *Massacre at Paris*. Sara Munson Deats argues that in the play's central plot "personifying majesty becomes synonymous with personifying masculinity"; *Sex, Gender, and Desire in the Plays of Christopher Marlowe* (Newark: University of Delaware Press, 1997).

The consistent counter to the emphasis on manly battle is Mycetes, whom Marlowe associates with evasive maneuvers. See, for example, 1.1.57–61; 2.2.59–71; and 2.4.20–22.

80. Thomas Wilson, 142–43.

81. Quoted in Thomas Cartelli, *Marlowe, Shakespeare, and the Economy of Theatrical Experience* (Philadelphia: University of Pennsylvania Press, 1991), 115.

82. See also Mycetes' lines (treated ironically by Marlowe) as he faces Cosroe's ridicule: "O where is duty and allegiance now?" (1.1.101).

83. In emphasizing a shared language of battle through which affiliations are mediated, Marlowe differs from his contemporary historical situation, in which "English" war was a multinational and multilingual activity. See Nick De Somogyi, "Marlowe's Maps of War," in *Christopher Marlowe and English Renaissance Culture*, ed. Darryll Grantley and Peter Roberts (Hants: Scolar Press, 1996), 96–109.

84. On the complexities of interpreting early modern representations of same-sex relationships and the social meanings of "sodomy," see: Alan Bray, *Homosexuality in Renaissance England* (London: Gay Men's Press, 1982); Jonathan Goldberg, *Sodometries: Renaissance Texts, Modern Sexualities* (Stanford, Calif.: Stanford University Press, 1992); Bruce Smith, *Homosexual Desire in Shakespeare's England: A Cultural Poetics* (Chicago: University of Chicago Press, 1991); Gregory Bredbeck, *Sodomy and Interpretation: Marlowe to Milton* (Ithaca, N.Y.: Cornell University Press, 1991); Valerie Traub, *Desire and Anxiety: Circulations of Sexuality in Shakespearean Drama* (London: Routledge, 1992); and Stephen Orgel, *Impersonations: The Performance of Gender in Shakespeare's England* (Cambridge: Cambridge University Press, 1996).

Marlowe's work in general, and *Edward II* in particular, have drawn attention.

See Michael Hattaway, "Christopher Marlowe: Ideology and Subversion," in *Christopher Marlowe and English Renaissance Culture*, ed. Darryll Grantley and Peter Roberts (Hants: Scolar Press, 1996), 198–223; Mario DiGangi, "Marlowe, Queer Studies, and Renaissance Homoeroticism," in *Marlowe, History, and Sexuality: New Critical Essays on Christopher Marlowe*, ed. Paul Whitfield White (New York: AMS Press, 1998), 195–212; Lawrence Normand, " 'What Passions Call You These?': *Edward II* and James VI," in *Christopher Marlowe and English Renaissance Culture*, ed. Darryll Grantley and Peter Roberts (Hants: Scolar Press, 1996), 172–97. Simon Shepherd argues for seeing Marlowe's texts "as problematising the male and masculinity (much of which has been hidden by the 'explanation' of sodomy)" (179).

For a discussion of representations of women in relation to shifting meanings of male friendship and service, see Lorna Hutson, *The Usurer's Daughter: Male Friendship and Fictions of Women in Sixteenth-Century England* (London: Routledge, 1994).

85. Traub, 111–14.

86. Both Phyllis Rackin ("Historical Difference," 40–41) and Bruce Smith (171) have noted that male friendship often was perceived as enhancing rather than detracting from manliness.

Among additional specific claims to friendship in this play are the following: Tamburlaine tells Theridamas: "These are my friends, in whom I more rejoice, / Than doth the king of Persia in his crown" (1.2.240–41). Tamburlaine invites his men to ride to Persepolis: "What says my other friends? Will you be kings?" (2.5.67). And Techelles responds to Tamburlaine's vision of the "sweet fruition of an earthly crown": "that made us, the friends of Tamburlaine, / To lift our swords against the Persian king" (2.7.17–35).

87. Castiglione, 137–38.

88. Howell, 1153.

89. The scene is often interpreted as a "wooing" scene. See, for example, Simon Shepherd's reading of it as "the sexualising of the male" in "the temptation of Theridamas" that results in an implied "betrothal" (202).

90. Orgel, 25. Orgel is explaining the perception that women are dangerous to men "because sexual passion for women renders men effeminate: this is an age in which sexuality itself is misogynistic, as the love of women threatens the integrity of perilously achieved male identity. . . . The fear of effeminization is a central element in all discussions of what constitutes a 'real man' in the period, and the fantasy of the reversal of the natural transition from woman to man underlies it" (26).

91. Mark Breitenberg argues that gender instability is the basis of male subjectivity: "If masculine identity is largely constructed as a desiring subject, a subject in pursuit, then the very condition of the masculinity is also the source of its potential destruction. Or, in other terms, desire is the basis of masculinity *and* emasculation, the form of differentiating a masculine subjectivity *and* the potential source of its dissolution into nothing" (*Anxious*, 166).

On the relationships between masculine identity and repudiations or idealizations of women, see: Rubin, "The Traffic," 157–210; Sedgwick, *Between Men*; and Coppélia Kahn, *Man's Estate: Masculine Identity in Shakespeare* (Berkeley: University of California Press, 1981).

92. David Daiches focuses on desire and language in this scene: "This disparity between desire and achievement is for Marlowe part of the human condition, and this

being so, it is in the expression of desire rather than in accomplishing the achievement that man reveals his most striking qualities"; "Language and Action in Marlowe's *Tamburlaine*," in *More Literary Essays* (Edinburgh: Oliver and Boyd, 1968), 46.

93. Marlowe returns to this issue of mutual relations between place and character in *Edward II*. From Gaveston's powerful imaging of the city of London—"The sight of London to my exiled eyes / Is as Elysium to a new-come soul; / Not that I love the city or the men, / But that it harbors him I hold so dear" (1.1.10–13)—to Edward's resignation in the play's final scene—"Whither you will, all places are alike, / And every earth is fit for burial" (5.1.145–46)—Marlowe develops a complex representation of the ways the presence of characters (including their presence to each other) organizes meaningful space. See also, for example, 1.1.152–53; 1.4.48–50; 1.4.117; 2.2.218–20; 2.4.17–18; and 5.1.2.

94. Greenblatt, *Renaissance*, 197. Contextualizing *Tamburlaine* among ethnographic discourses, Bartels (56–57) refutes Greenblatt's emphasis on the cosmic homelessness of Marlowe's figures. For a reading of *Tamburlaine*'s travel issues as reflecting the interests of merchants and the recapitalization of joint stock companies, see Richard Wilson, "Visible Bullets: *Tamburlaine the Great* and Ivan the Terrible," in *Christopher Marlowe and English Renaissance Culture*, ed. Darryll Grantley and Peter Roberts (Hants: Scolar Press, 1996), 51–69.

95. Gillies, "Marlowe, the *Timor* Myth, and the Motives of Geography," in *Playing the Globe: Genre and Geography in English Renaissance Drama*, ed. John Gillies and Virginia Mason Vaughan (Madison, N.J.: Fairleigh Dickinson University Press, 1998), 203 and 207. For additional comments on the relationships between the motif of cartographic expansion and a set of more ritually-based paradigms of spatial practice, see Gillies "Introduction: Elizabethan Drama and the Cartographizations of Space" (40) in the same edition.

96. Thomas Wilson, 45–46. Wilson is expanding on Quintilian's rules for praising. This kind of link between character and place afforded rhetoricians such as Wilson an opportunity to expand on the relations between particular soils and the men they produce. In discussing ways to prove things by conjecture, he declares: "The countrey where the man was borne declares sometime his natural inclination, as if he wer borne or brought up emong the Tindale, and Riddesdale menne, he may the soner be suspected" (193). Following this with his example of "oration judiciall" about a solider accused of a heinous crime, he writes: "Neither is he onelye knowen universallye to be nought, but his soyle also (where he was borne) giveth him to be an evill man: consideringe he was bredde and brought up emong a denne of theves, emonge the men of Tindale and Ryddesdale, where pillage is good purchase, and murderynge is counted manhood" (197).

97. Such key terms as "country," "empire," "Persia," and "Africa" are conveniently surveyed in *A Concordance to the Plays, Poems, and Translations of Christopher Marlowe*, ed. Robert J. Fehrenbach, Lea Ann Boone, and Mario A. Di Cesare (Ithaca, N.Y.: Cornell University Press, 1982).

98. On contemporary fears of foreign insurgencies and *Edward II* see Mark Thornton Burnett, "*Edward II* and Elizabethan Politics," in *Marlowe, History, and Sexuality: New Critical Essays on Christopher Marlowe*, ed. Paul Whitfield White (New York: AMS Press, 1998), 91–107.

There was considerable government anxiety about disaffected itinerant soldiers.

In 1586 and 1587, the Privy Council associated soldiers returning from Leicester's troops in the Netherlands with a potentially threatening aimlessness. By 1587, although the captains serving in the Netherlands had been paid, Elizabeth's treasury was thin, and the captains defrauded their men. "'Great numbers of private soldiers,' it was reported from England, 'come over in lamentable case, alleging for their defense, when they are charged as vagabonds and threatened to be punished . . . that their captains have paid them neither wages nor lendings, but have also disarmed them, and sent them away without any food, money or passport'"; quoted in J. E. Neale, *Essays in Elizabethan History* (New York: St. Martin's Press, 1958), 198.

99. Among other related meanings, the *OED* includes: "inclined to stray or gad about without proper occupation; leading an unsettled, irregular, or disreputable life; good-for-nothing; rascally; worthless"; "characteristic of a homeless wanderer"; "roving, straying, not subject to control or restraint." The term's second primary meaning is: "One who has no fixed abode or home, who wanders about from place to place, *specifically* one who does this without regular occupation or obvious means of support; an itinerant beggar, idle loafer, or tramp; a vagrant."

100. Gillies, "Marlowe," 210–11.

101. Yi-Fu Tuan, 4–5.

102. Yi-Fu Tuan, 162.

Chapter 4: Secrecy and the Epistolary Self

1. Neale, *Essays*, 117.

2. Howell, *Cobbett's*, 1195. Responding to news that the Commission had pronounced her guilty, Mary said: "That the English had many time slaughtered their kings; no marvel, therefore, if they now also shew their cruelty upon me, that am issued from the blood of their kings" (Howell, 1201). Abbott writes that Edmund Plowden reportedly advised Justice Anthony Browne in the preparation of two books written on behalf of Mary's claim to the English throne (*Law Reporting*, 200).

3. Full texts of the indictments are printed in Howell, 1141–42; and Lockyer, *Tudor*, 179. See also Holinshed, *Chronicles*, 923–25; and Jayne Lewis, *The Trial of Mary Queen of Scots: A Brief History with Documents* (New York: St. Martin's Press, 1999).

4. Scholars associate this shift with such historical changes as the development of printing presses, reforms in religion, and rises in literacy. See, for example, Walter J. Ong, *The Presence of the Word: Some Prolegomena for Cultural and Religious History* (New Haven, Conn.: Yale University Press, 1967); and Barbara J. Shapiro, *A Culture*.

5. Howell, 1145.

6. Lacey Baldwin Smith, *Treason in*, 44.

7. A convenient overview of letters among other stage props is in Frances Teague, *Shakespeare's Speaking Properties* (Lewisburg, Pa.: Bucknell University Press, 1991), Appendix A, 158–93.

8. Discussions of *The Spanish Tragedy* have generally focused on the play as a model of revenge tragedy, as an early modern example of Senecan drama, and as the introduction of the first Machiavel to the English stage. See J. R. Mulryne, "Introduction" to Thomas Kyd, *The Spanish Tragedy*, New Mermaids, 2nd. ed (London: A & C

Black, 1989), xviiff.; and Fredson T. Bowers, *Elizabethan Revenge Tragedy* (Princeton, N.J.: Princeton University Press, 1940). In these discussions, what Thomas McAlindon (*English Renaissance Tragedy* [Vancouver: University of British Columbia Press, 1986]), terms "quite the most important single play in the history of English drama" (55) is generally assimilated into a tradition of generic concerns.

9. See MacCaffrey, *Elizabeth I*, 342.

10. MacCaffrey, 351.

11. Mary became the focus of political and religious discontent: in the 1560's the Northern Rebellion developed; in 1570 the Pope issued a bull deposing Elizabeth which effectively pitted international Catholicism against Protestant England; beginning with the Ridolfi plot of 1572, Mary was connected to plan after plan allegedly made to assassinate Elizabeth; the St. Bartholomew's Day massacre in France in 1572, in which Catholics overthrew the Protestant rulers, lent renewed fervor to fears among the English of widespread anti-Elizabethan conspiracies (Neale, *Essays*, 117–18). A summary of treason legislation that seems spurred at least in part by Mary is in Bellamy, *Tudor Law*, 68–73.

12. Howell, 1153.

13. Howell, 1162. In her first speech (November 12, 1586) to the Parliamentary petitioners urging Mary's execution, Elizabeth acknowledges the bond "most thankfully," recognizes the "singular zeal and affection" of the signatories, and assures Parliament that she "never knew of it until three thousand hands with seals thereof were brought and showed unto [her] at Hampton Court"; see *Elizabeth I: Collected Works*, ed. Leah S. Marcus, Janel Mueller, and Mary Beth Rose (Chicago: University of Chicago Press, 2000), 189. The emphasis on speaking with a collective identity is apparent also in the Commissioners' advice to Elizabeth to execute Mary following the trial: "judging that both the welfare and hurt of the prince belongeth to all, [they] concurred again with one voice in the same opinion," that Mary must be executed; they advised Mary's execution "with one voice and mind making humble and instant suit for the same" (Howell, 1195, 1198).

14. That not all members of Parliament shared this position is evidenced by William Parry's fate. After speaking out against a law inspired by the Bond, Parry was arrested, tried, found guilty of treason, and executed March 2, 1585; see Neale, *Elizabeth I*, 39.

15. Howell, 1168. See also MacCaffrey, 344.

16. Howell, 1162. A description of the complicated formula employed in selecting the special commissioners in the Scots case is in Bellamy, *Tudor Law*, 123.

17. Howell, 1197–98.

18. Howell, 1169. Throughout her captivity, she "could not enjoy the protection or benefit of the laws of England; nay, I could never yet understand from any man, what manner of laws those were" (Howell, 1169).

19. Howell, 1169. Howell reports Mary's additional comments: "That she was no subject, and rather would she die a thousand deaths, than acknowledge herself a subject, considering, that by such an acknowledgement, she should both prejudice the height of regal majesty, and withal confess herself to be bound by all the laws of England, even in matter of religion" (1169). Mary refuses (rightfully, according to most historians) to recognize the authority of the unique act under which she is being ac-

cused: "the authority of their delegation was founded upon a late law made to intrap" her, she claimed (Howell, 1171).

20. Quoted in Stefan Zweig, *Mary Queen of Scotland and the Isles*, trans. Eden and Cedar Paul (New York: Viking, 1935), 325. These are absolutist ideas from "an absolute queen" about the sanctity of monarchy, and Mary's evocations of them again mark her as an alien, allying her more closely with the Scots notion of the monarch's superior authority than with the English notion of the monarch's relative prerogatives; see Sommerville, *Royalists*, 51.

21. See Kantorowicz, *The King's*, 7–23. Kantorowicz aims to clarify "sometimes confusing distinctions between the *K*ing's sempiternity and the *k*ing's temporariness, between his immaterial and immortal body politic and his material and mortal body natural" (20–21). Marie Axton argues that "the development and popularization of the theory [of the King's two bodies] are inextricably connected with the Elizabethan succession question, with its polemics and with its reflection in dramatic art" (x). See Axton, *The Queen's*.

22. Howell, 1171. Echoing the repeated theme of moots in assimilating and repelling the stranger, English treason legislation anticipated the stranger's appearance in national betrayals. In April 1557, Englishman Thomas Stafford landed at Scarborough, seized the castle, and announced his claim to the throne. With him had come a Frenchman, John Sherlles. When the legal question arose whether Sherlles could be tried for treason, the judges had decided that "an alien, born in a country at peace with England at the time of his offense, who should levy war alongside English traitors, had in fact committed treason"; see Bellamy, *Tudor Law*, 60.

23. Howell, 1173–74.

24. Howell, 1174.

25. See Jerome McGann, *A Critique of Modern Textual Criticism* (1983; rpt. Charlottesville: University of Virginia Press, 1992), 90.

26. Howell, 1174.

27. Howell, 1176–1177. Mary continues: "Babington might confess what he list, but it was an open lye, that she had devised such means to escape."

28. See, for example, Henderson and McManus, *Half Humankind*.

29. Thomas Wilson, *Arte*, 46.

30. Howell, 1178. On conventional gender lines and women's familiarity with martial strategies, see Castiglione, *The Book*, 216–17.

31. Howell, 1181–82.

32. Alison Plowden, *The Elizabethan*, 100. J. B. Black describes Walsingham's method of intercepting the letters, which involved wrapping them in "a waterproof case, inserted through the bung into a cask of ale"; *The Reign of Elizabeth, 1558–1603* (Oxford: Clarendon Press, 1936), 328–29. Walsingham's role in the conspiracy has been long debated. What seems evident is that he refused to allow Anthony Babington to leave the country a few weeks earlier, when Babington applied to him for a license to leave. And he was instrumental in arranging the passage and interception of Mary's correspondence during the time leading up to the Babington plot; see MacCaffrey, 345–46.

33. Howell, 1177.

34. Howell, 1180.

35. Patterson, *Censorship*, 216.

36. Howell, 1174.

37. Erasmus, *De recta Graeci et Latini sermonis pronunciatione*, in *Scribes and Sources: Handbook of the Chancery Hand in the Sixteenth Century: Texts from the Writing Masters*, ed. A. S. Osley (Boston: David R. Godine, 1980), 30; quoted in Jonathan Goldberg, *Writing Matter: From the Hands of the English Renaissance* (Stanford, Calif.: Stanford University Press, 1990), 278. Subsequent notes indicate my debt to Goldberg's *Writing Matter*, which considers how "the history of the secretaryship participates" in "the production of the individual as something accomplished through writing within its differentiated domains" (257). See also Michel Foucault, "What Is an Author?" in *Language, Counter-Memory, Practice*, ed. Donald F. Bouchard, trans. Donald F. Bouchard and Sherry Simon (Ithaca, N.Y.: Cornell University Press, 1977), 113–38. Annabel Patterson's chapter, "Letters to Friends: The Self in Familiar Form" (*Censorship*, 211–40), traces shifting meanings of letters in the sixteenth and early seventeenth centuries.

38. Goldberg, *Writing*, 266, citing Angell Day, *The English Secretary*, 101–133.

39. Goldberg, *Writing*, 248.

40. Erasmus, *De recta Graeci*, 30; quoted in Goldberg, *Writing*, 277. See also David Aers, *Culture and History, 1350–1660: Essays on English Communities, Identities, and Writing* (Detroit: Wayne State University Press, 1992).

41. William Fulwood, *The Enemy of Idlenesse* (London, 1621), 1–2; quoted in Goldberg, *Writing*, 249.

42. Foucault, "What Is an Author?" 115.

43. Angell Day, *The English Secretary* (1599), 1; quoted in Goldberg, *Writing*, 251. Day writes: "A Letter . . . is that wherein is expreslye conveied in writing, the intent and meaning of one man, immediately to passe and be directed to another, and for the certaine respects thereof, is termed the messenger and familiar speeche of the absent" (Goldberg, *Writing*, 251). For the "new criticism" statement on intentionality in writing, see W. K. Wimsatt and Monroe C. Beardsley, "The Intentional Fallacy," in *Critical Theory Since Plato*, ed. Hazard Adams, rev. ed. (New York: Harcourt, 1992), 944–951.

44. Howell, 1183. Mary continues: "The circumstances may be proved but never the fact; Her integrity depended not upon the credit and memory of her Secretaries, though she knew them to be honest and sincere men. Yet if they have confessed any thing out of fear of torments or hope of reward and [?], it was not to be admitted, for just causes, which she would alledge elsewhere. . . . Letters may be directed to others, than those to whom they are written, and many things have been often inserted, which she never dictated. If her papers had not been taken away, and she had her Secretary, she could better confute the things objected against her" (Howell, 1183).

She later attacks her secretaries' allegiance and claims that their subjectivity is compromised by their betrayal: "As for her Secretaries, seeing they had done contrary to their duty and allegiance sworn unto her, they deserved no credit. Neither did these men think themselves bounden by any oath whatsoever in court of conscience, forasmuch as they had sworn their fidelity and secrecy to her before, and were no subjects of England" (Howell, 1187).

For a discussion of the ways accusations of treason could disrupt the conventional apprentice-master hierarchy within the family, see Craig A. Bernthal, "Treason in the Family: The Trial of Thumpe v. Horner," *Shakespeare Quarterly* 42,1 (Spring 1991): 44–54.

45. Howell, 1208.

46. For an overview of Renaissance interpretations of presence in writing, see Ong. On fidelity and transcription, see Parker, *Shakespeare*, 149–84. Mary's physical presence seems to be a recurring problem. It is a submerged theme in Elizabeth's speech to Parliament in November 1586 explaining "why [she] did not deal by the course of the common law of the realm" with Mary: "I know very well the same to be sufficient, for God forbid that the ancient law should be defective to punish a person which should offend in so high a degree. But you, my masters of the law, are so fine—you regard so much the words, syllables, and letters thereof more than the true sense and meaning indeed—that oftentimes you make the same to seem absurd. For if I should have followed that course of the commonlaw, forsooth, she must have been indicted by a jury of twelve men in Staffordshire. She must have held up her hand and openly been arraigned at a bar, which had been a proper manner of proceeding with a woman of her quality! (I mean her quality by birth and not by conditions.) Yet this way I might have used according to the common course of the law, as I was assured by the judges of the realm who showed it me written in their books. I mean not the pettifoggers of the law, who look more on the outside of their books than study them within. But I thought it much better and more fit to have her tried by the most honorable and ancient nobility of the realm, against whom and whose proceedings no exceptions might or can be taken" (Marcus, *Elizabeth I*, 188).

47. Joseph Lowenstein, "The Script in the Marketplace," in *Representing the English Renaissance*, ed. Stephen Greenblatt (Berkeley: University of California Press, 1988), 265. See also Elizabeth Eisenstein, *The Printing Press as an Agent of Change*, 2 vols. (Cambridge: Cambridge University Press, 1979).

48. The trial consisted largely of reiterated affirmations by the Commissioners that the documents constituted evidence of Mary's guilt and of her denials that she had written the passages for which she was condemned; the word of Phelippes, the professional forger and decipherer, was taken as true and he was not called for questioning; the depositions of Naw and Curle were accepted and they were not called for questioning; and the confessions of the Babington conspirators were presented as true, their authors having been executed. No original letter or document was produced at the trial. See Andrew Dakers, *The Tragic Queen: A Study of Mary Queen of Scots* (New York: Houghton Mifflin, 1931), 257.

49. Howell, 1189. The question of Mary's precise knowledge of the Babington plot continues to trouble historians. J. H. Pollen believes Mary guilty of full knowledge of the conspiracy (*Mary Queen of Scots*, Appendix I, 32). Conyers Read concludes Mary was guilty of complicity with Babington (*Mr. Secretary Walsingham*, 2:44). J. B. Black writes that "Mary's *knowledge* of the plot . . . is now generally admitted" (*The Reign*, 330, n.1). An overview of the Scots threat, the trial, and the execution is in Black, 328–36.

50. James Howell, Letter to Sir J. C., *Epistolae*, 2:658; quoted in Patterson, *Censorship*, 217.

51. On character and inscription in Shakespeare, see Harry Berger Jr., "What Did the King Know and When Did He Know It? Shakespearean Discourses and Psychoanalysis," *South Atlantic Quarterly* 88 (1989): 811–62; Margreta De Grazia and Peter

Stallybrass, "The Materiality of the Shakespearean Text," *Shakespeare Quarterly* 44,3 (Fall 1993): 255–83; and Jonathan Goldberg, "Hamlet's Hand," *Shakespeare Quarterly* 39,3 (Fall 1988): 307–27.

52. On discourse and the body, see Judith Butler, *Bodies That Matter: On the Discursive Limits of "Sex"* (New York: Routledge, 1993).

53. Mary's arrival is usually dated May or July 1568. From her arrival until her execution in 1587 she was kept in continual captivity. A detailed description of her execution is printed in Zweig, *Mary*, 349–53. For a study of relations among women's executions, agency, and spirituality, see Dolan, "Gentlemen," 157–78.

54. Alison Plowden, 2–3. Born in Scotland on December 9, 1542, Mary was the daughter of James V of Scotland and his wife, the French Marie De Guise-Lorraine. She was six days old when she became queen of Scotland upon her father's death, and she was at the center of matrimonial bidding wars throughout her life. She was contracted to Francis II of France, son of the ruling monarch, and left Scotland for France in August 1548. She married for the first time in April 1558 to Francis II, who died in December 1560. In August 1561 she returned to reclaim Scotland, where after some marital skirmishes with Elizabeth, she married Henry Stuart, Lord Darnley in July 1565, and she gave birth to her son in June 1566. Darnley was killed in an explosion in December 1567. Soon after, Mary married Bothwell (see Zweig, esp. 3–95). On possible relations between Mary's marriage to Bothwell and divorce law reforms of the mid-sixteenth century, see Powell, *English Domestic Relations*, 64.

55. H. F. Diggle, *The Casket Letters of Mary Stuart: A Study in Fraud and Forgery* (London: R. Ackrill, n.d.), 6.

56. The letters remain subjects of dispute. Edward Parry (*The Persecution of Mary Stuart* [London: Cassell and Co., 1931]) summarizes some sources of skepticism about Mary's relationship to the letters: "The story is that when Mary was in Lochleven, Morton [Moray's surrogate] discovered a casket of hers containing letters of a shameless character, written by her to Bothwell. No person now alive ever saw these alleged letters. Few were ever allowed to see them when they existed. And as the originals must have been written in French, the so-called copies existing today, whether in Latin, Scots or French, are merely translations of copies, or of copies of copies" (300). For views sympathetic to Mary that focus on inconsistencies in Moray's version of finding the casket letters, and on questions of authorship, forgery, and fraud, see: Parry, 300–319; Dakers, 125–35; and Diggle. Diggle argues that even positive attribution of authorship to Mary (something that cannot be achieved), which would solve the question of forgery, would not solve the question of "fraud" in that a genuine letter was adapted to a different set of circumstances (11). For discussions that take the letters as true revelations of Mary's character, see Zweig, 157–62; and Jenny Wormald, *Mary Queen of Scots: A Study in Failure* (London: George Philip, 1988), 178.

57. Parry, 304.

58. Parry, 305. "Maitland himself could imitate Mary's writing, and so could other people. It was one thing to write out letters in a feigned hand, and quite another thing actually to forge a royal signature. . . . The mere act of writing a letter in a feigned hand was not a criminal offence. Forgery in England was only a misdemeanour at this date. . . . But forgery of the the Great Seal, or a royal decree, was treason" (305). The next time the letters are referred to in a Parliamentary document, on December 15, they are described as "Privy Letters wholly written with her own hand" (306).

59. Parry, 306.

60. Parry, 315–16.

61. Diggle, 36–37.

62. Printed in Diggle, 32.

63. Printed in Diggle, 36–37. Among the issues Diggle raises regarding the long Glasgow letter are: 1) who Mary is addressing throughout; 2) what elements prove a motive for murder; 3) whether it proves a conspiracy to murder Darnley; 4) how much of it was genuine and written from Glasgow; 5) how much of it may be interpolations of earlier letters; and 6) the impossible time frame within the letter (if it is one letter).

64. The first mention of the sonnets is in a receipt given by Moray to his ally Morton for the casket and its contents just before the York conference at which they reportedly showed the letters to the assembled Parliament. Later, Morton assured the English commissioners that the sonnets had been found with the other documents in June 1567, though they had not been mentioned at that time (Diggle, 107). Sonnets 1, 2, 8, and 9 are addressed to "him," while the remainder are addressed to "you." On the editorial changes to pronouns in sonnets during the sixteenth century, see De Grazia and Stallybrass, 270–71.

65. Printed in Zweig, 162.

66. Printed in Zweig, 165.

67. Zweig, 242. "Although [Moray] had promised both Elizabeth and Mary to safeguard the latter's honour, on December 15, 1567, he had the compromising documents found in the silver casket, the letters and sonnets, read aloud in the Scottish parliament, examined by those assembled, and unanimously declared to be in the dethroned queen's handwriting. Four bishops, fourteen abbots, twelve earls, and somewhere near fifty of the lesser lights of the nobility and gentry . . . swore to the genuineness of the letters and the sonnets" (242).

68. Alison Plowden, 45.

69. Alison Plowden, 42.

70. Alison Plowden, 7–8.

71. Parry, 316. For Elizabeth's fascinating letters to Mary and speeches about her throughout Mary's difficulties in Scotland and residency in England, see Marcus, *Elizabeth I*, 114–25, 186–204; on those they exchanged between 1569 and 1587, see Lewis, *The Trial*, 78–90.

72. For arguments that female writing is perceived as a blot on a woman's character, see Wendy Wall, *The Imprint of Gender: Authorship and Publication in the English Renaissance* (Ithaca, N.Y.: Cornell University Press, 1993); and Eve Sanders, *Gender and Literacy on Stage in Early Modern England* (Cambridge: Cambridge University Press, 1998), 138–39. On women's writings more generally, see: Constance Jordan, *Renaissance Feminism*; Mary Ellen Lamb, *Gender and Authorship in the Sidney Circle* (Madison: University of Wisconsin Press, 1990); Margaret P. Hannay, ed., *Silent But For The Word: Tudor Women as Patrons, Translators, and Writers of Religious Works* (Kent, Oh.: Kent State University Press, 1985); and Barbara Kiefer Lewalski, *Writing Women in Jacobean England* (Cambridge, Mass.: Harvard University Press, 1993).

73. Alison Plowden, 45, 47. For a brief look at how the evidence in the Scots case reveals "conventions shaping representations of the adulterous, murderous wife," see Dolan, *Dangerous Familiars*, 42–45.

74. Holinshed, 926. In addition, Holinshed prints his version of letters from Parliament to Elizabeth arguing for Mary's execution: "As she hath already by her allurements brought to destruction more noblemen and their houses, together with a greater multitude of the commons of this realm, during her being here, than she should have been able to do if she had been in possession of her own crown" (932).

75. Thomas Kyd, *The Spanish Tragedy*, ed. J. R. Mulryne, New Mermaids, 2nd ed. (London: A & C Black, 1989), 4.1.113–15. Subsequent references are to this edition.

76. For a biography of Kyd, see Arthur Freeman, *Thomas Kyd: Facts and Problems* (Oxford: Clarendon Press, 1967); and Mulryne, xi–xiii.

77. The lord is variously identified as Henry, fourth earl of Sussex, or Ferdinando Stanley, Lord Strange (Mulryne, xi).

78. For an overview of claims about the English use of torture, see McIlwain, *Constitutionalism*, 118–20.

79. All Mulryne, xii.

80. For Kyd's other writings, see Mulryne, xii–xiii.

81. A brief overview of proposed dates is in Mulryne, xiv. James Shapiro seems to assume a date after 1586, as he discusses Kyd's having seen the Babington executions in "Tragedies naturally performed," 99–113.

82. Mulryne points out that the play "is unusual among Elizabethan plays in having no major narrative source" (xv). Though he cites several possible sources for individual episodes, no longer narrative pattern emerges. However, the incident of the death of Pedringano by Lorenzo may have several sources. One of these is the anonymous *A Copie of a Letter* (1584), "which tells how the Earl of Leicester rid himself of an unwanted accomplice, a thief called Gates, by affecting to be his protector while actually arranging his death" (Mulryne, xv).

83. See Zweig, 114–22. According to Zweig, the Scottish nobles were jealous of the privileges Mary permitted Rizzio, so they targeted him, plotting a violent end and recruiting Darnley, who was estranged from Mary, as head and protector of their conspiracy; as titular king of Scotland, he transformed the assassination from crime into valor. The conspiracy culminated in Rizzio's being ambushed and murdered during an evening in Mary's company; she witnessed the attacks, and was physically prevented from intervening by her husband, who held her back. After Rizzio's death, Bothwell became the man Mary relied on, and Darnley fled to his family estate in Glasgow, fearing retribution by both his wife and the conspirators who had used him.

84. On the relationship between arranged marriage, erotic desire, and the aristocratic female body, see Tennenhouse, *Power On Display*, esp. 17–36.

85. Quoted in Eve Sanders, 171. Sanders reproduces a series of letters from 1574 between Mercy Harvey and a married nobleman. Her brother Gabriel Harvey, who claims to have copied them into his commonplace book, said he intercepted them by accident. Sanders takes the exchange and commentary as instances of a wide-spread cultural association between women's writing and promiscuity (165–69).

86. Howell, 1183.

87. Howell, 1183.

88. For a focus on the representation of voices of the "common people," see Nina Levine, "Lawful Symmetry: The Politics of Treason in 2 *Henry VI*," in *Renaissance Drama and the Law*, ed. Frances E. Dolan, special issue of *Renaissance Drama* n.s. 25 (1994): 197–218.

89. Quoted in Steven R. Smith, "The London Apprentices as Seventeenth-Century Adolescents," *Past and Present* 61 (1973): 150.

90. On the go-between as "the covert author of the event" in *Twelfth Night*, see Eagleton, *William Shakespeare*, 31.

91. Frank Ardolino, "The Hangman's Noose and the Empty Box: Kyd's Use of Dramatic and Mythological Sources in *The Spanish Tragedy (III, iv)*," *Renaissance Quarterly* 30 (1977): 339; Barbara Baines, "Kyd's Silenus Box and the Limits of Perception," *Journal of Medieval and Renaissance Studies* 10 (1980): 41–51.

92. Mulryne, 53, n.23.

93. Mulryne, xxxii.

94. Belsey finds that the letter "begins the constitution and isolation of Hieronimo as a knowing subject" (*The Subject*, 77).

95. Howell, 1181–82.

96. Goldberg, *Writing*, 248.

97. Goldberg, "Hamlet's," 313.

98. Marlowe among other playwrights uses this coupling to great effect in *Edward II*. As Edward shreds a document ordering a change of his guard, he hopes, "Well may I rend his name [Mortimer's] that rends my heart. / This poor revenge hath something eased my mind, / So may his limbs be torn as is this paper" (5.1.139–42). For a perceptive discussion of how the letter Lady Margaret receives from Gaveston (2.1.1) in *Edward II* is situated ironically in same-sex and courtly love discourses, see Normand, "What Passions," 172–97.

99. The stage directions read, "Red ink," which Mulryne takes as "probably an author's note that the letter should be seen to have been written in red" (53, n.25). For a reading of early modern women's bodies in terms of their fluids, see Gail Paster, *The Body Embarrassed*.

100. See Jayne Lewis, *Mary Queen of Scots: Romance and Nation* (London: Routledge, 1998), 44.

101. In the Scots case, "every scrap of writing that [Mary] had possessed pertaining to the accusation with which she was charged had been taken from her rooms at Chartley," as was any means to write. "If her papers had not been taken away, and she had her Secretary, she could better confute the things objected against her" (Howell, 1183).

102. Holinshed, 921.

103. Goldberg, *Writing*, 263.

104. Castiglione, 92.

105. On sources and interpretations of Hieronimo's tongue-biting, see Jonas Barish, "*The Spanish Tragedy*, or The Pleasures and Perils of Rhetoric," in *Elizabethan Theatre*, ed. J. R. Brown and B. A. Harris, Stratford-on-Avon Studies 9 (London: Edward Arnold, 1966), 59–86; and S. F. Johnson, "*The Spanish Tragedy* or Babylon Revisited," in *Essays on Shakespeare and Elizabethan Drama in Honor of Hardin Craig*, ed. Richard Hosley (Columbia: University of Missouri Press, 1962), 23–36.

106. A penknife was a small knife used originally for making or mending quill pens. Contemporary usage (1549) included at least one example of it having been used as a weapon: "Caesar . . . got 23 strikes with a pen knife in the capitol" (*OED*, 2120).

107. Vives, "Scripto," *Linguae Latinae Exercitatio* (1538), Ninth Dialogue, 70; trans. by Claudius Desainliens as *Campo Di Fior* in 1583; quoted in Goldberg, *Writing*,

63. Goldberg characterizes the displacement by which open violence is resituated in the pen as a crucial aspect of early modern pedagogy of handwriting (63).

Conclusion

1. A convenient overview of some of the questions associated with Shakespeare's play is Jeanne T. Newlin, ed., *Richard II: Critical Essays* (New York: Garland, 1984). See also Arthur F. Kinney, "Essex and Shakespeare versus Hayward," *Shakespeare Quarterly* 44 (1993): 464–66; and John Hayward, *The First Part of the Life and Raigne of King Henrie the IIII* (1599; Norwood, N.J.: Walter J. Johnson, 1975).

Works Cited

Abbott, L. W. *Law Reporting in England, 1485–1585*. London: Athlone Press, 1973.

Abercrombie, M. L. J. "Face to Face—Proximity and Distance." In *Rules and Meanings: The Anthropology of Everyday Knowledge*, ed. Mary Douglas. Baltimore: Penguin, 1973. 92–94.

Aers, David. *Culture and History, 1350–1600: Essays on English Communities, Identities, and Writing*. Detroit: Wayne State University Press, 1992.

Agnew, Jean-Christophe. *Worlds Apart: The Market and the Theater in Anglo-American Thought, 1550–1750*. Cambridge: Cambridge University Press, 1986.

Althusser, Louis. "Ideology and Ideological State Apparatuses (Notes Towards an Investigation)." In *Lenin and Philosophy and Other Essays*. Trans. Ben Brewster. New York: Monthly Review Press, 1971.

Altman, Joel B. "'Preposterous Conclusions': Eros, *Enargeia*, and the Composition of *Othello*." *Representations* 18 (1987): 129–57.

———. *The Tudor Play of Mind: Rhetorical Inquiry and the Development of Elizabethan Drama*. Berkeley: University of California Press, 1978.

Amussen, Susan. *An Ordered Society: Gender and Class in Early Modern England*. Oxford: Blackwell, 1988.

Ardolino, Frank. "The Hangman's Noose and the Empty Box: Kyd's Use of Dramatic and Mythological Sources in *The Spanish Tragedy (III, iv)*." *Renaissance Quarterly* 30 (1977): 334–40.

Aristotle. *Aristotle's Treatise on Rhetoric*. Ed. Theodore Buckley. London: Bell and Sons, 1894.

———. *Metaphysics*. Trans. W. D. Ross. In *Introduction to Aristotle*, ed. Richard McKeon. New York: Modern Library, 1947. 239–96.

———. *Poetics*. Trans. Ingram Bywater. In *Introduction to Aristotle*, ed. Richard McKeon. New York: Modern Library, 1947. 619–67.

Axton, Marie. *The Queen's Two Bodies: Drama and the Elizabethan Succession*. London: Royal Historical Society, 1977.

Bacon, Francis. *Essays*. Introduction by Michael J. Hawkins. London: Dent, 1972.

Baines, Barbara. "Kyd's Silenus Box and the Limits of Perception." *Journal of Medieval and Renaissance Studies* 10 (1980): 41–51.

Bakeless, John. *The Tragicall History of Christopher Marlowe*. 2 vols. Cambridge, Mass.: Harvard University Press, 1942.

Baker, J. H. "The Inns of Court and Legal Doctrine." In *Lawyers and Laymen*, ed. T. M. Charles-Edwards, Morfydd E. Owen, and D. B. Walters. Cardiff: University of Wales Press, 1986. 274–86.

———. *An Introduction to English Legal History*. London: Butterworths, 1990.

Baker, J. H., and Samuel Thorne, eds. *Readings and Moots at the Inns of Court in the Fifteenth Century*. Vol. 2, *Moots and Readers' Cases*. London: Seldon Society, 1990.

Bakhtin, Mikhail. *The Dialogic Imagination*. Ed. Michael Holquist. Trans. Michael Holquist and Caryl Emerson. Austin: University of Texas Press, 1981.

———. *Rabelais and His World*. Trans. Helene Iswolsky. Bloomington: Indiana University Press, 1984.

Barbour, Richmond. "Britain and the Great Beyond: *The Masque of Blackness* at Whitehall." In *Playing the Globe: Genre and Geography in English Renaissance Drama*, ed. John Gillies and Virginia Mason Vaughan. Madison, N.J.: Fairleigh Dickinson University Press, 1998. 129–53.

Barish, Jonas. "*The Spanish Tragedy*, or The Pleasures and Perils of Rhetoric." In *Elizabethan Theatre*, ed. J. R. Brown and B. A Harris, Stratford-on-Avon Studies 9. London: Edward Arnold, 1966. 59–86.

Barker, Francis. *The Tremulous Private Body: Essays on Subjection*. New York: Methuen, 1984.

Bartels, Emily. *Spectacles of Strangeness: Imperialism, Alienation, and Marlowe*. Philadelphia: University of Pennsylvania Press, 1993.

Baugh, Albert C. et al., eds. *A Literary History of England*. New York: Appleton-Century-Crofts, 1948.

Bellamy, John. *The Law of Treason in England in the Later Middle Ages*. Cambridge: Cambridge University Press, 1970.

———. *The Tudor Law of Treason*. London: Routledge and Kegan Paul, 1979.

Belsey, Catherine. *The Subject of Tragedy: Identity and Difference in Renaissance Drama*. London: Methuen, 1985.

Bennett, H. S. *English Books and Readers, 1475–1557*. Cambridge: Cambridge University Press, 1970.

———. *English Books and Readers, 1603–1640*. Cambridge: Cambridge University Press, 1970.

Berger, Harry, Jr. "What Did the King Know and When Did He Know It? Shakespearean Discourses and Psychoanalysis." *South Atlantic Quarterly* 88 (1989): 811–62.

Bernthal, Craig. "Treason in the Family: The Trial of Thumpe v. Horner." *Shakespeare Quarterly* 42,1 (Spring 1991): 44–54.

Bevington, David. *From "Mankind" to Marlowe: Growth of Structure in the Popular Drama of Tudor England*. Cambridge, Mass.: Harvard University Press, 1962.

Black, J. B. *The Reign of Elizabeth, 1558–1603*. Oxford: Clarendon Press, 1936.

Boas, Frederick S. *Christopher Marlowe: A Biographical and Critical Study*. Rev. ed. Oxford: Clarendon Press, 1953.

Bourdieu, Pierre. "The Force of Law: Toward a Sociology of the Juridical Field." Trans. Richard Terdiman. *Hastings Law Journal* 38 (July 1987): 805–53.

Bowers, Fredson T. *Elizabethan Revenge Tragedy*. Princeton, N.J.: Princeton University Press, 1940.

Bowman, Mary. "'she there as Princess rained': Spenser's Figure of Elizabeth." *Renaissance Quarterly* 43,3 (Autumn 1990): 509–28.

Bray, Alan. *Homosexuality in Renaissance England*. London: Gay Men's Press, 1982.

Bredbeck, Gregory. *Sodomy and Interpretation: Marlowe to Milton*. Ithaca, N.Y.: Cornell University Press, 1991.

Breight, Curt. "'Treason doth never prosper': *The Tempest* and the Discourse of Treason." *Shakespeare Quarterly* 41,1 (Spring 1990): 1–28.

Breitenberg, Mark. *Anxious Masculinity in Early Modern England*. Cambridge: Cambridge University Press, 1996.

Brooke, C. F. Tucker. *The Life of Marlowe and the Tragedy of Dido Queen of Carthage*. London: Methuen, 1930.

Buck, Sir George. "The Third University of England." Appendix. *Chronicle of England*, by John Stow. London, 1615.

Burnett, Mark Thornton. "*Edward II* and Elizabethan Politics." In *Marlowe, History, Sexuality: New Critical Essays on Christopher Marlowe*, ed. Paul Whitfield White. New York: AMS Press, 1998. 91–107.

Butler, Judith. *Bodies That Matter: On the Discursive Limits of "Sex"*. New York: Routledge, 1993.

Campbell, John Lord. *Shakespeare's Legal Acquirements Considered*. 1859. Rpt. New York: Appleton, 1972.

Cartelli, Thomas. *Marlowe, Shakespeare, and the Economy of Theatrical Experience*. Philadelphia: University of Pennsylvania Press, 1991.

Castan, Nicole. "The Public and the Private." In *A History of Private Life*, ed. Roger Chartier, trans. Arthur Goldhammer. Vol. 3, *Passions of the Renaissance*. Cambridge, Mass.: Harvard University Press, 1989. 403–45.

Castiglione, Baldesar. *The Book of the Courtier*. Trans. George Bull. Rev. ed. New York: Penguin, 1976.

Chambers, E. K. *The Mediaeval Stage*. Oxford: Oxford University Press, 1903. Vol. 2.

Cicero. *Works: English and Latin*. London: W. Heinemann. 28 vols. Cambridge, Mass.: Harvard University Press, 1913- 1977. Vol. 2, *De Inventione. De optimo genere oratorum Topica*.

Clark, Eleanor Grace. *Ralegh and Marlowe: A Study in Elizabethan Fustian*. New York: Russell & Russell, 1965.

Clark, Glenn. "The 'Strange Geographies' of *Cymbeline*." In *Playing the Globe: Genre and Geography in English Renaissance Drama*, ed. John Gillies and Virginia Mason Vaughan. Madison, N.J.: Fairleigh Dickinson University Press, 1998. 230–59.

Coddon, Karin S. "'Suche Strange Desygns': Madness, Subjectivity, and Treason in *Hamlet* and Elizabethan Culture." In *Hamlet*, ed. Susanne L. Wofford. New York: Bedford, 1994. 380–402.

Coke, Edward. "Coke on Littleton." In *Institutes of the Laws of England*. Part 1. 15th ed. 3 vols. 1794.

———. *The Reports of Sir Edward Coke*. 2nd ed. London, 1680.

———. *The Third Part of the Institutes of the Laws of England*. 1797. Rpt. Buffalo, N.Y.: Hein, 1986.

Collomp, Alain. "Families: Habitations and Cohabitations." In *A History of Private Life*, ed. Roger Chartier, trans. Arthur Goldhammer. Vol. 3, *Passions of the Renaissance*. Cambridge, Mass.: Harvard University Press, 1989. 493–529.

Cook, Ann Jenalie. *The Privileged Playgoer of Shakespeare's London, 1576–1642*. Princeton, N.J.: Princeton University Press, 1981.

Correll, Barbara. "Malleable Material, Models of Power: Women in Erasmus's 'Marriage Group' and *Civility in Boys*." *English Literary Renaissance* 57 (1990): 241–62.

Cressy, David. *Literacy and the Social Order: Reading and Writing in Tudor and Stuart England*. Cambridge: Cambridge University Press, 1980.

Critical Inquiry. "Questions of Evidence." 17,4 (Summer 1991); 18,1 (Autumn 1991); 18,2 (Winter 1992).

Cunningham, Karen. "Renaissance Execution and Marlovian Elocution: The Drama of Death." *PMLA* 105,2 (March 1990): 209–22.

Daiches, David. "Language and Action in Marlowe's *Tamburlaine*." In *More Literary Essays*. Edinburgh: Oliver and Boyd, 1968. 42–69.

Dakers, Andrew. *The Tragic Queen: A Study of Mary Queen of Scots*. New York: Houghton Mifflin, 1931.

Daston, Lorraine. "Marvelous Facts and Miraculous Evidence in Early Modern Europe." *Critical Inquiry* 18,1 (Autumn 1991): 93–124.

Davis, Natalie Zemon. *Fiction in the Archives*. Stanford, Calif.: Stanford University Press, 1987.

Day, Angell. "Of the partes, place, and Office of a Secretary." In *The English Secretary*, ed. Robert O. Evans. Gainesville, Fla.: Scholars' Facsimiles and Reprints, 1967. 101–33.

Deats, Sara Munson. *Sex, Gender, and Desire in the Plays of Christopher Marlowe*. Newark: University of Delaware Press, 1997.

De Grazia, Margreta, and Peter Stallybrass. "The Materiality of the Shakespearean Text." *Shakespeare Quarterly* 44,3 (Fall 1993): 255–83.

Denton, William. *Records of St. Giles' Cripplegate*. London: George Bell, 1883.

De Somogyi, Nick. "Marlowe's Maps of War." In *Christopher Marlowe and English Renaissance Culture*, ed. Darryll Grantley and Peter Roberts. Hants: Scolar Press, 1996. 96- 109.

Devecmon, William C. *"In Re" Shakespeare's Legal Acquirements*. New York: Shakespeare Press, 1899. Rpt. AMS Press, 1971.

DiGangi, Mario. "Marlowe, Queer Studies, and Renaissance Homoeroticism." In *Marlowe, History and Sexuality: New Critical Essays on Christopher Marlowe*, ed. Paul Whitfield White. New York: AMS Press, 1998. 195–212.

Diggle, H. F. *The Casket Letters of Mary Stuart: A Study in Fraud and Forgery*. London: R. Ackrill, n.d.

Dobie, Rowland. *History of the United Parishes of St. Giles-in- the-Fields and St. George, Bloomsbury*. London: Henry Bickers Press, 1834.

Dolan, Frances E. *Dangerous Familiars: Representations of Domestic Crime in England, 1550–1700*. Ithaca, N.Y.: Cornell University Press, 1994.

———. "'Gentlemen, I have one thing more to say': Women on Scaffolds in England, 1563–1680." *Modern Philology* 92,4 (November 1994): 157–78.

———, ed. *Renaissance Drama and the Law*. Special issue of *Renaissance Drama* n.s. 25 (1994).

Dollimore, Jonathan. "Introduction: Shakespeare, Cultural Materialism, and the New Historicism." In *Political Shakespeare: New Essays in Cultural Materialism*, ed. Jonathan Dollimore and Alan Sinfield. Ithaca, N.Y.: Cornell University Press, 1985. 2–17.

———. *Radical Tragedy: Religion, Ideology and Power in the Drama of Shakespeare and His Contemporaries*. Brighton: Harvester Press, 1984.

———. "Transgression and Surveillance in *Measure for Measure*." In *Political Shakespeare: New Essays in Cultural Materialism*, ed. Jonathan Dollimore and Alan Sinfield. Ithaca, N.Y.: Cornell University Press, 1985. 72–87.

Douglas, J. D., ed. *The New Bible Dictionary*. Grand Rapids, Mich.: Eerdmans, 1962.

Douglas, Mary. *Cultural Bias*. London: Royal Anthropological Institute of Great Britain and Ireland, 1978.

———. *Purity and Danger: An Analysis of Concepts of Pollution and Taboo*. New York: Frederick Praeger, 1966.

Dugdale, William. *Origines Juridiciales*. 1666. 3rd ed. London, 1680.

Dworkin, Ronald. *Law's Empire*. Cambridge, Mass.: Belknap Press, 1986.

Eagleton, Terry. *William Shakespeare*. Oxford: Blackwell, 1986.

Earle, John. *Micro-Cosmographie*. London, 1628.

Eisenstein, Elizabeth. *The Printing Press as an Agent of Change*. 2 vols. Cambridge: Cambridge University Press, 1979.

Elton, G. R. *Policy and Police: The Enforcement of the Reformation in the Age of Thomas Cromwell*. Cambridge: Cambridge University Press, 1992.

———. "The Rule of Law in Sixteenth-Century England." In *Tudor Men and Institutions*, ed. Arthur J. Slavin. Baton Rouge: Louisiana State University Press, 1972. 265–94.

———. "The Sessional Printing of Statutes, 1484–1547." In *Wealth and Power in Tudor England*, ed. E. W. Ives, R. J. Knecht, and J. J. Scarisbrick. London: Althone, 1978. 68–76.

———, ed. *The Tudor Constitution*. Cambridge: Cambridge University Press, 1960.

Erasmus. *De recta Graeci et Latini sermonis pronunciatione*. In *Scribes and Sources: Handbook of the Chancery Hand in the Sixteenth Century: Texts from the Writing Masters*, ed. A. S. Osley. Boston: David R. Godine, 1980.

Fehrenbach, Robert J., Lea Ann Boone, and Mario A. DiCesare, eds. *A Concordance to the Plays, Poems, and Translations of Christopher Marlowe*. Ithaca, N.Y.: Cornell University Press, 1982.

Finkelpearl, Philip J. *John Marston of the Middle Temple*. Cambridge, Mass.: Harvard University Press, 1969.

Fish, Stanley. *Doing What Comes Naturally: Change, Rhetoric, and the Practice of Theory in Literary and Legal Studies*. Durham, N.C.: Duke University Press, 1989.

———. "Normal Circumstances, Literal Language, Direct Speech Acts, the Ordinary, the Everyday, the Obvious, What Goes Without Saying, and Other Special Cases." 1978. In *Critical Theory Since Plato*, ed. Hazard Adams. Rev. ed. New York: Harcourt, 1992. 1200–09.

———. *Self-Consuming Artifacts: The Experience of Seventeenth-Century Literature*. Berkeley: University of California Press, 1972.

Fitzpatrick, Peter, and Alan Hunt, eds. *Critical Legal Studies*. Oxford: Blackwell, 1987.

Fortescue, Sir John. *On the Laws and Governance of England*. Ed. Shelley Lockwood. Cambridge: Cambridge University Press, 1997.

Foucault, Michel. *Discipline and Punish: The Birth of the Prison*. Trans. Alan Sheridan. New York: Vintage, 1979.

———. "Discourse on Language." Appendix. In *The Archeology of Knowledge*, trans. A. M. Sheridan Smith. New York: Pantheon, 1972. 215–37.

———. *The History of Sexuality*. Trans. Robert Hurley. New York: Vintage, 1980.

———. "What Is an Author?" In *Language, Counter-Memory, Practice*, ed. Donald F. Bouchard, trans. Donald F. Bouchard and Sherry Simon. Ithaca, N.Y.: Cornell University Press, 1977. 113–38.

Freeman, Arthur. *Thomas Kyd: Facts and Problems*. Oxford: Clarendon Press, 1967.

Fulwood, William. *The Enemy of Idlenesse*. London, 1621.

Fumerton, Patricia. *Cultural Aesthetics: Renaissance Literature and the Practice of Social Ornament*. Chicago: University of Chicago Press, 1991.

Gassner, John, ed. *Medieval and Tudor Drama*. New York: Applause, 1987.

Geertz, Clifford. *The Interpretation of Cultures*. New York: Basic Books, 1973.

———. *Local Knowledge: Further Essays in Interpretive Anthropology*. New York: Basic Books, 1983.

Gifis, Stephen. *Law Dictionary*. 3rd. ed. Hauppauge, N.Y.: Barron's Educational Series, 1991.

Gillies, John. "Introduction: Elizabethan Drama and the Cartographizations of Space." In *Playing the Globe: Genre and Geography in English Renaissance Drama*, ed. John Gillies and Virginia Mason Vaughan. Madison, N.J.: Fairleigh Dickinson Unversity Press, 1998. 19–45.

———. "Marlowe, the *Timur* Myth, and the Motives of Geography." In *Playing the Globe: Genre and Geography in English Renaissance Drama*, ed. John Gillies and Virginia Mason Vaughan. Madison, N.J.: Fairleigh Dickinson University Press, 1998. 203–29.

Godshalk, William. *The Marlovian World Picture*. The Hague: Mouton, 1974.

Goldberg, Jonathan. "Hamlet's Hand." *Shakespeare Quarterly* 39,3 (Fall 1988): 307–27.

———. *James I and the Politics of Literature*. Baltimore: Johns Hopkins University Press, 1983.

———. *Sodometries: Renaissance Texts, Modern Sexualities*. Stanford, Calif.: Stanford University Press, 1992.

———. *Writing Matter: From the Hands of the English Renaissance*. Stanford, Calif.: Stanford University Press, 1990.

Graham, Kenneth J. E. *The Performance of Conviction: Plainness and Rhetoric in the Early English Renaissance*. Ithaca, N.Y.: Cornell University Press, 1994.

Green, Richard Firth. *A Crisis of Truth: Literature and Law in Ricardian England*. Philadelphia: University of Pennsylvania Press, 1999.

Green, Thomas Andrew. *Verdict According to Conscience*. Chicago: University of Chicago Press, 1985.

Greenblatt, Stephen. *Renaissance Self-Fashioning: From More to Shakespeare*. Chicago: University of Chicago Press, 1980.

———. *Shakespearean Negotiations: The Circulation of Social Energy in Renaissance England*. Berkeley: University of California Press, 1988.

———. *Sir Walter Ralegh: The Renaissance Man and His Roles*. New Haven, Conn.: Yale University Press, 1973.

———, ed. *The Forms of Power and the Power of Forms in the Renaissance*. Norman: University of Oklahoma Press, 1982.

Greg, W. W., ed. *Gesta Grayorum, 1688*. Malone Society Reprints. Oxford: Clarendon Press, 1914.

Gurr, Andrew. *Playgoing in Shakespeare's London*. Cambridge: Cambridge University Press, 1987.

Hall's Chronicle; Containing the History of England, During the Reign of Henry the Fourth, and the Succeeding Monarchs, to the End of the Reign of Henry the Eighth, in which are Particularly Described the Manners and Customs of those Periods. London: J. Johnson et al., 1809. Rpt. New York: AMS Press, 1965.

Hannay, Margaret P., ed. *Silent But for the Word: Tudor Women as Patrons, Translators, and Writers of Religious Works*. Kent, Oh.: Kent State University Press, 1985.

Hanson, Elizabeth. *Discovering the Subject in Renaissance England*. Cambridge: Cambridge University Press, 1998.

Harrison, William. *The Description of England*. London, 1577. Ed. Georges Edelen. Ithaca, N.Y.: Cornell University Press, 1968.

Hartwig, Joan. *Shakespeare's Tragicomic Vision*. Baton Rouge: Louisiana State University Press, 1972.

Hattaway, Michael. "Christopher Marlowe: Ideology and Subversion." In *Christopher Marlowe and English Renaissance Culture*, ed. Darryll Grantley and Peter Roberts. Hants: Scolar Press, 1996. 198–223.

Hayward, John. *The First Part of the Life and Raigne of King Henrie IIII*. 1599. Norwood, N.J.: Walter J. Johnson, 1975.

Heinemann, Margot. "Shakespearean Contradictions and Social Change." *Science and Society* 41 (1977): 7–16.

Helgerson, Richard. *Forms of Nationhood: The Elizabethan Writing of England*. Chicago: University of Chicago Press, 1992.

Helly, Dorothy O., and Susan M. Reverby, eds. *Gendered Domains: Rethinking the Public and Private in Women's History*. Ithaca, N.Y.: Cornell University Press, 1992.

Henderson, Katherine Usher, and Barbara McManus. *Half Humankind: Contexts and Texts of the Controversy About Women in England, 1540–1640*. Urbana: University of Illinois Press, 1985.

Herrup, Cynthia B. *The Common Peace: Participation and the Criminal Law in Seventeenth Century England*. Cambridge: Cambridge University Press, 1987.

Hobbes, Thomas. *Leviathan*. Ed. C. B. Macpherson. Harmondsworth: Penguin, 1968.

Holdsworth, William. *A History of English Law*. 5th ed. London: Methuen, 1942. Vol. 3.

Holinshed, Raphael. *Holinshed's Chronicles of England, Scotland, and Ireland*. 6 vols. London, 1587. Rpt. London, 1808. Vol. 4.

Hopwood, Charles H., ed. *Middle Temple Records*. 4 vols. London: Butterworths, 1904–5. Vol. 1.

Horace. "Art of Poetry." In *Critical Theory Since Plato*, ed. Hazard Adams. Rev. ed. New York: Harcourt, Brace, Jovanovich, 1992. 67–74.

Howard, Jean E. "The New Historicism in Renaissance Studies." *English Literary Renaissance* 16 (1986): 13–43.

———. "Renaissance Anti-Theatricality and the Politics of Gender and Rank in *Much Ado About Nothing*." In *Shakespeare Reproduced*, ed. Jean E. Howard and Marion F. O'Connor. New York: Methuen, 1987. 163–87.

———. "Scholarship, Theory, and More New Readings: Shakespeare for the 1990's." In *Shakespeare Study Today*, ed. Georgianna Ziegler. New York: AMS Press, 1986. 127–31.

———. "Scripts and/versus Playhouses: Ideological Production and the Renaissance Public Stage." In *The Matter of Difference: Materialist Feminist Criticism of Shakespeare*, ed. Valerie Wayne. Ithaca, N.Y.: Cornell University Press, 1991. 221–36.

———. *The Stage and Social Struggle in Early Modern England*. New York: Routledge, 1994.

Howell, Thomas B., ed. *Cobbett's Complete Collection of State Trials*. 33 vols. London: R. Bagshaw, 1809–1826.

Hume, Martin. *The Wives of Henry the Eighth*. New York: Brentano's, n.d.

Hutson, Lorna. *The Usurer's Daughter: Male Friendship and Fictions of Women in Sixteenth-Century England*. London: Routledge, 1994.

Jameson, Fredric. *The Political Unconscious: Narrative as a Socially Symbolic Act*. Ithaca, N.Y.: Cornell University Press, 1981.

Jardine, David, ed. *Criminal Trials . . . During the Reigns of Queen Elizabeth and James I*. 2 vols. London: M. A. Nattalie, 1947. Vol. 2.

Jerrold, Walter. *Henry VIII and His Wives*. New York: Doran, n.d.

Johnson, S. F. "*The Spanish Tragedy* or Babylon Revisited." In *Essays on Shakespeare and Elizabethan Drama in Honor of Hardin Craig*, ed. Richard Hosley. Columbia: University of Missouri Press, 1962. 23–36.

Jonson, Ben. *Every Man Out of His Humour*. Ed. F. P. Wilson. London: Oxford University Press, 1920.

———. *Volpone, or the Fox*. Ed. Jonas Barish. Arlington Heights, Ill.: AHM Press, 1958.

Jordan, Constance. *Renaissance Feminism: Literary Texts and Political Models*. Ithaca, N.Y.: Cornell University Press, 1990.

———. *Shakespeare's Monarchies: Ruler and Subject in the Romances*. Ithaca, N.Y.: Cornell University Press, 1997.

Judson, Margaret Atwood. *The Crisis of the Constitution*. New Brunswick, N.J.: Rutgers University Press, 1949.

Kahn, Coppélia. *Man's Estate: Masculine Identity in Shakespeare*. Berkeley: University of California Press, 1981.

———. "The Rape in Shakespeare's *Lucrece*." *Shakespeare Studies* 9 (1976): 45–72.

Kahn, Victoria. *Rhetoric, Prudence, and Skepticism in the Renaissance*. Ithaca, N.Y.: Cornell University Press, 1985.

Kantorowicz, Ernst. *The King's Two Bodies: A Study in Mediaeval Political Theology*. Princeton, N.J.: Princeton University Press, 1957.

Kaplan, M. Lindsay, and Katherine Eggert. "'Good Queen, my lord, good queen': Sexual Slander and the Trials of Female Authority in *The Winter's Tale*." In *Renaissance Drama and the Law*, ed. Frances E. Dolan. Special issue of *Renaissance Drama* n.s. 25 (1994): 89–118.

Khare, R. S. "The Other's Double—The Anthropologist's Bracketed Self: Notes on Cultural Representation and Privileged Discourse." *New Literary History* 23,1 (Winter 1992): 1–23.

Kinney, Arthur F. "Essex and Shakespeare versus Hayward." *Shakespeare Quarterly* 44 (1993): 464–66.

Klein, Joan Larsen, ed. *Daughters, Wives, and Widows: Writings by Men About Women and Marriage in England, 1500–1640*. Urbana: University of Illinois Press, 1992.

Knafla, Louis A. "The Matriculation Revolution and Education in the Inns of Court in Renaissance England." In *Tudor Men and Institutions*, ed. Arthur J. Slavin. Baton Rouge: Louisiana State University Press, 1972. 232–64.

Knight, G. Wilson. *The Crown of Life: Essays in Interpretation of Shakespeare's Final Plays*. 1947. Rpt. New York: Barnes and Noble, 1966.

Knight, W. Nicholas. *Shakespeare's Hidden Life: Shakespeare at the Law 1585–1595*. New York: Mason & Lipscomb, 1973.

Kyd, Thomas. *The Spanish Tragedy*. Ed. J. R. Mulryne. New Mermaids. 2nd ed. London: A & C Black, 1989.

Lamb, Mary Ellen. *Gender and Authorship in the Sidney Circle*. Madison: University of Wisconsin Press, 1990.

Langbein, John H. *Torture and the Law of Proof*. Chicago: University of Chicago Press, 1977.

Larner, Christina. *Witchcraft and Religion: The Politics of Popular Belief*. Oxford: Blackwell, 1984.

Lehmberg, Stanford E. "Sir Thomas Audley: A Soul as Black as Marble?" In *Tudor Men and Institutions*, ed. Arthur J. Slavin. Baton Rouge: Louisiana State University Press, 1927. 3–31.

Letters and Papers of the Reign of Henry VIII. 21 vols. London, 1862–1932.

Levack, Brian P. *The Civil Lawyers in England, 1603–1641*. Oxford: Clarendon Press, 1973.

Levin, Harry. *The Overreacher: A Study of Christopher Marlowe*. Cambridge, Mass.: Harvard University Press, 1952.

Levine, Nina. "Lawful Symmetry: The Politics of Treason in *2 Henry VI*." In *Renaissance Drama and the Law*, ed. Frances E. Dolan. Special issue of *Renaissance Drama* n.s. 25 (1994): 197–218.

Lewalski, Barbara Kiefer. *Writing Women in Jacobean England*. Cambridge, Mass.: Harvard University Press, 1993.

Lewis, Jayne Elizabeth. *Mary Queen of Scots: Romance and Nation*. London: Routledge, 1998.

———. *The Trial of Mary Queen of Scots: A Brief History with Documents*. New York: St. Martin's Press, 1999.

Little, David. *Religion, Order and Law: A Study in Pre-Revolutionary England*. Oxford: Blackwell, 1970.

Lockyer, Roger. *Tudor and Stuart Britain, 1471–1714*. New York: St. Martin's Press, 1985.

Loftus, Elizabeth, and Katherine Ketchum. *Witness for the Defense*. New York: St. Martin's Press, 1991.

Lowenstein, Joseph. "The Script in the Marketplace." In *Representing the English Renaissance*, ed. Stephen Greenblatt. Berkeley: University of California Press, 1988. 265–78.

Lowenthal, David. *The Past Is a Foreign Country*. Cambridge: Cambridge University Press, 1986.

Luther, Martin. *The Babylonian Captivity of the Church*. 1520. In *Martin Luther: Selections from His Writings*, ed. John Dillenberger. New York: Doubleday, 1961.

MacCaffrey, Wallace. *Elizabeth I*. London: Edward Arnold, 1993.

Macfarlane, Alan, ed. *Witchcraft in Tudor and Stuart England*. London: Routledge and Kegan Paul, 1970.

Maclure, Millar. *Marlowe: The Critical Heritage, 1588–1896*. London: Routledge and Kegan Paul, 1979.

Marcus, Leah. "*Cymbeline* and the Unease of Topicality." In *The Historical Renaissance*, ed. Heather Dubrow and Richard Strier. Chicago: University of Chicago Press, 1988. 134–68.

Marcus, Leah, Janel Mueller, and Mary Beth Rose, eds. *Elizabeth I: Collected Works*. Chicago: University of Chicago Press, 2000.

Marlowe, Christopher. *The Complete Plays of Christopher Marlowe*, ed. Irving Ribner. New York: Odyssey Press, 1963.

Maus, Katharine Eisaman. "Horns of a Dilemma: Jealousy, Gender, and Spectatorship in English Renaissance Drama." *English Literary History* 54 (1987): 561–83.

———. *Inwardness and Theater in the English Renaissance*. Chicago: University of Chicago Press, 1995.

———. "Taking Tropes Seriously: Language and Violence in Shakespeare's 'Rape of Lucrece.'" *Shakespeare Quarterly* 37 (1986): 66–82.

McAlindon, Thomas. *English Renaissance Tragedy*. Vancouver: University of British Columbia Press, 1986.

McCoy, Richard C. *The Rites of Knighthood: The Literature and Politics of Elizabethan Chivalry*. Berkeley: University of California Press, 1989.

McEachern, Claire. *The Poetics of English Nationhood, 1590–1612*. Cambridge: Cambridge University Press, 1996.

McGann, Jerome. *A Critique of Modern Textual Criticism*. 1983. Rpt. Charlottesville: University of Virginia Press, 1992.

McIlwain, Charles Henry. *Constitutionalism Ancient and Modern*. Rev. ed. Ithaca, N.Y.: Cornell University Press, 1947.

Miller, Anthony. "Domains of Victory: Staging and Contesting the Roman Triumph in Renaissance England." In *Playing the Globe: Genre and Geography in English Renaissance Drama*, ed. John Gillies and Virginia Mason Vaughan. Madison, N.J.: Fairleigh Dickinson University Press, 1998. 260–87.

Miola, Robert S. "*Cymbeline*: Shakespeare's Validiction to Rome." In *Roman Images*, ed. Annabel Patterson. Baltimore: Johns Hopkins University Press, 1984. 51–63.

Montrose, Louis Adrian. "'Shaping Fantasies': Figurations of Gender and Power in Elizabethan Culture." In *Representing the English Renaissance*, ed. Stephen Greenblatt. Berkeley: University of California Press, 1988. 31–64.

More, Sir Thomas. *Utopia*. Trans. Paul Turner. Harmondsworth: Penguin, 1961.

Mullaney, Steven. *The Place of the Stage: License, Play and Power in Renaissance England*. Chicago: University of Chicago Press, 1998.

Mulryne, J. R. "Introduction." *The Spanish Tragedy*. By Thomas Kyd. 2nd. ed. London: A & C Black, 1989. xi–xxxiv.

Neale, J. E. *Elizabeth I and Her Parliaments, 1584–1601*. London: Jonathan Cape, 1957.

———. *Essays in Elizabethan History*. New York: St. Martin's Press, 1958.

Newlin, Jeanne T., ed. *Richard II: Critical Essays*. New York: Garland, 1984.

Newman, Karen. *Fashioning Femininity and English Renaissance Drama*. Chicago: University of Chicago Press, 1991.

Nicholl, Charles. "'At Middleborough': Some Reflections on Marlowe's Visit to the

Low Countries in 1592." In *Christopher Marlowe and English Renaissance Culture*, ed. Darryll Grantley and Peter Roberts. Hants: Scolar Press, 1996. 38–50.

———. "'Faithful Dealing': Marlowe and the Elizabethan Intelligence Service." In *Marlowe, History, and Sexuality: New Critical Essays on Christopher Marlowe*, ed. Paul Whitfield White. New York: AMS Press, 1998. 1–13.

———. *The Reckoning: The Murder of Christopher Marlowe*. Chicago: University of Chicago Press, 1992.

Nichols, James, ed. *The Church History of Britain*. London, 1840. Vol. 3.

Normand, Lawrence. "'What Passions Call You These?': *Edward II* and James VI." In *Christopher Marlowe and English Renaissance Culture*, ed. Darryll Grantley and Peter Roberts. Hants: Scolar Press, 1996. 172–97.

Nosworthy, J. M., ed. Introduction to *Cymbeline*, by William Shakespeare. Arden Edition. Cambridge, Mass.: Harvard University Press, 1955.

Ong, Walter J. *The Presence of the Word: Some Prolegomena for Cultural and Religious History*. New Haven, Conn.: Yale University Press, 1967.

Orgel, Stephen. *Impersonations: The Performance of Gender in Shakespeare's England*. Cambridge: Cambridge University Press, 1996.

———. "Making Greatness Familiar." In *The Forms of Power and the Power of Forms in the Renaissance*, ed. Stephen Greenblatt. Norman: University of Oklahoma Press, 1982. 41–48.

Orlin, Lena Cowen. *Private Matters and Public Culture in Post-Reformation England*. Ithaca, N.Y.: Cornell University Press, 1994.

Parker, Patricia. *Literary Fat Ladies: Rhetoric, Gender, Property*. London: Methuen, 1987.

———. *Shakespeare From the Margins: Language, Culture, Context*. Chicago: University of Chicago Press, 1996.

Parry, Edward. *The Persecution of Mary Stewart*. London: Cassell and Co., 1931.

Paster, Gail. *The Body Embarrassed: Drama and the Disciplines of Shame in Early Modern England*. Ithaca, N.Y.: Cornell University Press, 1993.

Patterson, Annabel. *Censorship and Interpretation: The Conditions of Writing and Reading in Early Modern England*. Madison: University of Wisconsin Press, 1984.

———. *Reading Holinshed's "Chronicles"*. Chicago: University of Chicago Press, 1994.

Perkins, William. *Christian Oeconomie*. 1618. In *Works*, trans. Thomas Pickering. Vol. 3.

Peterson, Douglas. *Time, Tide, and Tempest*. San Marino, Calif.: Huntington Library, 1973.

Plowden, Alison. *The Elizabethan Secret Service*. New York: St. Martin's Press, 1991.

Plowden, Edmund. *The Commentaries, or Reports*. 2 Parts. London: S. Brooke, 1816.

Pollen, John Hungerford. *Mary Queen of Scots and the Babington Plot*. Publications of the Scottish History Society. 3rd ser. 3 Edinburgh: University Press, 1922.

Ponet, John. "A Short Treatise of Politic Power." In *John Ponet (1516?-1566): Advocate of a Limited Monarchy*, ed. Winthrop S. Hudson. Chicago: University of Chicago Press, 1942.

Posner, Richard. *Law and Literature: A Misunderstood Relation*. Cambridge, Mass.: Harvard University Press, 1998.

Powell, Chilton Latham. *English Domestic Relations, 1487–1653*. New York: Columbia University Press, 1917.

Prest, Wilfrid R. *The Inns of Court under Elizabeth I and the Early Stuarts, 1590–1640.* London: Longman, 1972.

Pritchard, Arnold. *Catholic Loyalism in Elizabethan England.* Chapel Hill: University of North Carolina Press, 1979.

Pye, Christopher. *The Regal Phantasm.* London: Routledge, 1990.

Quintilian. *The Institutio Oratoria of Quintilian.* Trans. H. E. Butler. Cambridge, Mass.: Harvard University Press, 1959–63.

Rackin, Phyllis. "Historical Difference/Sexual Difference." In *Privileging Gender in Early Modern England*, ed. Jean R. Brink. Sixteenth Century Essays & Studies 23 (1993): 37–63.

———. *Stages of History: Shakespeare's English Chronicles.* Ithaca, N.Y.: Cornell University Press, 1990.

Ranum, Orest. "The Refuges of Intimacy." In *A History of Private Life*, ed. Roger Chartier. Trans. Arthur Goldhammer. Vol. 3, *Passions of the Renaissance.* Cambridge, Mass.: Harvard University Press, 1989.

Read, Conyers. *Mr. Secretary Walsingham and the Policy of Queen Elizabeth.* 3 vols. Oxford: Clarendon Press, 1925.

Rezneck, Stephen. "The Trial of Treason in Tudor England." In *Essays in Honor of C. H. McIlwain.* Cambridge, Mass.: Harvard University Press, 1936. 258–88.

Riggs, David. "Marlowe's Quarrel with God." In *Marlowe, History and Sexuality*, ed. Paul Whitfield White. New York: AMS Press, 1998. 15–37.

Roberts, Peter. "The 'Studious Artizan': Christopher Marlowe, Canterbury and Cambridge." In *Christopher Marlowe and English Renaissance Culture*, ed. Darryll Grantley and Peter Roberts. Hants: Scolar Press, 1996. 17–37.

Rubin, Gayle. "The Traffic in Women: Notes on the 'Political Economy' of Sex." In *Toward an Anthropology of Women*, ed. Rayna R. Reiter. New York: Monthly Review Press, 1975. 157–210.

Said, Edward. *Orientalism: Western Concepts of the Orient.* New York: Vintage Books, 1978.

Sanders, Eve. *Gender and Literacy on Stage in Early Modern England.* Cambridge: Cambridge University Press, 1998.

Sanders, Norman et al. *The Revels History of Drama in English.* Vol. 2, *1500–1576.* London: Methuen, 1980.

Sanford, Rhonda Lemke. "A Room Not One's Own: Feminine Geography in *Cymbeline.*" In *Playing the Globe: Genre and Geography in English Renaissance Drama*, ed. John Gillies and Virginia Mason Vaughan. Madison, N.J.: Fairleigh Dickinson University Press, 1998. 63–85.

Scarry, Elaine. *The Body in Pain: The Making and Unmaking of the World.* New York: Oxford University Press, 1985.

Sebek, Barbara. "'Strange Outlandish Wealth': Transglobal Commerce in *The Merchant's Mappe of Commerce* and *The Fair Maid of the West, Parts I and II.*" In *Playing the Globe: Genre and Geography in English Renaissance Drama*, ed. John Gillies and Virginia Mason Vaughan. Madison, N.J.: Fairleigh Dickinson University Press, 1998. 176–202.

Sedgwick, Eve Kosofsky. *Between Men: English Literature and Male Homosocial Desire.* New York: Columbia University Press, 1985.

Shakespeare, William. *The Complete Works of Shakespeare*, ed. David Bevington. 3rd ed. Glenview, Ill.: Scott, Foresman, 1980.

Shapiro, Barbara J. *A Culture of Fact: England, 1550–1720*. Ithaca, N.Y.: Cornell University Press, 2000.

Shapiro, James. "'Tragedies Naturally Performed': Kyd's Representation of Violence." In *Staging the Renaissance: Reinterpretations of Elizabethan and Jacobean Drama*, ed. David Kastan and Peter Stallybrass. New York: Routledge, 1991. 99–113.

Sharpe, J. A. *Crime in Early Modern England, 1550–1750*. London: Longman, 1984.

———. "'Last Dying Speeches': Religion, Ideology and Public Execution in Seventeenth Century England." *Past and Present* 107 (May 1985): 144–67.

Shepherd, Simon. *Marlowe and the Politics of Elizabethan Theatre*. London: Harvester Press, 1986.

Sidney, Sir Philip. "An Apology for Poetry." 1583; 1595. In *Critical Theory Since Plato*, ed. Hazard Adams. Rev. ed. New York: Harcourt, Brace, Jovanovich, 1992. 142–62.

Siemon, James E. "Noble Virtue in *Cymbeline*." *Shakespeare Survey* 29 (1976): 51–61.

Smith, Alan Gordon. *The Babington Plot*. London: Macmillan, 1936.

Smith, Barbara Herrnstein. "Belief and Resistance: A Symmetrical Account." *Critical Inquiry* 18,1 (Autumn 1991): 125–39.

Smith, Bruce. *Homosexual Desire in Shakespeare's England: A Cultural Poetics*. Chicago: University of Chicago Press, 1991.

Smith, Lacey Baldwin. "English Treason Trials and Confessions in the Sixteenth Century." *Journal of the History of Ideas* 15 (1954): 471–98.

———. *Treason in Tudor England: Politics and Paranoia*. Princeton, N.J.: Princeton University Press, 1986.

———. *A Tudor Tragedy: The Life and Times of Catherine Howard*. New York: Pantheon, 1961.

Smith, Philip. *A History of Education for the English Bar*. London: Butterworths, 1860.

Smith, Steven R. "The London Apprentices as Seventeenth-Century Adolescents." *Past and Present* 61 (1973): 149–61.

Smith, Thomas. *De Republica Anglorum*. London, 1583.

Sommerville, J. P. *Royalists and Patriots: Politics and Ideology in England 1603–1640*. 2nd ed. London: Longman, 1999.

Stallybrass, Peter. "Patriarchal Territories: The Body Enclosed." In *Rewriting the Renaissance*, ed. Margaret W. Ferguson, Maureen Quilligan, and Nancy J. Vickers. Chicago: University of Chicago Press, 1986. 123–42.

Stapleton, Thomas. *The Life and Illustrious Martyrdom of Sir Thomas More*. Part 3 of "Tres Thomae." Douai, 1588. Trans. Philip E. Hallet. London: Burnes, Oates, and Washburn, 1928.

Stephen, H. L., ed. *State Trials: Political and Social*. 2 vols. London: Duckworth, 1899.

Stimpson, Catherine. "Shakespeare and the Soil of Rape." In *The Woman's Part: Feminist Criticism of Shakespeare*, ed. Carolyn Ruth Swift-Lenz, Gayle Green, and Carol Thomas Neely. Urbana: University of Illinois Press, 1980.

Stone, Lawrence. *The Crisis of the Aristocracy, 1558–1641*. Oxford: Clarendon Press, 1965.

Swander, Homer. "*Cymbeline* and the 'Blameless Hero.'" *English Literary History* 30 (1964): 259–70.

Teague, Frances. *Shakespeare's Speaking Properties*. Lewisburg, Pa.: Bucknell University Press, 1991.

Tennenhouse, Leonard. *Power on Display: The Politics of Shakespeare's Genres*. New York: Methuen, 1986.

Thomas, Brook. "Reflections on the Law and Literature Revival." *Critical Inquiry* 17,3 (Spring 1991): 510–39.

Thomas, Donald, ed. *State Trials: Treason and Libel*. London: Routledge and Kegan Paul, 1972.

Thomas, Keith. "The Meaning of Literacy in Early Modern England." In *The Written Word: Literacy in Transition*, ed. Gerd Baumann. Oxford: Clarendon Press, 1986.

Thomas, Keith, and Donald Pennington, eds. *Puritans and Revolutionaries: Essays in Seventeenth Century History Presented to Christopher Hill*. Oxford: Clarendon Press, 1978.

Todd, Barbara J. "The Remarrying Widow: A Stereotype Reconsidered." In *Women in English Society 1500–1800*, ed. Mary Prior. London: Methuen, 1985. 54–92.

Traub, Valerie. *Desire and Anxiety: Circulations of Sexuality in Shakespearean Drama*. London: Routledge, 1992.

Tuan, Yi-Fu. *Space and Place: The Perspective of Experience*. Minneapolis: University of Minnesota Press, 1977.

Udall, Nicholas. *Ralph Roister Doister*. In *Medieval and Tudor Drama*, ed. John Gassner. New York: Applause, 1987. 263- 345.

Vickers, Nancy J. "Diana Described: Scattered Women and Scattered Rhyme." *Critical Inquiry* 8 (1981).

Vives, Juan Luis. *Instruction of a Christian Woman*. 1529. In *Daughters, Wives, and Widows: Writing by Men About Women and Marriage in England, 1500–1640*, ed. Joan Larsen Klein. Urbana: University of Illinois Press, 1992.

———. "Scripto." *Linguae Latinae Exercitatio* (1538). Ninth Dialogue. Trans. Claudius Desainliens as *Campo Di Fior* (1583).

Wall, Wendy. *The Imprint of Gender: Authorship and Publication in the English Renaissance*. Ithaca, N.Y.: Cornell University Press, 1993.

Warner, J. Christopher. *Henry VIII's Divorce: Literature and the Politics of the Printing Press*. Woodbridge: Boydell Press, 1998.

Wayne, Valerie. "Historical Differences: Misogyny and *Othello*." In *The Matter of Difference: Materialist Feminist Criticism of Shakespeare*, ed. Valerie Wayne. Ithaca, N.Y.: Cornell University Press, 1991. 153–79.

Whitaker, William. *A Disputation on Holy Scripture*. 1588. Ed. William Fitzgerald. Parker Society 45. Cambridge: Cambridge University Press, 1849.

Wickham, Glynne. *Early English Stages, 1300–1600*. Vol. 3, *Plays and Their Makers to 1576*. London: Routledge and Kegan Paul, 1981.

Williams, Raymond. *Marxism and Literature*. Oxford: Oxford University Press, 1977.

Wilson, Richard. "Visible Bullets: *Tamburlaine the Great* and Ivan the Terrible." In *Christopher Marlowe and English Renaissance Culture*, ed. Darryll Grantley and Peter Roberts. Hants: Scolar Press, 1996. 51–69.

Wilson, Thomas. *Arte of Rhetorique*. Ed. Thomas J. Derrick. New York: Garland, 1982.

Wimsatt, W. K., and Monroe C. Beardsley. "The Intentional Fallacy." In *Critical Theory Since Plato*, ed. Hazard Adams. Rev. ed. New York: Harcourt, 1992. 944–951.

Woodbridge, Linda. *Women in the English Renaissance: Literature and the Nature of Womankind, 1540–1620*. Urbana: University of Illinois Press, 1984. 224–43.

Wormald, Jenny. *Mary Queen of Scots: A Study in Failure*. London: George Philip, 1988.

Wriothesley, Charles. *A Chronicle of England During the Reigns of the Tudors, From A.D. 1485 to 1559*. 2 vols. Ed. William Douglas Hamilton. 1875. Rpt. New York: Johnson Reprint Corporation, 1965.

Ziegler, Georgianna. "'My Lady's Chamber': Female Space, Female Chastity in Shakespeare." *Textual Practice* 4,1 (Spring 1990): 71–90.

Zweig, Stefan. *Mary Queen of Scotland and the Isles*. Trans. Eden Paul and Cedar Paul. New York: Viking, 1935.

Index

Abbott, L. W., 38, 152 nn.64, 66–70, 153 n.72, 158 n.59, 160 n.17, 177 n.2
Abercrombie, M. L. J., 33, 157 n.35
Aers, David, 180 n.40
affiliation: in the Babington trials, 80–82; and courtiership, 98–99, 128–29, 174 n.83; character and place in, 86–87, 94; and Inns of Court, 32–39; and male friendship, 21, 78, 84–85, 99–104, 108; in moot cases, 24, 32; and Scots prosecution, 113–14. *See also* association; Bond of Association; households
Agnew, Jean-Christophe, 67, 145 n.4, 166 n.96
allegiance: and the Babington defendants, 21, 81, 94; and conscience, 92; and male friendship, 19, 112; in Marlowe, 21; renunciation of, 21, 83–84; in *Tamburlaine I*, n.82; and traitors, 6, 108, 171 n.43. *See also* affiliation; association; fidelity; loyalty
All's Well That Ends Well (Shakespeare), 111
Althusser, Louis, 148 n.36
Altman, Joel B., 155 n.13, 164 n.70, 170 n.33
Amussen, Susan, 14, 151 nn.55–57, 157 n.35
"Apology for Poetry, An." *See* Sidney, Sir Philip
Ardolino, Frank, 131, 183 n.91
Aristotle, 44, 147 n.16, 160 n.14
Arte of Rhetorique, 147 n.15, 165 n.84, 169 n.19, 179 n.29; character and place in, 105–6, 113; "the country" in, 91; and eyewitnessing, 62; female weakmindedness in, 116; legal examples in, 19; manhood and danger in, 81, 98; poets and truth in, 4
As You Like It (Shakespeare), 24, 89.
Ascham, Roger, 38
association: among men, 11, 104; among women, 52–56, 77. *See also* affiliation; Babington trials; Bondof Association; households; Howard attainder
attainder: and *Cymbeline*, 68–69, 72–74; defined, 42, 159 n.4; and female fidelity, 75–77; of Katherine Howard, 9, 13, 19–22, 41–45, 49, 60, 164 n.69; of Mary, Queen of Scots, 22; and *Ralph Roister Doister*, 60–64, 164 n.78. *See also* Howard attainder
Audley, Thomas, 42, 44, 159 n.5, 161 n.25
Axton, Marie, 145 n.5, 179 n.21

Babington (Anthony), trials: and Catholicism, 170 n.32; and conscience, 90, 92–93; and "the country," 80–81; and courtiership, 81–83; and *diffidatio*, 83; and fabricated evidence, 19, 179 n.32; and formulaic rhetoric, 91; and imagination, 10; and intention, 13; indictments of, 80, 168 n.11; and the lawful, 87–90, 150 n.44; and legal identity, 93; and male friendship, 21, 83–84; and Marlowe, 21, 95–96, 173 n.71; and Mary, Queen of Scots, 110, 112, 113, 115–17, 119, 126, 153 n.76, 168 n.10, 181 n.49; and masculine identity, 21, 77–78, 85–86, 169 n.23; and national identity, 77; and plain speech, 14; and rootlessness, 86–87, 93–94; scaffold speeches in, 94–95; and self-commemoration, 168 n.12; and *The Spanish Tragedy*, 128, 135, 184 n.91; and *Tamburlaine I*, 77–78, 96, 102–4, 108–19
Bacon, Francis, 24, 32, 38, 39, 87, 157 n.33, 171 n.42
Baines, Barbara, 131, 185 n.91
Baines, Richard, 173 n.67
Bajazeth (*Tamburlaine I*), 97, 99, 106, 107
Bakeless, John, 95, 173 n.67
Baker, J. H., 23–26, 29, 32, 154 nn.2–6, 9, 155 nn.10, 11, 13–15, 156 nn.18, 24–27, 157 nn.32, 34, 38, 39, 171 n.42
Bakhtin, Mikhail, 48, 146 n.11, 158 n.56, 161 n.30
Ballard, John, 79, 80, 82, 86–89, 93, 94, 168 n.11, 173 n.71
Barbour, Richmond, 171 n.38

Barish, Jonas, 155 n.12, 185 n.105
Barker, Francis, 145 n.4
Bartels, Emily, 173 n.75, 176 n.94
Baugh, Albert C., 146 n.6, 164 n.71
Beardsley, Monroe C., 180 n.43
Beaumont, Francis, 38
belief: and corroboration, 46–47, 136–38; in *Cymbeline*, 70–75; in the Howard attainder, 44; and interpretation, 91–92, 120, 127, 132; as rhetorical effect, 15. *See also* corroboration; credibility; evidence; proof
Bel-imperia (*The Spanish Tragedy*), 127, 129–31, 133–35, 137, 139
Bellamy, John, 8, 147 n.24, 148 nn.28–35, 149 nn.39, 40, 150 nn. 44–46, 50, 159 nn.1, 2, 4, 170 nn.25, 26, 172 n.46, 178 nn.11, 16, 179 n.22
Belsey, Catherine, 145 n.4, 153 n.83, 162 n.41, 172 n.57, 185 n.94
Bennett, H. S., 151 n.57, 152 n.64
Berger, Harry, Jr., 181 n.51
Bernthal, Craig, 180 n.44
Bevington, David, 149 n.37, 174 n.77
Black, J. B., 179 n.32, 180 n.49
Boas, Frederick, 173 n.67
Boleyn, Anne, 8–9, 40, 42–43, 159 n.2, 160 n.9, 165 n.93
Bond of Association: 112–13, 178 n.14. *See also* affiliation; association; evidence; Mary, Queen of Scots
Book of the Courtier, The. *See* Castiglione, Baldesar
Bothwell, James, Earl of, 122–25, 182 n.54, 182 n.56, 184 n.83
Bourdieu, Pierre, 145 n.2
Bowers, Fredson T., 177 n.8
Bowman, Mary, 168 n.4
Bray, Alan, 174, n.84
Bredbeck, Gregory, 174 n.84
Breight, Curt, 146 n.9
Breitenberg, Mark, 58–59, 164 n.76, 175 n.91
Brooke, C. F. Tucker, 173 n.67
Browne, William, 38
Buck, Sir George, "The Third University of England," 157 n.41, 158 n.55
Burnett, Mark Thornton, 176 n.98
Butler, Judith, 182 n.52

Calvin, John, 30, 151 n.51, 171 n.43
Camden, William, 3
Campbell, John, Lord, 146 n.6
Campion, Thomas, 38
Carew, Thomas, 38
Cartelli, Thomas, 174 n.81
Castan, Nicole, 162 n.46, 165 nn.85, 88, 89, 91
Castiglione, Baldesar, *The Book of the Courtier*, 167 n.103, 175 n.87, 185 n.104; courtiership in, 81, 169 n.18; gender and martial strategies in, 179 n.30; and letters versus arms, 138; male friendship in, 100, 102; writing in, 71
Catholicism: and the Babington trials, 78–79, 170 n.32; and the Henrician dissolution, 40; and the Howard attainder, 42, 45, 51, 160 n.6; at Inns of Court, 158 n.60; and itinerancy, 171 n.39; and Marlowe, 95–96, 173 n.71; and the Scots prosecution, 110, 178 n.11
Chambers, E. K., 164 n.72
Chaucer, Geoffrey, 38
Christmas Prince revels, 37, 158 n.58
Christopherson, John, *Exhortation to all menne to take hede and beware of rebellion*, 15
Cicero, 5, 82, 150 n.49, 169 n.20
Clark, Eleanor Grace, 174 n.77
Clark, Glenn, 27, 54, 156 n.19, 163 n.69, 166 n.99
Cleves, Anne of, 42, 48, 69, 161 n.32
Coddon, Karin S., 149 n.38
Coke, Edward, 3, 152 n.65, 153 nn.73, 74, 75, 161 n.29; and common versus civil law, 19, 87, 153 n.78, 171 n.42; on eyewitnessing, 48, 62; and law reporting, 16–19, 152 n.66; on overt act, 150 n.47; and Ralegh* 14
Collomp, Alain, 163 n.56
Comedy of Errors, The (Shakespeare), 64
Commentaries; or Reports. *See* Plowden, Edmund
common law: and civil, 149 n.39, 153 n.78, 171 n.42; defined, 7; and Inns of Court, 23, 154 n.5; and intention, 11, 149 n.39; and limited monarchy, 7; and overt act, 12–13; and the Scots prosecution, 181 n.46; and treason, 10, 148 n.28, 172 n.46; and witnesses, 12, 150 n.44. *See also* Coke, Edward; treason
Congreve, William, 38
Cook, Ann Jenalie, 151 n.63
Correll, Barbara, 78, 168 nn.4, 5
corroboration: in *Cymbeline*, 71–72; in the Howard attainder, 46–47, 49; as legal effect, 47; in *The Spanish Tragedy*, 131, 133, 136–38. *See also* belief; credibility; evidence

Cosroe (*Tamburlaine I*), 97–99, 102, 106–8, 174 nn.76, 82
courtiership: and the Babington trials, 21, 78, 81–83, 86, 94; and the Scots prosecution, 124; in *The Spanish Tragedy*, 129; in *Tamburlaine I*, 98, 99, 108. *See also* affiliation; Castiglione
Cranmer, Thomas, 41, 44–45, 49, 61, 160 n.20, 161 n.33
credibility: in the Babington trials, 85; and credit, 14–15; in *Cymbeline*, 71–74; in *Doctor Faustus*, 67; in the Howard attainder, 47–49; and intention, 47; and plain speech, 14; in *Ralph Roister Doister*, 65–66; in the Scots prosecution, 116; in *The Spanish Tragedy*, 129–31; and written evidence, 44–45. *See also* belief; corroboration; evidence
Cressy, David, 151 n.57
Cromwell, Thomas, 42, 58, 83, 153 n.80, 160 n.6
Culpeper, Thomas, 43, 46, 49–52, 56, 57, 60, 63, 160 n.7, 161nn.25, 35, 164 n.78
Cunningham, Karen, 146 n.9, 173 n.66
Custance, Christian (*Ralph Roister Doister*), 21, 41, 57–66, 71
Cymbeline (Shakespeare): 156 n.19; and bodily evidence, 71, 74; and British unification, 166 n.99; and *Doctor Faustus*, 73; evidence and motive in, 69, 70, 71, 72–73, 74; female fidelity in, 66–76; and female identity, 70–71, 73–74; and the Howard attainder, 21, 41, 69, 72, 73, 75, 76; Imogen in, 68; legalisms in, 166 n.98; and material evidence, 72–73, 167 n.107; Posthumus in, 166 n.97; and *Ralph Roister Doister*, 21, 41, 68, 70, 72, 75, 76; relativity of virtue in, 69; report in, 70; and sexual violence, 166 n.101, 167 n.108; and simulated evidence, 68, 75; and unstable evidence, 71, 72, 73. *See also* names of individual characters

Daiches, David, 175 n.92
Dakers, Andrew, 181 n.48, 182 n.56
Darnley, Henry Stuart, Lord, 122–25, 128, 182 n.54, 183 n.63, 184 n.83
Daston, Lorraine, 150 n.50
Davenant, William, 38
Davies, John, 38
Davis, Natalie Zemon, 160 n.20
Day, Angell, 45, 118, 119, 160 n.19, 180 nn.38, 43
Deats, Sara Munson, 174 n.79
De Grazia, Margreta, 181 n.51, 183 n.64
de Mendoza, Bernardine, 80, 86
Denham, John, 38
Denton, William, 173 n.64
Dereham, Francis, 43, 46, 47, 49, 53, 55–57, 60, 160 n.7, 161 nn.25, 35, 163 n.55
De Somogyi, Nick, 174 n.83
Devecmon, William C., 146 n.6
diffidatio, 83. *See also* allegiance; Babington trials
DiGangi, Mario, 174 n.84
Diggle, H. F., 182 nn.55, 56, 183 nn.61–64
Dobie, Rowland, 173 n.64
Doctor Faustus (Marlowe), 163 n.60; and blood, 135; and bodily evidence, 67–68, 73; character and place in, 54–55; and theatrical evidence, 67–68
documentary evidence. *See* evidence
Dolan, Frances E., 145 n.5, 162 n.41, 165 n.93, 182 n.53, 183 n.73
Dollimore, Jonathan, 145 n.4, 153 n.83, 156 n.30, 172 n.53, 173 n.71
Donne, John, 38
Douglas, J. D., 172 n.57
Douglas, Lady Margaret, 9, 40
Douglas, Mary, 6, 26, 147 n. 23, 155 nn.16, 17, 156 nn.25, 31
Drayton, Michael, 3
Duchess of Malfi, The (Webster), 111
Dugdale, William, *Origines Juridiciales*, 157 n.43, 158 n.55
Dworkin, Ronald, 147 n.23

Eagleton, Terry, 146 nn.5, 8, 185 n.90
Earle, John, *Micro-Cosmographie*, 157 n.45
Education of a Young Gentlewoman, The, 130
Edward II (Marlowe): character and space in, 176 n.93; and treason, 173 n.76; and foreign insurgency, 176 n.98; and homosociability, 174 n.84; and letters, 111, 185 n.98; and proprietorship, 97
Edward III: and common law treason, 10, 148 n.28; and constructive treason, 7–8; and imagining, 10; and witnessing, 12
Egerton, Sir Thomas, 14, 70, 88, 89
Eggert, Katherine, 160 n.9
Eisenstein, Elizabeth, 181 n.47
Elizabeth I, 17, 146 n.10, 167 n.108; and the Babington trials, 79–80, 168 n.10, 171 n.43, 172 n.49; and the Bond of Association, 112–13, 178 n.13; and gender anxiety, 78;

Elizabeth I (*continued*)
and Inns of Court, 20; and itinerant soldiers, 176 n.98; and the Lopez plot, 141; and the Scots prosecution, 22, 110, 112, 114, 123, 125, 126, 135, 153 n.80, 178 n.11, 181 n.46, 183 nn.67, 71; and the Statute of Silence, 79. *See also* Mary, Queen of Scots
Elton, G. R., 148 n.30, 152 n.64, 153 n.80, 160 n.6
Erasmus, 78, 118, 119, 131, 133, 180 nn.37, 40
Essex, Earl of, 13, 35, 141, 142, 186 n.1
Every Man Out of His Humour (Jonson), 39, 159 n.64
evidence, 3; bodily, 13, 47–49, 51, 67, 73–74, 161 n.32; courtroom versus theater, 67, 75; documentary, 44–49, 132–34, 161 n.20, 181 n.48; and economics, 14; epistolary, 22, 116–23, 136–39; eyewitness, 62, 67; fabrication of, 19; and "fact," 151 n.50; fact versus perception, 126; gifts as, 59–60, 65; and intention, 11–13, 89; material, 69–75; material versus oral, 160 n.18; and memory, 167 n.105; and rhetoric, 113, 150 n.49; variability of, 13. *See also* belief; corroboration; credibility; knowledge
executions: of the Babington defendants, 93–94; in Holinshed, 18; of Katherine Howard, 49–51; of Mary, Queen of Scots, 178 n.13, 181 n.49, 182 n.53; 184 n.74; of a monarch, 153 n.80; as public rituals, 3, 146 n.9; and scaffold speeches, 162 n.41

fee simple, 27
fee tail, 27
Fehrenbach, Robert J., 176 n.97
felony: and intention, 11; in moot cases, 26, 30; versus treason, 8
fidelity: in the Babington trials, 77–78; in *Cymbeline*, 21, 41, 66, 68–72; and homeland, 86–87, 107; in the Howard attainder, 50; in law and theater, 2, 142; and male friendship, 21, 84–86, 101–2, 108–9; in matrimonial treasons, 40–41; in *Ralph Roister Doister*, 41, 57–63, 64–66; in the Scots prosecution, 124, 130–31, 180 n.44; in *The Spanish Tragedy*, 22, 111, 136; in *Tamburlaine I*, 77–78; and travel, 86–87; and wager plots, 166 n.97; and women, 55, 75. *See* also affiliation; allegiance; association; friendship
Finkelpearl, Philip J., 35, 38, 146 n.6, 157 n.40, 157 nn.43, 48, 50, 158 nn.51, 52, 55, 57, 60, 63
Fish, Stanley, 47, 147 n.23, 151 nn.52, 62, 161 nn.22, 26, 28
Fitzpatrick, Peter, 153 n.82
Ford, John, 38
forfeiture, 7, 147 n.24
forgery, 182 n.58
Fortescue, Sir John, 35, 37, 154 n.9, 157 nn.41, 42, 49, 158 n.55
Foucault, Michel, 15, 119, 146 n.9, 151 n.60, 154 n.1, 156 n.22, 157 n.36, 167 n.112, 180 nn.37, 42
Fraunce, Abraham, 38
Freeman, Arthur, 184 n.76
friendship: versus allegiance, 19, 21, 94, 109, 112; in culture and theater, 174 n.84; and manliness, 175 n.86; among men, 83–86, 94, 77–78, 99–104, 108, 175 n.86; among women, 52. *See also* affiliation; association; courtiership; fidelity; loyalty
Fulwood, William, 119, 134, 180 n.41
Fumerton, Patricia, 145 n.4

Gardiner, Stephen, 42
Gascoigne, George, 38
Gassner, John, 65–66, 158 n.62, 164 nn.73, 77, 165 n.92
Geertz, Clifford, 147 n.22, 156 n.29
gender: in discourses of treason, 1, 3, 6, 19; in moot cases, 27–28; and national identity, 66, 75. *See also* affiliation; association; courtiership; fidelity; households; sexuality; individual trials and plays
Gifis, Stephen, 156 n.21
Gillies, John, 105, 107, 176 n.95, 177 n.100
Gismonde of Salerne, 39
Godshalk, William, 174 n.77
Goldberg, Jonathan, 118, 134, 145 n.4, 154 n.1, 174 n.84, 180 nn.37–41, 43, 181 n.51, 185 nn.96, 97, 103, 107
Goodluck, Gawyn (*Ralph Roister Doister*), 58–61, 63–66, 71
Googe, Barnabe, 38
Gorboduc (Sackville and Norton), 2, 39
Gosynhill, Edward, *Mulierum Paean*, 55
Gower, John, 38
Graham, Kenneth J. E., 14, 151 nn.51, 52
Green, Richard Firth, 11, 149 n.39
Green, Thomas Andrew, 172 n.52
Greenblatt, Stephen, 105, 145 n.4, 146 n.9,

147 n.19, 154 n.1, 166 n.94, 172 n.53, 176 n.94
Greg, W. W., 158 n.58
Gurr, Andrew, 151 n.63

Hakluyt, Richard, 3
Hall's Chronicle; Containing the History of England, 44, 159 n.4, 160 n.13*
Hamlet (Shakespeare), 48, 111, 129, 134, 135, 149 n.37
Hannay, Margaret P., 183 n.72
Hanson, Elizabeth, 149 n.38
Harington, John, 38
Harrison, William, *The Description of England*, 36, 149 n.42, 157 n.47
Hartwig, Joan, 166 n.97
Hattaway, Michael, 174 n.84
Hatton, Sir Christopher, 83, 84, 90–93, 96, 102, 115, 168 n.9, 172 n.32
Hayward, John, 186 n.1
Heinemann, Margot, 151 n.63
Helgerson, Richard, 3, 83, 145 n.5, 146 n.10, 168 n.2, 170 n.24, 171 n.42
Helly, Dorothy O., 163 n.61
Henderson, Katherine Usher, 55, 163 n.62, 170 n.35
Henry IV, Part 1 (Shakespeare), 111
Henry VIII, 17; and divorce literature, 159 n.1, 164 n.71; and Katherine Howard, 20, 41, 77; and Inns of Court, 20, 23; and matrimonial treason, 8–9, 40, 148 n.33, 165 n.93; and treason legislation, 148 n.30; and Nicholas Udall, 57
Herrup, Cynthia B., 2, 146 n.7, 151 n.58
Hieronimo (*The Spanish Tragedy*), 127, 132–39, 185 n.94
Hobbes, Thomas, 15, 151 n.61
Holdsworth, William, 149 n.39
Holinshed, Raphael, *Chronicles of England, Scotland, and Ireland*, 149 n.42, 150 n.8, 169 n.22, 172 n.58, 173 nn.68, 69, 185 n.102; and the Babington trials, 82, 92, 95, 135, 153 n.76, 168 nn.10, 11, 169 n.23, 170 n.31; Catholicism and treason in, 170 n.32; and intention, 13; and legal stories, 18; and the Scots prosecution, 126, 153 n.76, 177 n.3, 184 n.74; and the Throckmorton trial, 10; and treasonous thought, 11
homeland: and female fidelity, 75; versus homelessness, 87, 94, 98, 104–9, 176 n.94; in the Howard attainder, 42, 51; and Inns of Court, 36, 39; and legal history, 90; in moot cases, 24, 26, 30; in the Scots prosecution, 114; in *The Spanish Tragedy*, 129; in treason trials, 1, 3, 5, 6, 80, 141; and "woman," 66. *See also* place; vagabondage
"Homily on Marriage, The," 85, 170 n.35
homosociability. *See* affiliation; association; Bond of Association; courtiership; friendship; households
Hooker, Richard, 3, 149 n.42
Hopwood, Charles H., 158 n.58
Horace, 5, 147 n.17
households: in *Cymbeline*, 72; in the Howard attainder, 52–58, 163 nn.50, 55; the king's, 37; and marriage, 52; in *Ralph Roister Doister*, 63–65; and rhetorical order, 165 n.93; and servants, 130; women's, 20, 66, 77
Howard, Jean E., 148 n.36, 153 n.83, 165 n.86
Howard (Katherine), attainder: and bodily evidence, 13, 47–48; character and space in, 52–55; corroboration in, 46–47; and female fidelity, 19–21, 41–57, 164 n.78; and female identity, 49, 162 n.42; indictments, 159 n.4, 160 nn.7, 8; and national identity, 42, 44, 160 n.6, 161 n.21, 161 n.25; and premarital sexuality, 43, 162 n.47; and *Ralph Roister Doister*, 63–64, 68, 69, 72–76, 77; and relativity of virtue, 46, 161 n.32; and reputation, 44; scaffold speeches, 49–50, 167 n.113; and treason legislation 9, 40, 43, 153 n.80, 161 n.35, 164 n.69; and women's households, 51, 55–57, 63–64, 160 n.12; writing in, 44–45, 160 n.20. See also *Cymbeline*
Howard, Thomas, Lord, 9, 40
Howell, Thomas B., 151 n.53 and passim
Hume, Martin, 159 n.4, 160 nn.7, 12, 161 nn.32, 35, 162 nn.42, 47, 163 nn.50, 164 nn.69, 78 and passim
Hutson, Lorna, 174 n.84

Iachimo (*Cymbeline*), 21, 41, 68, 70–75
Imogen (*Cymbeline*), 21, 66, 68–75, 167 n.108
inner assent, 65, 116
Inns of Court: and characterization of space, 157 n.5; and Christmas Prince revels, 34–35, 158 n.58; and court-centered authority, 17, 20, 23; histories of, 157 n.41; and law reports, 16, 152 n.66; legal influence of, 154 n.3; members of, 158 n.52, 159 n.60; mooting in, 154 n.9; and production of

Inns of Court (*continued*)
literature, 38–39; and revels, 158 n.55; and status, 36; treason in, 35, 37, 38. *See* also affiliation; homeland; mooting
intention: in the Babington trials, 81, 88–89; in common versus civil law, 149 n.39; in *Cymbeline*, 69–71, 74; and evidence, 47, 150 n.50; in the Howard attainder, 161 n.35; in letters, 118–19, 180 n.43; in Plowden's *Commentaries*, 18; as treason, 11, 13, 149 n.39; and treason prosecutions, 8
interiority: 2, 70, 141, 149 n.38; and belief, 70; and divine point of view, 91; in early modern literature, 145 n.4; evidence of, 11–12, 13, 14, 47, 117; in Marlowe, 105; and matrimonial treason, 40; in moot cases, 31; and writing, 111. *See also* subjectivity; individual trials and plays

"Jacob and Esau," and moot cases, 25–28, 155 n.11. *See also* mooting
James I, 165 n.93
Jameson, Fredric, 153 n.83
Jardine, David, 173 n.71
Jerrold, Walter, 159 n.4, 160 n.6, 162 n.42, 163 nn.50, 55, and passim
Jew of Malta, The (Marlowe), 111, 141
Johnson, S. F., 185 n.105
Jonson, Ben, 39, 155 n.12, 159 n.64
Jordan, Constance, 145 n.5, 163 n.62, 166 n.97, 183 n.72
Judson, Margaret Atwood, 147 n.25

Kahn, Coppélia, 167 n.108, 175 n.91
Kahn, Victoria, 147 n.20, 155 n.13
Kantorowicz, Ernst, 148 n.28, 179 n.21
Kaplan, M. Lindsay, 160 n.9
Ketchum, Katherine, 167 n.105
Khare, R. S., 156 n.29
King Lear (Shakespeare), 111, 132
Kinney, Arthur F., 186 n.1
Klein, Joan Larsen, 164 n.79
Knafla, Louis A., 157 n.41
Knight, G. Wilson, 166 n.99
Knight, W. Nicholas, 146 n.6
knowledge: in *Cymbeline*, 68, 71–74; in the Howard attainder, 44, 48, 77; of law, 18, 19, 89–90; of minds, 2; oral versus written, 110–11, 115; in *Ralph Roister Doister*, 61–66; and revels, 158 n.55; in the Scots prosecution, 181 n.49; sexuality and, 58–59; as treason, 9, 148 n.35; of truth in poetry, 4; of women, 41, 165 n.85; written, 134, 136–38, 139–40
Kyd, Thomas, 1; biography, 184 n.76, 77, 80; and Marlowe, 127–28; and written evidence, 22, 111. See also *The Spanish Tragedy*

Lamb, Mary Ellen, 183 n.72
Langbein, John H., 150 n.50
Larner, Christina, 73, 167 n.109
law reporting, 15–18; and truth, 17–18; in Holinshed, 18–19
legal story-telling, 3, 38; in the *Arte of Rhetorique*, 19
Lehmberg, Stanford E., 160 n.5, 161 n.25
Letters and Papers of the Reign of Henry VIII, 49, 159 nn.4, 5, 162 nn.25, 38, 42
Levack, Brian P., 149 n.39, 153 n.78
Levin, Harry, 98, 174 n.79
Levine, Nina, 184 n.88
Lewalski, Barbara Kiefer, 183 n.72
Lewis, Jayne, 177 n.3, 183 n.71, 185 n.100
Little, David, 169, 172 n.57
Lockyer, Roger, 168 n.11, 177 n.3
Lodge, Thomas, 38, 127
Loftus, Elizabeth, 167 n.105
Lorenzo, 129–34, 136, 139, 184 n.82
Love's Labors Lost (Shakespeare), 111
Lowenstein, Joseph, 120, 181 n.47
Lowenthal, David, 174 n.78
loyalty: in the Babington trials, 81–84; and "the country," 21; in documentary form, 113–14; and homeland, 86–87, 107–8; in the Howard attainder, 164 n.78; and itinerancy, 171 n.39; and married women, 52; among men, 60–61, 66, 68, 83–84, 99, 102, 104; personal versus political, 21; of secretaries, 130; of servants, 131; in treason trials, 6, 141. *See also* individual trials and plays
Luther, Martin, *The Babylonian Captivity of the Church*, 13, 151 n.51

MacCaffrey, Wallace, 79, 168 nn.6, 8, 9, 170 n.32, 178 nn.9, 10, 15, 179 n.32
Macfarlane, Alan, 167 n.110
Maclure, Millar, 173 n.73
manhood: in the Babington trials, 19, 21, 77, 78, 84–86; and discourses of treason, 3; and male fidelity, 108–9. *See also* affiliation; *Arte of Rhetorique*; courtiership; individual trials and plays

Mannock, Henry, 43, 46–49, 53, 163 n.55
Marcus, Leah, 166 nn.98, 99, 178 n.13, 181 n.46, 183 n.71
Marlowe, Christopher, 1, 21; and blood, 135; character and space in, 54–55; and espionage, 173 n.71; and Kyd, 127–28; legal entanglements of, 173 n.67; letters in, 111; and manhood, 77–78; male friendship in, 78, 95–108; and rhetorical prowess, 175 n.92; theatrical evidence in, 67–68; and vagabondage, 176 n.94. *See also* names of individual characters and plays
Marston, John, 38, 146 n.6
Mary I, 5, 15, 17; and common law treason, 10, 150 n.44; and matrimonial treason, 66, 165 n.93; and Nicholas Udall, 57, 58
Mary, Queen of Scots: and absolute majesty, 114–16, 178 n.19, 179 n.20; and the Babington trials, 21–22, 79, 80, 168 nn.10, 12, 179 n.27, 181 n.49; and blood, 135, 177 n.2; and the Bond of Association, 112–13, 178 n.13; casket letters of, 123–24, 182 n.56, 183 n.63, 67; as discursive theme, 112, 141, 178 n.11; and epistolary evidence, 13, 19, 115–18, 181 nn.46, 48, 182 n.58; and Essex, 141; as femme fatale, 125, 184 n.74, 182 n.54; and scribal identity, 119, 120–28, 185 n.101; sonnets of, 124–25, 183 n.64; and *The Spanish Tragedy*, 128, 130–33, 184 n.83; and testimony of secretaries, 119–21, 180 n.44; and writing of secretaries, 118–19
Massacre at Paris, The (Marlowe), 111
matrimonial treason: 9, 40, 66, 77. *See also* Henry VIII; Howard attainder; treason
Maus, Katharine Eisaman, 145 n.4, 147 n.19, 149 n.38, 164 n.76, 166 n.94, 167 n.108
McAlindon, Thomas, 177 n.8
McCoy, Richard C., 169 n.21, 170 n.24
McEachern, Claire, 146 n.10
McGann, Jerome, 179 n.25
McIlwain, Charles Henry, 20, 148 n.25, 153 n.81, 171 n.42, 184 n.78
Merchant of Venice, The (Shakespeare), 141
Middle Temple: 2, 32, 38, 155 n.9, 157 n.48, 158 nn.55, 58, 60
Midsummer Night's Dream, A (Shakespeare), 52
Miller, Anthony, 169 n.23
Miola, Robert S., 166 n.101
Mirror for Magistrates, 39
Misfortunes of Arthur, The (Hughes), 39
mobility, *See* homeland; travel; treason
monarchy: in the Babington trials, 81; and ciphering, 177; in civil versus common law, 171 n.42; in *Edward II*, 97; and lawful dissent, 171 n.43; limited versus absolute, 7, 153 n.78, 179 n.20; and secretaries, 120; in *Tamburlaine I*, 100; and treason legislation, 138 n.34
Montrose, Louis Adrian, 168 n.4
mooting: the abbot in, 29; blood in, 28, 135; and court-centered authority, 20, 152 n.70, 154 n.3; defined, 25, 154 n.2, 155 nn.9, 11; and the Howard attainder, 51; the husband-father in, 28; and imaginative discourses, 24–25, 39; pedagogical practices of, 32–34; and property, 154 n.5; and proprietorship, 23; and "the realm," 31–32; ritual and improvisation in, 31–34; the stranger in, 30–31, 179 n.22; the wife-mother in, 28–29. *See also* Inns of Court; "Jacob and Esau"
More, Sir Thomas, 11, 42, 169 n.18
Much Ado About Nothing (Shakespeare), 24
Mullaney, Steven, 170 n.32
Mulryne, J. R., 132, 177 n.8, 184 nn.75
Mycetes (*Tamburlaine I*), 97, 98, 102, 108, 174 n.79

national identity: 3; and the Babington trials, 77, 80–87, 92–94, 104; and female fidelity, 75–76, 77; and female sexuality, 69; and heroic service, 169 n.73; and the Howard attainder, 42, 46, 50, 51, 57; and legal history, 16; and male friendship, 77–78; and mooting, 31, 34; and the Scots prosecution, 115, 121–22, 126; and *Tamburlaine I*, 21, 97, 108; and treason, 2–3, 5–6, 11, 141–42
Neale, J. E., 110, 147 n.25; 176 n.98, 177 n.1, 178 n.11, 14
Newlin, Jeanne T., 186 n.1
Newman, Karen, 162 n.41, 167 n.110
Nicholl, Charles, 95, 173 nn.67, 70–73
Nichols, James, 158 n.60
Norfolk, Duchess of, 43, 52, 53, 55, 56
Normand, Lawrence, 174 n.84, 185 n.98
Norton, Thomas, 2, 38, 39, 146 n.6
Nosworthy, J. M., 166 n.97

Ong, Walter J., 177 n.4, 181 n.46
Orgel, Stephen, 103, 168 n.4, 174 n.84, 175 n.90
Orlin, Lena Cowen, 53, 54, 162 n.49, 163 nn.56, 57, 65, 165 nn. 81, 88

Othello (Shakespeare), 166 n.94
overt act, 12, 13; in Coke, 150 n.47. *See also* evidence

Parker, Patricia, 5, 73, 147 nn.19, 20, 165 n.93, 166 n.94, 167 n.108, 181 n.46
Parry, Edward, 123, 182 nn.56–58, 183 nn.59, 60, 71
Parry, William, 178 n.14
Paster, Gail, 73, 166 n.95, 167 n.110, 185 n.99
Patterson, Annabel, 18, 118, 145 n.5, 153 nn.77, 79, 180 nn.35, 37, 181 n.50
Pedringano (*The Spanish Tragedy*), 129–32, 136, 137, 184 n.82
Perkins, William, *Christian Oeconomie*, 92, 172 n.57
Peterson, Douglas, 166 n.97
place: and allegiance, 104–9; in the *Arte of Rhetorique*, 105–6, 96; in the Babington trials, 82, 86–87, 93; and the Bond of Association, 113–14; character and, 20; in *Doctor Faustus*, 54; in *Edward II*, 176 n.93; in the Howard attainder, 54–55; and land transmission, 31–32; of origin, 36; in *Ralph Roister Doister*, 63–65; in *Richard II*, 169 n.16; and status, 31–33. *See also* homeland; household, space, vagabondage
Plato, 121, 131
Pleasant Historie of the Conquest of West India, 98
Plowden, Alison, 169 n.17, 179 n.32, 182 n.54, 183 nn.68–70, 73
Plowden, Edmund, *Commentaries*, 152 n.66, 153 n.71 of; and law reporting, 17–18; and legal truth, 44, 160 n.16; and Mary, Queen of Scots, 177 n.2
Pollen, John Hungerford, 168 nn.6, 7, 181 n.49
Ponet, John, 5–6, 147 n.21
Posner, Richard, 147 n.23
Posthumus (*Cymbeline*), 68–73, 166 nn.97, 99
Powell, Chilton Latham, 164 n.71, 182 n.54
Prest, Wilfrid R., 155 n.12, 157 nn.44–46
Pritchard, Arnold, 171 n.39, 173 n.71
proof: conflicting, 69; constructed, 21, 41, 150 n.50; and dramatic structure, 155 n.13; epistolary, 117; of malice, 11; of patrimony, 106; from servants, 119; of sexual activity, 72–75; simulated, 41, 75; speech as, 13, 160 n.18; visible, 48; of willfulness, 43, 57; and witnessing, 88. *See also* evidence; witnessing
property: and blood, 28–30, 135; and bodily evidence, 48; and common law, 154 n.5; and duty, 60–61; and dynasty, 51; in moot cases, 20, 23, 27–30
proprietorship: 20; in the Bond of Association, 113; in moot cases, 23–27, 35, 39; in the Scots prosecution, 114–15; in *Tamburlaine I*, 78, 96–97. *See also* courtiership; mooting; individual trials and plays
Protestantism: and the Babington trials, 79, 81; and "ease," 169 n.23; and Katherine Howard, 41–42; and Mary, Queen of Scots, 178 n.11; and plain speech, 13–14; and resistance to monarchs, 171 n.43
Pye, Christopher, 50, 162 n.41

Quarles, Francis, 38
Quintilian, 5, 150 n.49, 176 n.96

Rackin, Phyllis, 149 n.42, 153 n.83, 156 n.23, 162 n.45, 172 n.53, 175 n.86
Ralegh, Sir Walter, 38; and evidence, 11, 13, 45, 160 n.18; and rhetorical skill 14; and Tamburlaine, 174 n.77
Ralph Roister Doister (Udall), 20, 57–58, 65–66, 164 n.77; character and space in, 57, 63–64, 66; classical influences in, 164 n.72; and *Cymbeline*, 41, 68, 70, 72, 75–76; and epistolary betrayal, 111; and female fidelity, 59–66; gifts in, 59–60, 65; and the Howard attainder, 41, 57, 63–64, 72, 75–76; interpreting Custance in, 58–59, 61–62; "knowing" women in, 61–62, 66; and male loyalty, 60–61, 66; and male testimony, 57, 60, 65; and matrimonial treason, 57; and Bopinion, 63; and treason legislation, 61; and women's households, 57, 58, 63–64
Ranum, Orest, 52, 60, 65, 163 nn.51, 57, 61, 165 nn.81, 90
Read, Conyers, 173 n.70, 181 n.49
report: and eyewitnessing, 60–63, 165 n.82; false, 70–72; and female sexuality, 77; at Inns of Court, 38; law (genre), 16–18, 152 n.66, 70; and overt act, 13; and testimony, 5, 21. *See also* Edward Coke; law reporting; Edmund Plowden
Rezneck, Stephen, 145 n.1
rhetoric: of alternativity, 69; as assault, 70; of chivalry, 81–83, 99; and evidence, 13, 14, 15; and exploratory comedy, 155 n.13; forensic versus mimetic, 4–5, 147 n.16;

and household order, 165 n.93; and the Howard attainder, 44–46; and "knowing" women, 41; and legal persuasion, 4–6, 91, 97, 150 n.49; of loyalty, 60–61; and manhood, 98; of place and space, 54, 105–7, 176 n.96; of promiscuity, 87, 104; of rootlessness, 104–5; and truth-telling, 4, 13, 20; of weakmindedness, 85. *See also Arte of Rhetorique*; individual trials and plays

Richard II (Shakespeare), 1, 2, 142, 169 n.16; 186 n.1

Riggs, David, 170 n.32

Ridolfi plot, 112, 125, 126, 178 n.11

Roberts, Peter, 96, 158 n.53, 168 n.12, 173 nn.72, 73

rootlessness: and infidelity, 21, 77–78, 87; in *Tamburlaine I*, 96, 104–7. *See* also Babington trials; homeland; vagabondage

Rubin, Gayle, 165 n.82, 175 n.91

Sackville, Thomas, 2, 38, 39, 146 n.6

Said, Edward, 156 n.29

Sanders, Eve, 183 n.72, 184 n.85

Sanders, Norman, 58, 164 nn.72, 74, 75

Sanford, Rhonda Lemke, 167 n.108

Scarry, Elaine, 162 n.41, 167 n.106

Schoolhouse of Women, 55, 163 n.62

Sebek, Barbara, 171 n.40

Sedgwick, Eve Kosofsky, 165 n.82, 175 n.91

Seneca, 39; and *The Spanish Tragedy*, 177 n.8

sexuality: fear of women's, 175 n.90; men's, 58, 84–85, 99–100; in moot cases, 24, 28–29; in same-sex relationships, 174 n.84; women's, 19, 28, 43, 50, 53–56, 68–69, 125, 130, 142; women's and legislation, 77. *See also* affiliation; association; fidelity; friendship; individual trials and plays

Shakespeare, William, 1, 2, 3; character and inscription in, 181 n.51; and the law, 146 n.6. *See also* names of individual characters and plays

Shapiro, Barbara J., 149 n.39, 150 n.50, 177 n.4

Shapiro, James, 146 n.9, 184 n.91

Sharpe, J. A., 146 n.7, 162 n.41

Shepherd, Simon, 174 n.77, 174 n.84, 175 n.89

Shirley, James, 38

Sidney, Sir Philip, 147 nn.12, 14, 18, 158 n.61, 169 n.23; on lawyers, 147 n.13; legal versus poetic truth, 3–5, 38; similitudes and persuasion in, 147 n.16

Siemon, James E., 166 n.97

Smith, Alan Gordon, 168 n.10, 172 n.49

Smith, Barbara Herrnstein, 71, 91–92, 167 n.104, 172 n.56

Smith, Bruce, 174 n.84, 175 n.86

Smith, Lacey Baldwin, 111, 145 n.1, 151 n.59, 155 n.13, 159 n.4, 161 nn.21, 35, 162 nn.41, 42, 167 n.113, 177 n.6

Smith, Philip, 154 nn.2, 5, 7, 157 nn.32, 33, 37, 41, 47, 49, 158 n. 54

Smith, Steven R., 185 n.89

Smith, Thomas, *De Republica Anglorum*, 37, 158 n.53

Sommerville, J. P., 148 n.26, 154 nn.5, 8, 168 n.6, 171 n.43, 179 n.20

space: and cartography, 176 n.95; and character, 20, 63–66; ideology of, 55, 77; and lawlessness, 93; meanings of, 109; in moot cases, 26, 33; and presence, 176 n.93; and privacy, 163 n.61; and sexuality, 52–55. *See also* households; place; individual trials and plays

Spanish Chronicle of Henry VIII, 50, 159 n.4

Spanish Tragedy, The (Kyd), 184 nn.75, 79, 81–82, 185 n.91; betrayal by letter in, 111; and blood, 135–36, 139, 185 n.99; casket letters in, 131–32; confederacy of knowledge in, 111, 129, 136, 137; and corroboration, 136–37; courtiership in, 128–29, 138–39; and documentary theory, 134–35; and early modern drama, 177 n.8; and epistolary interpretation, 111, 132–33; and eyewitnessing, 137–38; and forgery, 131, 133–34; and Kyd, 128; and prior belief, 111, 127, 137; and the Scots prosecution, 127, 128, 139–40; and the secretary, 130; and the servant, 130–32; writing and interiority in, 111, 131, 133–35, 139–40; writing and revenge in, 185 nn.92,93; writing and sexuality in, 129–30, 134; writing and truth in, 110, 127, 129–30; and written evidence, 22, 111, 132, 139. *See also* Mary, Queen of Scots; individual characters

Speed, John, 3

Spenser, Edmund, 3, 127, 168 n.4

Stallybrass, Peter, 162 n.49, 181 n.51, 183 n.64

Stapleton, Thomas, 149 n.41

Stephen, H. L., 149 n.43 and passim

Stimpson, Catherine, 167 n.108

Stone, Lawrence, 168 n.6, 172 n.52

stranger, the: as archetype, 94; in Inns of Court, 36–37; in moot cases, 28, 29–31, 39, 156 n.26; in treason legislation, 179 n.22

subjectivity: and conscience, 92; in law and

subjectivity (*continued*)
literature, 2; in matrimonial treasons, 40; in men, 175 n.91; of secretaries, 180 n.44; and service, 131; and writing, 125–26; in treason trials, 11; in women, 40, 66. *See also* interiority; individual trials and plays
Suckling, John, 38
Suresby, Sim (*Ralph Roister Doister*), 59–63, 66, 71, 165 n.82
Swander, Homer, 166 n.97, 167 n.107

Tamburlaine I (Marlowe), 77, 174 n.79, 175 n.92, 176 n.94; and blood, 102–3; character and space in, 104–7, 109; "the country" in, 78, 96–98; courtiership in, 98–99; and Edward II, 173 n.76; and fidelity, 100; homeland in, 98; homosocial identity in, 99–100, 103–4; and the lawful, 107–8; and male friendship, 99–104, 175 n.86; and Marlowe, 78, 95–97; vagabondage in, 107; and women, 103–4. *See* also affiliation; Babington trials; courtiership; friendship
Tamburlaine (*Tamburlaine I*), 98–109; ambiguity of, 174 n.77
Teague, Frances, 177 n.7
Techelles (*Tamburlaine I*), 99–101, 175 n.86
Tennenhouse, Leonard, 154 n.1, 184 n.84
testimony: and "the country," 80–81; and credibility, 14; and eyewitnessing, 167 n.105; fabricated, 21; female, 45–46, 49–50, 114–15, 116; and honesty, 70; male, 21, 57, 65, 75; oral versus material, 160 n.18; oral versus written, 44, 110, 161 n.20; personal knowledge versus fact, 66; and prior belief, 91; and report, 5; ritual form of, 91; of secretaries, 120–21; of servants, 131; and truth, 145 n.1; written, 12. *See also* evidence; individual trials
Theridamas (*Tamburlaine I*), 101, 102, 106, 175
Thomas, Brook, 147 n.23
Thomas, Donald, 160 nn.9 and passim
Thomas, Keith, 151 n.57, 156 n.28
Throckmorton, Francis, 112
Throckmorton, Nicholas, 10, 17–18, 93
Titchburne, Chidiock, 79–81, 84–86, 94–95, 103, 168 n.11; in Holinshed, 170 n.31
Todd, Barbara J., 163 n.66, 164 n.74
Traub, Valerie, 99, 174 n.84, 175 n.85
travel: ambivalent representations of, 170 n.38; and character, 170 n.38; and Imogen, 167 n.108; and promiscuity, 21; and trade, 176 n.94. *See also* Babington trials; homeland; Tamburlaine I; vagabondage
treason: and adultery, 40; and anti-papal sentiment, 93, 170 n.32, 171 n.39; in *Arte of Rhetorique*, 172 n.54; and Christmas Prince revels, 35; common law, 7, 10, 148 n.28, 179 n.22; and *diffidatio*, 83; and executions, 146 n.9; and *Edward II*, 173 n.76; female versus male, 77; and forfeiture, 147 n.24; imagining as, 2, 8, 10, 11; and lawful action, 87; legislation, 7–9, 148 nn.30, 32, 34, 35, 164 n.69, 165 n.93, 178 n.11; and Marlowe, 95–96, 97, 173 n.71; matrimonial, 9, 40, 66, 77, 148 n.33, 159 n.2; and monarchy, 7; and overt act, 12–13, 150 n.47; in print, 152 n.64; prosecutions, 1; relativity of, 5–6, 81; and witchcraft, 67. *See* also affiliation; fidelity; law reporting; loyalty; treason trials; individual trials and plays
treason trials: agency in, 47; versus attainder, 42, 159 n.4; character and space in, 54; and competitive proprietorship, 109; conscience in, 92; and credibility, 14–15, 47; cultural bias in, 22; as discourse, 3, 6; of Duke of Buckingham, 11; and English law, 87–90, 108, 153 n.80; evidence in, 13; female fidelity in, 40–41, 50, 61, 75, 124, 130–31; female versus male, 85–86; and formulaic rhetoric, 90–91, 162 n.41; as historical processes, 3, 87–90, 81; and honest speech, 14; of imagination, 13; and intention, 11, 149 n.39; invisible action in, 11; male friendship in, 21, 84, 104, 108–9, 112; and moot cases, 20; of Thomas More, 11; and national identity, 3, 6, 20, 121, 141–43; and overt act, 12; and protocols of "truth," 15, 44–45; public consumption of, 1; publicizing, 1; of Walter Ralegh, 13, 70; and subjectivity, 6, 10–11, 13, 49, 59, 92, 109, 126–27; and theater, 2, 6–7; themes, 1, 2, 3, 143; of Nicholas Throckmorton, 10, 18–19; travel in, 86–87, 104; and witness-accusers, 12, 150 n.44, 172 n.46. *See also* individual trials
Trusty, Tristram (*Ralph Roister Doister*), 60, 65, 66
truth-telling: in *Arte of Rhetorique*, 4; in drama, 3, 66; and intention, 41; in law versus literature, 3–4; and male testimony, 41; and theatrical simulation, 41. *See also* evidence; *Arte of Rhetorique*; Sir Philip Sidney

Tuan, Yi-Fu, 109, 169 n.16, 177 nn.101, 102
Turberville, George, 38
Twelfth Night (Shakespeare), 111, 185 n.90
Two Gentlemen of Verona (Shakespeare), 111

Udall, Nicholas, 1; *Ralph Roister Doister*, 57–66, 164 n.77

vagabondage, 107, 176 n.98. *See also* homeland; place; rootlessness
Vickers, Nancy J., 162 n.49, 167 n.108
Vives, Juan Luis: *Instruction of a Christian Woman*, 59, 60, 164 n.79, 165 n.81; *Linguae Latinae Exercitatio*, 139, 185 n.107
Volpone (Jonson), 25, 155 n.12

Wall, Wendy, 183 n.72
Walsingham, Francis: and the Babington trials, 79, 168 n.9, 10, 12, 169 n.17; and Marlowe, 21, 95, 96; and the Scots prosecution, 112, 117–18, 128, 179 n.32
Warner, J. Christopher, 159 n.1
Wayne, Valerie, 166 n.94
Webster, John, 111
Whitaker, William, *A Disputation on Holy Scripture*, 151 n.51
Wickham, Glynne, 164 n.72
widow, the: 163 n.66, 164 n.74, 79; and female-headed households, 56–58, 64, 163 n.55
wife, the: in early modern households, 165 n.88; in the Howard attainder, 43, 46, 48, 50, 56–57, 161 n.32; and loyalty among men, 61, 166 n.97; in moot cases, 26–31, 156 n.26; murderous, 183 n.73; in treason statutes, 8, 9
Williams, Raymond, 148 n.36
Wilson, Richard, 176 n.94
Wilson, Thomas, See *Arte of Rhetorique*
Wimsatt, W. K., 180 n.43
witchcraft: 67, 73, 167 n.110
Wither, George, 38
witnessing: versus accusing, 12; and conscience, 92; contradictory, 150 n.47; and corroboration, 45–48; and credibility, 14–15; by document, 139, 161 n.20; eyewitnessing, 48, 62, 68, 137; and intention, 13; legal history of, 12–14, 88–89, 150 n.44, 172 n.46; and memory, 157 n.105; and motive, 62; and plain speech, 13–14; by servants, 119–20, 126. *See also* evidence; report; testimony
womanhood: in discourses of treason, 3; and Katherine Howard, 51; and relativity of virtue, 46, 69, 161 n.32; and sexuality, 122. *See also* association; fidelity; individual trials and plays
Woodbridge, Linda, 56, 163 n.62, 164 n.67, 169 n.19
Wormald, Jenny, 182 n.56
Wriothesley, Charles, 42, 46, 77, 159 nn.3, 4

Yearbooks, 16, 38, 152 n.66

Zenocrate (*Tamburlaine I*), 101, 103, 104, 108
Ziegler, Georgianna, 166 n.102
Zweig, Stefan, 179 n.20, 182 nn.53, 54, 56, 183 nn.65–67

Acknowledgments

During the time I have been working on this book, I have benefited from the professional and personal support of many institutions, colleagues, and friends. I take great pleasure in acknowledging them here.

I have received much-appreciated material support from the Committee on Faculty Research and Creativity at the Florida State University in Tallahassee, the Committee on Faculty Sabbaticals, and the President's Travel Foundation. The School of Criticism and Theory at Dartmouth College, the Shelby Cullom Davis Center for Historical Research at Princeton University, and the Folger Shakespeare Library provided grants and fellowships that made my travel to libraries and participation in seminars possible. The staffs at the Humanities and Law Libraries at Florida State University, Princeton University, and the Universities of California at Santa Barbara and Los Angeles were unfailingly helpful and kind.

Earlier versions of parts of Chapter 2 appeared in "Female Fidelities on Trial: Proof in the Howard Attainder and *Cymbeline*," *Renaissance Drama* n.s. 24 (1994), and are reprinted by permission of Northwestern University Press. Many of the ideas in individual chapters took shape as talks at various conferences, and I want to thank the audiences for their comments, many of which made their way into this book.

I am grateful to Annabel Patterson, who provided an early opportunity at a Renaissance Society of America convention to test some of my thinking about trials. While at Princeton, I incurred a special debt to Natalie Zemon Davis, Barbara Herrnstein Smith, and Bonnie G. Smith. I herewith deliver on my promise. Richard Helgerson, Gail Kern Paster, Frances E. Dolan, Arthur F. Kinney, and Katharine Eisaman Maus have shown a sustained interest in my work that I deeply appreciate. Stanley Fish, Sara Munson Deats, Lee Bliss, and Constance Jordan have all made contributions that kept this project on track.

Mihoko Suzuki and Cynthia Marshall have perhaps had to listen too often to too much about the early modern traitor, which they have done with great generosity. At Florida State University, I want to thank Anne Rowe,

Laura Rosenthal, Helen Burke, James O'Rourke, Ralph Berry, and Sally Warner. Elsewhere, I have benefited from the friendship of Mark Rose, Garrett Stewart, Natasa Durovicova, Everett Zimmerman, and Muriel Zimmerman.

My greatest debt is to Gary Karasik, without whom this book would not have been imagined.